Choreography.

80% of a choreographer's work is knowing your craft!

Most choreographic techniques work regardless of the choreographer's own dance skills.

Dance.

Like music, dance permits us to participate in the sensations and moods of the soul. Dancers do not perform like a musicians – they inhabit existence in the moment of movement. Like music, musicians capable of throwing light into the gaps between emotional states, which would otherwise remain hidden within human beings. Dance can comprehend things of the soul and magnify them until they become visible – it is capable of expressing heaven on earth. Its substance is an intermingling of knowledge and the non-verbal that no academic treatise can define. There lies an unfathomable mystery in dance which we may musicians approach at a moment of movement. Within the essence of dance,, there is a core which exudes a fascination we can locate emotionally as we encircle it. Dance is the seeking after this inner core, in order to come closer to the mystery – within movement.

Konstantin Tsakalidis

Choreography
craft and vision

Developing and Structuring Dance

for Solo, Duet and Groups

Publisher:

Stage Verlag – Tanz-Zentrale
Erich-Zeigner-Allee 64b
04229 Leipzig, Germany

info@choreo-book.com
www.choreo-book.com

Dancer on Cover: Verena Sommerer
Book Design: Alf Ruge | www.alf-ruge.de

Translation: Simone Kick

Photos:
Rolf Wrobel, Alf Ruge, Betty Pabst, Bernd Hänisch, Vera
Bandeira, Holger Vocke, Hai Vu Nguyen, Florian Bornträger,
Konstantin Tsakalidis, Felix Alexander Neudeck, Celine
Weigt, Ulf Leuteritz, Nina Niestroy, Bernhard Mohr, Sophie
Krabbe

Copyright (2020) by Konstantin Tsakalidis.
ISBN 978-3-9821187-3-4
BOD Softcover
Originally published in German in 2010:
"Choreographie - Handwerk & Vision"

Acknowledgements

I thank all the dancers who feature in the photographs in this book.

My thanks go to my teachers at the Laban Centre in London, from whom I learned a lot about choreographing; and also to the tutors at the Tanzwerkstatt Konstanz who invested much patience and love in their dance students. I would also like to thank Erwin Schumann and my teachers in Zurich, in whose classes I discovered the existential in dance.

Also, my thanks go to the directors and choreographers with whom I have worked.
I am grateful to the many students who gave me their trust and tried out the studies and exercises I developed for this book. My thanks also go to Jeanette Neustadt for proofreading the first draft, and to Dr Christiana Rosenberg-Ahlhaus for revising the second draft. I am very grateful to Werner Nater for the countless hours he spent on the third draft. Thank you to my editor, Bärbel Philipp, and to my graphic designer, Alf Ruge.

Thanks to Annett Walter and Sophia Loth for their support.

Thanks to my translator Simone Kick and thanks to Betty Pabst, Bernd Hänisch, Rolf Wrobel, Alf Ruge, Vera Bandeira, Holger Vocke, Hai Vu Nguyen, Florian Bornträger, Felix Alexander Neudeck, Celine Weigt, Ulf Leuteritz, Nina Niestroy, Bernhard Mohr, Sophie Krabbe for the wonderful photos.

I am indebted to my wife, Luise, whose great interest has informed both my performances and my writing of this book. Her patience and attentive support have greatly contributed to my work.

Studies		16
Exercises		17

0 Introduction — 20

Becoming a choreographer		22
	From dancer to choreographer	22
	Career changers	22
	To what degree can I learn to be a choreographer?	23
	Chapters	26

1 Sub-text and spirit — 28

Drawing on internal resources		30
Intention		31

2 Theme – Structure – Dramaturgy — 34

Theme and material		36
	Structuring a dance piece	44
The dramatic arc		47
	Experiencing time within a dramatic composition	47
	Progression	52
	Turning points	53
	Building up to a turning point	54
	Retardation	59
	Parameters of intensity	61
	Example: Storyboard	62
Structuring source material		66
	Transitional scenes	69

3 Design principles — 72

Direction — 73
    Focus — 78
    Structuring pathways based on literary sources, plays, musicals or opera — 81
    Personal space — 84
    A technical break-down of personal space — 85
    The limits of internal and external space — 89
    Metre — 91

Music and movement — 91
    What role does music play in choreography? — 98

4 Thematic development — 106

Connections between theme and dancer — 108

Repertoire — 108
    Working with the third dimension — 112

Manipulating available movements — 116
    Framework — 116
    Manipulation parameters — 117
    Developing manipulation parameters by transferring the essence of a movement onto a group or body parts — 117
    Manipulation parameters from extreme changes in dimension — 121
    Manipulation parameters from movement quality — 121
    Transferring movement segments from one point in space to another — 132
    Changing the dance space changes the performance — 133
    Manipulation using temporal aspects: Rhythm and tempo — 136
    Manipulation using complementary elements — 138
    Developing movements for a theme — 139
    The indirect approach — 140
    The direct approach — 141
    Definitions — 144
    Synonyms on movement level — 144
    Non-verbal and emotional links between theme and movement — 146
    Image — 146

Music 148

Sculpture 148

Inner substance and evocative setting 152

Using visualisation to develop movements specific to a theme 161

Working with elusive themes – abstraction and focus 164

Summary of approaches to
choreographic material 167

5 Arrangement and composition 170

Internal components 171

Internal and superordinate form 172

Structures 174

The language of space 176

Implied emotion in an empty space 179

Balance points in space 181

Places and spaces 183

Change of perspective and 'black holes' 186

Directing attention in overlapping actions 188

Spatial arrangement 205

Space within the arrangement 207

Establishing relationships 213

Levels 216

Composition and its elements 221

Unisono 223

Opposition 226

Generating movement through axes 231

Motif, counter-motif and counterpoint 232

Symmetry – Asymmetry 234

Intensity 237

Position – flow – transition 242

Rhythm 245

Compositional variation 252

The solo in contemporary dance 255

   Choreography and development 255

   Where do I start? 255

A basic choice of approaches 261

Technical approaches: Gesture, manipulation, opposition, movement quality, and composition 262

   Examples for spatial approaches 264

   Examples for qualitative approaches 282

The connection between emotion and body 286

Developing a character 290

   1. Approach 290

   2. Vita 291

   3. Interview 293

   4. Improvisations and Approaches 293

   5. Dream and Strength 293

   6. Shapes 298

   7. Interview 298

   The character develops 299

   Identification and empathy after Lee Strasberg 302

   Impulse points in your hands 306

   Gestures 309

   Costume or object 309

   Walking and moving 313

   Movement quality 313

   Body parts 314

   Developing solos 315

   Systemic constellation 315

IV. Autobiographical solo: important stepping stones and emotional, life-changing experiences collected in a dance 316

Translating music into dance 318

   Movement synonyms 318

7 Pedagogical aspects — 332

8 Acting, language and dance — 336

Dance as an interlude in a play — 340

9 Dance and film — 344

10 Stage design — 350

Experience – association – feeling – understanding – connection — 360

11 Lighting — 364

Lighting parameters — 365
Colours — 367
Perception — 368

Stage lighting — 369
Floodlights — 369
Spotlights — 370
Profile spots — 372
PAR lights — 372
Dimmer — 373

Light design — 376

12 Study and exercises — 382

Epilogue — 412

About the author — 413

Notes — 414

Studies

1   Relationship between source material and interpretation.........67
2   Transitions 71
3   Tension between audience and performance space 77
4   Directions between dancers in relation to the audience...........77
5   Focus I..79
6   Focus II...79
7   Focus III..80
8   Focus IV 80
9   Mapping a literary source..83
10 20 different directions 87
11 Counts and accents in music 94
12 Musical interpretation.. 102
13 Implementing turning points and dynamic units of time 111
14 Turning points and dynamic units 113
15 External, relational manipulation parameters 119
16 Developing manipulation parameters.............................. 119
17 Reverse phrasing... 120
18 Transforming individual sequences 120
19 Manipulation parameters 120
20 Manipulation parameters from dimension 120
21 Effort defined by material 125
22 Manipulations using separate elements 128
23 Transferring movements within the body 128
24 Free and constrained manipulations.............................. 128
25 Manipulations with energetic changes 129
26 Manipulating space within the kinesphere........................ 131
27 Translating movements from one spatial level into another 131
28 The influence of the dance space on choreography 135
29 Manipulation using tempo and rhythm 137
30 Devising complementary elements 137
31 Accumulation 137
32 Linking theme and movement via synonyms...................... 145
33 Theme and structure.. 149
34 Constructing a thematic setting 158
35 Using visualisation... 163
36 Abstraction and basic components 168
37 ABA structure and canon 175
38 The potential of space... 177
39 The effect of different positions in space 180
40 Different arrangements of balance points in space 182

41   Settings in landscapes 185
42   Connection and isolation in space and in emotion 195
43   Spatial tension 197
44   Movement to the motif of 'closeness – distance' 201
45   Negative Space 209
46   Spatial relationships within the arrangement 210
47   Islands and paths of focus within an arrangement 215
48   The living climbing frame 219
49   Transforming medium level movements i 220
50   Compositions of space 222
51   Synchronicity in relation to dynamics 225
52   Opposing attributes 233
53   Developing a piece from a gesture 233
54   From symmetry to asymmetry 236
55   Tighten and expand 240
56   Setting up positions in a movement flow 243
57   New paths into familiar positions 244
58   Phrasing with different parameters 251
59   Mini plays 342
60   Film 348
61   Stage design 362

Exercises

I.   The internal spaces of the body 384

1   Hearing 384
2   Partner work – divided attention 385
3   Different circles of attention 385
4   Guided improvisation – composition – group exercise 386
5   Inner spaces – mental journey 390
6   Visualisation 391
7   Subtext 'Mama' 392

II.   Structure and dynamics 392

8   Exercise for structure and dramatic arc 392

III. Stage spaces 393

    9   Spatial tension 393
    10   Spatial tension – stationary 393
    11   Spatial tension through movement quality and tempo 394
    12   Different relations between action and reaction 394

IV. Structure and dynamics 395

    13   Exercise for structure and dramatic arc 395

V. Scene, language, and dance 395

    14   Plot 395
    15   Storytelling 395
    16   Gestures 395
    17   Image 396
    18   Poem 396
    19   Personal story 396
    20   Colours 396

VI. Music 397

    21   Movement combination 397

VII. Relationships 397

    22   Impulses 397
    23   Towel impulses 398
    24   Mirroring 398
    25   Rolling Point 398
    26   Obstacles 398
    27   Taking weight 399
    28   Absorb - divert 399
    29   Support 399
    30   Nodes 400
    31   Connection 400
    32   Snapping 400
    33   Push and release 400
    34   Balls – Trio 401

VIII. Movement quality 401

35 Light and heavy 401
36 Rolling and gliding 401
37 Chinese letters – developing into partner or trio exercise 402
38 Waves 402
39 Twister 403

IX. Group dynamics 403

40 Switching leaders 403
41 Collective decisions and reactions 403
42 Walking in a circle 404

X. Music and movement 405

43 Relationship between beat and dance 405
44 Approaching a composition using graphical notes 405
45 Verbally defining a piece of music 405
46 Transferring musical structures to dance 405
47 The music plays with the choreography 406
48 Dialogue: musician - dancer 406
49 Sounds 406
50 Vowels 407

XI. Rhythm 407

51 Body percussion 407
52 Vocal rhythms 407
53 Rhythmical structure 408
54 Vocal rhythms dominating the movement rhythms 408
55 Rhythmic transformations 408
56 Rhythmic observation and transfer 409
57 Breaks 409
58 Accents and inner impulses 409
60 Translating two-dimensional rhythms 410
59 Impulses 410
61 Musical lyrics and complementary elements 411

Introduction

A great number of choreographers are self-taught. Many arrive at dance by a roundabout route, bypassing dance training and entering the dance world directly as choreographers. In dance training, on the other hand, dance students are rarely taught any sound choreographic techniques. At best, those who are interested in choreography will have the opportunity of putting their work up for discussion, but they are hardly ever given insight into different methods of how to develop a piece of dance, simply because many teachers do not follow a specific method themselves. The examination of what makes a piece a success or a failure is rarely included in dance training.

Many of the themes discussed in this book are addressed in practice and theory as part of choreography courses offered at some universities. These educational institutes differ in terms of how they divide up the individual elements that comprise the subject of choreography, sometimes considerably, and they differ as to where the focus will lie in their particular course.

This is a book for dancers, choreographers, directors, performers and teachers. It offers comprehensive insight into a variety of approaches that can be applied in the development of contemporary choreography, providing choreographic tools with which dance pieces can be adapted and analysed. It is, so to speak, an overview of the methods you can use to transform an idea into its realisation, the stageproduction.

Further, I will address the process of structuring a dance piece and the theme-related development of movements, as well as elementary components of dance pieces such as composition, movement qualities and spatial laws. Some of the individual chapters, such as those discussing set design, film and lighting go beyond the subject of choreography, examining these fields of expertise so close and important to the staging of dance.

If you are not a dancer, reading this book will give you an insight into the choreographic process and thus offer you the opportunity of developing a closer understanding of the world of dance.

Each chapter contains field-tested exercises that are useful for dancers as well as actors or other performative artists whose main focus isn't dance.

Becoming a choreographer

From dancer to choreographer

Most dancers who have been dancing all their lives, always focused on their own bodies, will at some point begin to choreograph. The step from dancing to choreographing presents a radical change in a dancer's working methods. Whereas before they were busy checking their shoulder placement, their turnout and their pointe, now as choreographers they are confronted with things outside of the body. From one day to the next, they have to shift their attention from their internal space to what is around them. They have to see things from different points of view, develop a vision, research a theme, and withstand the pressures of production.

The change of focus from inside to outside alone requires an immense amount of strength. As a choreographer, you are the decision-making authority in the piece. As a dancer, you are told what is right and what is wrong. Jumping in at the deep end as a young choreographer, it usually doesn't take long until you find yourself overwhelmed, and even if you are outrageously talented, you may find that no-one is born a master choreographer.

Career changers

In the experimental theatre scene (whose techniques often also inspire the more established theatres), you will find directors who do not have the slightest idea of the nature of dance, let alone about how to harness the potential of dancers in the staging of a multidisciplinary performance.

They will have an idea, a mental image of their dance scene; what they lack, however, is a methodical approach towards developing that scene. Visualising a scene takes place in the mind's eye, it is made up of intertwining emotions and abstract sensations that are hard to unravel, and has nothing to do whatsoever with real people treading the real boards in a real theatre.

It doesn't matter how well you describe your vision to your dancers - they will never see what you see. They will always see their own mental images. Flesh out your ideas as you may, what your listeners visualise will always be something different; it is always their own image. Rehearsals are usually swarming with different mental images, and there is an infinite number of ways how to translate an idea into a scene – every dance troupe has to approach this in their own way.

Some of these approaches I will describe in this book. They serve as building blocks for making and developing choreographies. The building blocks will change as your work progresses, and you will add others into the mix. You will have to find your own way of combining the blocks in order to develop your own dance language.

To what degree can I learn to be a choreographer?

Inevitably, a large part of the art of making choreography defies definition - which is why there are so few books on the subject, despite the numbers of technical approaches having grown substantially in the last decades of the 20th century. The spectrum of available choreographic techniques expanded enormously as modern dance forms emerged, Eastern energy work was integrated and an increased understanding about theatre and performance was drawn from experimental theatrical forms. This not only changed and improved our understanding of dance and choreography, but also raised the number of techniques for analysing and staging dance.

Exactly which technique you choose is not important, since they all obey the same laws on the level of design. The same design impetus can be fed into any number of different techniques. To what degree you will learn the craft of choreography will depend on your willingness to work and how much you enjoy performing, on how you respond to the stimuli that you find in this book and in the wider world of dance, how you develop them, in analysis and experiment, and how you use them to create your own truth. The HOW is the thing - how you unfold your technical spectrum as a designer, how you observe it through a dramaturgical lens.

Dance begins where words fail. Dance is experienced through your senses, and they just are not verbal. That is one of the challenges of choreography: a balancing act between intuition and intellect. It means to work with something intangible, non-verbal, ephemeral, which, nonetheless, wants to be, and can be, studied intellectually. Intellectual analysis takes place on many levels. All of its integral components inform one another, so that they cannot be singled out, and must be seen in context with one another.

However valuable such analysis may be academically, it excludes the non-verbal and is thus only half of the story. Without the other half, it will never really make sense. Often, choreographers get obsessed with one of these halves. Many educational concepts are similarly one-sided. What would be desirable are educational approaches which successfully integrate both aspects. Dance is non-verbal, but it does need to be broken down intellectually during the choreographic process without losing its intuitive source.

As choreographers, we need to develop a creative mind-set which
allows us to interpose technical analysis into the impenetrable magic of dance without
losing touch with the intuitive.

There are tools which can combined with each other in the process of choreography.
These tools or aids take the form of practical techniques.

For your work to be a success, what will be decisive is how you are able to
adjust techniques to suit the given situation, and according to which criteria you select
them.

A choreographic technique is composed of four building blocks:

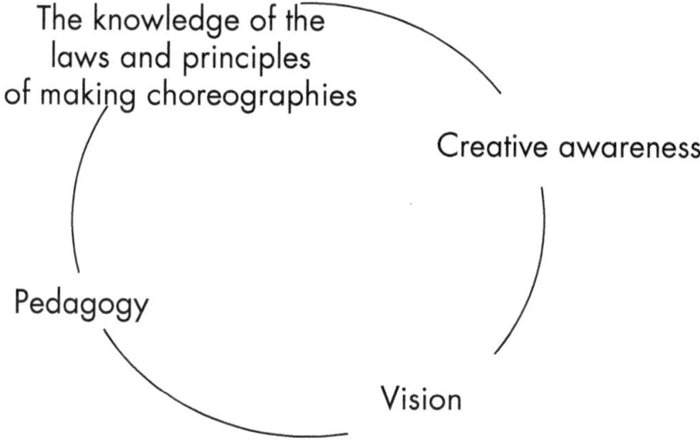

These umbrella terms are discussed in chapters, which are structured according to specific themes.

Chapters

Chapter 1   Sub-text and spirit
Chapter 2   Subject matter – structure – dramatic theory
Chapter 3   Design principles
Chapter 4   Thematic development
Chapter 5   Arrangement and composition
Chapter 6   Solo
Chapter 7   Educational aspects
Chapter 8   Drama, language and dance
Chapter 9   Dance and film
Chapter 10   Set design
Chapter 11   Lighting
Chapter 12   Studies and exercises

In order to grasp the connections between the building blocks of choreography, I recommend that you first read through all of the chapters so that you can link them intuitively.

The second step is to try out the studies and exercises. Let yourself be inspired rather than guided by the suggestions.

Develop your own research.

Don't work in a chronological fashion; let yourself be guided by your own interests.

May this book inspire you! May your dance enrich the world!

Sub-text and spirit

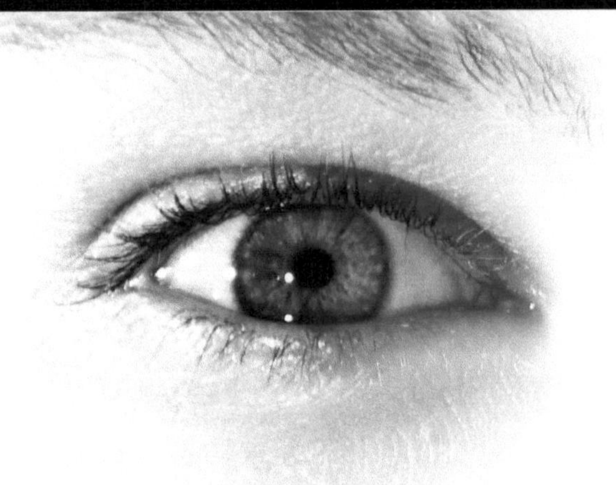

When we watch a dance piece, we see more than just human bodies. We perceive energy, spirit, soul in a dance performance – or the lack thereof. It is, therefore, worth asking how we, the choreographers, can fill a mere set of steps with a deeper meaning, a subtext that touches the audience. Without this subtext, the performance will seem disappointingly empty, no matter how sophisticated the choreography or how excellent the dancers. Spectators will walk out feeling unsatisfied, but unable to put their finger on what they were lacking, and the critics' reviews will be along the lines of 'Pretty, but predictable'.

It takes more than dance steps to provoke an emotional response in an audience. It takes more than dancers who play their part in the piece. What makes dance come alive is when we witness dancers feeling their movement. In a group piece, we will notice how each dancer experiences their steps differently, sometimes opposing another dancer's feeling, sometimes harmonising with it. Many choreographers expect their dancers to innately know the secret behind the dance steps and be able to share it with the audience through their 'expression'. Unfortunately, this hardly ever works. The dancers don't know what kind of expression is expected of them. I recently overheard two dancers talking about how they often didn't know what they were supposed to represent, and how difficult it was to dance expressively when they didn't really know what the dance was about. They worried about making mistakes, and they solved this problem by holding back their own emotion and just moving with 'general expression'. Is this what a choreographer really wants? 'General expression'? If that is not what you want, you will need to inspire your dancers. Let them feel. Encourage them to nurture and show emotion in their dance.

Drawing on internal resources

For many people, art is the expression of an inner conflict or tension. They draw from this tension when creating their art. Imagine, for instance, a man moving from Greenland to New York. He cannot get used to the confined spaces. Before his mind's eye, the houses are constantly overlaid by visions of wide-open spaces. His sense of constriction and his longing for open space create tension within him. From this tension emerges the desire to produce a dance piece expressing these thoughts, and to share his experience with other people living in New York.

If you want to use material from an internal conflict in a dance piece, you need to find a connection, an open channel between your inner reality and the outside world. Merely seeing images of wide, open spaces between skyscrapers doesn't make our Greenlander's experience a piece of art. He needs to be able to translate his sentiment into movement, and then check whether his translation truly expresses his experience. So our channel has to work in both directions – inside to outside, and outside to inside. Developing and refining this channel is key to any artistic work, because it is only with open, fine-tuned channels that we can connect to both our inner selves and the outside world, feel how we react to the world, and feel how it prompts us to create dance pieces.

Naturally, going through everyday life with our channel wide open also makes us vulnerable – without walls around our soul, unprotected, out in the open. You will feel when you are open, allowing the world inside, and when you are keeping it out. When you completely shut out all external impulses, you may notice that you keep choosing the same topics for your pieces, or you may feel as if you were running out of ideas altogether. In the end, it is our choice: either we can be satisfied living between constant repetition and total lack of material, or we decide to work on the connection between ourselves and the world, inside and outside.

Choreographers are always training their dancers. On one hand because better dancers means better dance pieces, and on the other because choreographers improve their own practice while training their dancers. So if you work with your dancers on developing their internal resources, you will benefit from it as well.

If you use one of the following approaches to your material, your dancers will
need to be familiar with the theme you want to develop:

Guided composition	The dancers improvise and react to directions from outside.
Visualisation	Basing movement on imagery.
Identification	Moving according to a previously outlined character sketch.
Emotion	Developing movements from a set emotion.

Intention

Whether you are putting together a show dance repertoire or developing artis-
tically authentic material as an expression of your innermost self, each movement, each set and each piece has an intention and an associated stylistic
form.

Connection between
intention as a whole and movement

∨

Overriding form

∨

Intention for the set

∨

Movement intention

Whenever you watch dance rehearsals or pieces at the theatre, ask yourself:

- Can you feel an intention in the dance sequences (even if you can't express it verbally)?

- In group pieces, do the intentions of the individual dancers complement or contrast each other when the dramatic arc requires it?

- Is there an overall intention and an associated stylistic form?

- Do you perceive a scenic intention?

- How do the dancers' movements show intention?

- What precisely expresses intention?

- Is there anything that seems replaceable?

Because it is difficult to express the intention for the dance in words, it is all the more important to keep in dialogue with the dancers. Convey to them WHAT IT IS. What is the piece about? What are we doing? If we can't answer these questions, if we don't feel where we are going before we start, we won't get anywhere.

The power of the choreographer's initial impetus to stage a piece often dwindles once the rehearsals become more and more complex. But growth ends when the roots are cut, and your intention is the root of your piece. Keep reminding yourself what your intention is. Your intention gives you and your dancers a point of reference. It tells you where you are going and what you are looking for, and if you succeed in sharing this with your troupe, it will give them a sense of direction and of meaning.

If you take commissions for choreographies on a certain theme, you will have to delve deep into the material until you discover something you can identify with, a personal intention in the given theme. You need to whet your appetite for creating a piece for and the only way to do this is to find the the point where your personality and the material meet. If you are asked to choreograph a dance for a play, it can be a challenge to meet the director's vision as well as identifying with the material.

Experiment with the following extremes to get a feeling for the connection between form and intention:

Intention

The dancers adhere to the intention.

At what point in the piece (which scene) do you deviate from the form?

How does the sequence change if the dancers still adhere to the intention?

Which parts of the movement material drop out if the dancers remain true to the intention?

Form

The dancers adhere to the form.

Where do movement and intention connect?

Which movements carry the intention?

What seems to be exchangeable?

When does the style of your choreography express your desired overall intention?

At which points does it depart from it?

2 Theme – Structure – Dramaturgy

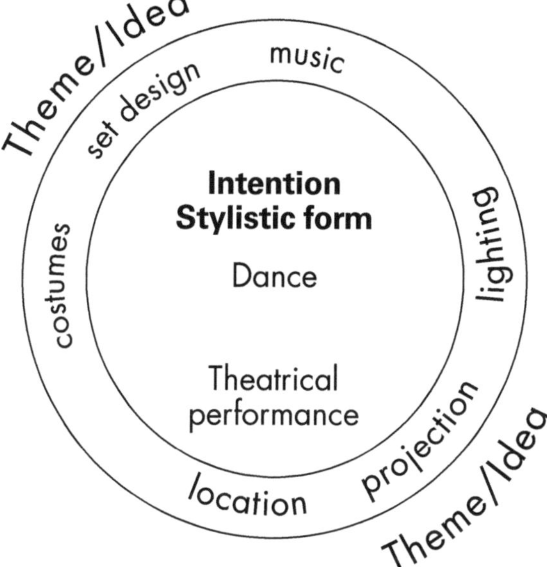

Even before a piece is created and staged, its energy is already there. It translates into the choreographer's impetus, seeking its expression. The form of the energetic expression is made up of different elements gathered around a central theme or idea.

You can choose any theme or idea: movement for movement's sake, the occupation of the Central African states, simple dancing to music, or experimentation, but you must have one, otherwise you have nothing to develop. Everything you bring together to create your performance, the dancers, the lighting, all the elements that are external to the choreographer, none of it exists unless you can develop an intention from an impetus.

Theme and material

In principle, you can create a good piece from any topic. It is what you make of your theme that counts, much more than the actual theme itself. However, if your subject matter is shallow in terms of content, it will take more blood, sweat and tears to turn it into a good piece than it otherwise would. Sometimes, a really promising theme turns out to be nothing but a bauble once you've started to work on it; sometimes, an idea that seemed nothing more than a trifle develops into an excellent theme that may stay with you for a long time. If you come across a topic and you can immediately specify how you are going to create a piece from it, it may well turn out that you have narrowed down the theme too early. Give your material time to develop. Don't feel guilty about putting it out of your mind or putting it aside. If it means something to you, it will return later on, pulling your sleeve and asking for attention.

If an idea seems promising because it illustrates the zeitgeist, but just does not evoke any images in you to translate into dance, decide whether this idea really has enough choreographic potential. If the idea doesn't speak to you, simply 'making a dance to this theme' will make it appear weaker and more superficial instead of revealing all its dimensions and deeper meaning.

When you are looking for themes, go for visual ones and those that awaken in you the feeling that you need to resolve them via the medium of dance. Notice how you react to each theme in terms of the images and thoughts that come to you. If you feel drawn to a story, consider the mythological aspects of the story – or whether it has an archaic component to it, a deep, non-verbal theme that speaks to you. In short, find something in it that you can only express through dance. Avoid using dance just to illustrate a story or plot.

The advantage of a story that can be told theatrically is that the audience will identify with the characters and get drawn into the story. As the narrative unfolds, the audience will forget the boundaries between reality and fiction. They will follow the characters through situations where they must rise above themselves. On their journey through the narrative, the protagonists often resolve a deep, unconscious conflict within themselves. They go through a kind of metamorphosis as they brave obstacles and tests, and their personality evolves into something larger or more resolved than it was at the start of the story.

Since narrative plots usually rely on verbal forms of expression, they don't easily translate into dance. It is difficult to create characters with whom the audience can identify just by means of dance. It is not in the nature of dance to serve as a mouthpiece for narratives that rely on plot and identification with characters. Dance is more about transforming a story and taking it to a higher level, closer to the emotional and spiritual than to the world of rational thought. Keep this in mind when you examine your idea. If you find that all you want to do is tell a story, consider whether it wouldn't be more efficient or appropriate to work with actors.

Using dance as a medium to develop a plot line is very difficult, and will hardly go beyond tedious pantomime. As the nature of dance is much closer to the allegorical than the narrative, it is best at revealing symbolic or allegorical aspects of a character or plot. Take care not to confuse plot and intention, however, as intentions can have narrative qualities. An example: A wants to approach B, but B cannot stand being close to A. The conflict is between the two characters, and it could be set up as a dramatic sequence, but it is not a plot yet, and certainly a long way from *Romeo and Juliet.*

Now, you might want to argue that you have seen profoundly touching dance interpretations of stories such as *Romeo and Juliet.* Ask yourself, however, whether it was really the story that touched you, or that the dance expressed something deeper that went beyond the mere narrative. Didn't the piece emphasise other aspects of the story than the plot?

This is basically what every novel that genuinely touches you does - it goes beyond the plot and opens the door to a deeper level of understanding or feeling. In literature, this is done via literary devices, and although we may think what touches us is the plot, it is them that add dimension and intensity to the story. If we just 'dance the story' without looking for a movement equivalent of the literary devices, we lose that extra depth.

If you want to create a piece from a story, make sure you not only understand it at plot level, but also be aware of its mythological level, the 'big stories' behind all fiction that give it more meaning and depth. Some authors deliberately base their stories on mythology, such as the *Cinderella* theme in *Pretty Woman,* or the triumph of the weak over the strong in *Rocky,* or love defying death.

In many stories, however, the mythological level manifests rather in a vague feeling of an extra dimension behind the story than a clearly identifiable myth. Take, for example, Heinz Strunk's *Fleisch ist mein Gemüse,* a novel about a musician who struggles to find his place in life, but finally finds a woman to love. Many readers will read the story with a sense of foreboding that all that awaits the characters is emptiness, that there is nothing to which they can look forward. Emptiness seems to lurk behind the protagonists and pervade the setting, tapping into the readers' own fear of the great void beyond earthly life. This is a theme with a mythological dimension, one that could well prove a fruitful source of inspiration for choreographic work. For other readers, the same story is much more about hope, the knowledge that even those who are struggling with relationships will finally meet the love of their life. There is mythological material in this theme that calls for expression beyond words, speaking to and about all the people living in loneliness and isolation who no longer dare to dream for themselves and yet, on a barely conscious, deep level, still cherish the hope that fate may have something wonderful in store for them.

Questions to ask of your theme:

- Is it possible to capture one essential aspect of the theme specifically through dance?

- What do you associate with the theme that is difficult to verbalise, but sparks dance imagery in you?

- Are there different ways of approaching the theme?

- Are there any sub-themes within the theme?

- What does the theme have to do with you? Does it provoke different emotions within you?

- Have you given the theme enough time to develop?

- What do you personally want to achieve with this piece?

The structure of a dance piece

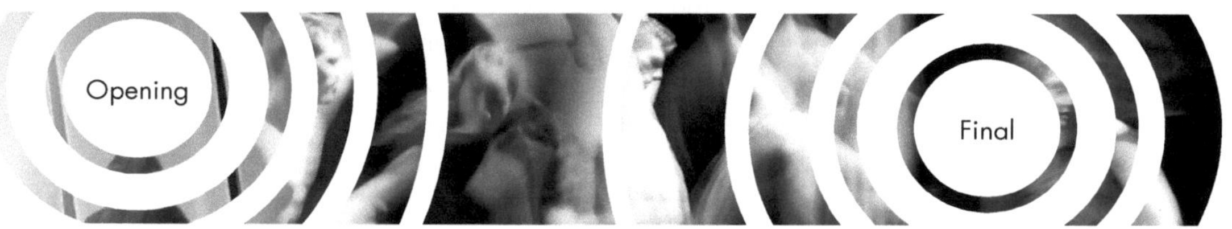

The structure of a piece extends from its opening right through to the finale.

Imagine that you are sitting inside a bubble of acrylic glass that is flying through a landscape. The bubble ducks and dives through a narrow thicket, branches whipping its sides, then plunges into a strange, sinister mass that silently oozes past. Your vehicle picks up speed, the mass through which you were struggling disappears, and you are shooting through wide open space towards to a funnel. Inside, you come upon a road and start to travel down it. But the bubble starts to skid, hurtling along out of control, until it bursts, and you land on soft, pillow-like ground.

The spectator is the traveller in the bubble; the piece you are choreographing is the landscape, and it is up to you how long the action stays in which part of your landscape. If you look at the whole journey, it is the shifting between environments that makes up the structure of the piece. If, several minutes into the piece, the audience get the impression that they are on an never-ending road, stretching into the distance, they will lose interest in that road, because they don't have to engage with what you are doing. They can engage if you structured the landscape accordingly so that they are caught up, effortlessly, in what is happening. To achieve this, you need to develop a sense for when your bubble has spent long enough in each respective environment, and what kind of environment you next need to plunge into. You design the landscape within your theme according to the journey you want to undertake with your audience, and you choose when to stop and where.

Example

If you want to stage a piece about war, this does not mean that you have to have 15 dancers running about and fighting like madmen. You could show a child walking along a road, or a lone figure sitting motionless. Perhaps you do want to go for the option with the 15 dancers. But will it capture your audience? The different faces of war are different parts of your landscape, and it is up to you to arrange them in a way that keeps your audience interested.

Subtext – Theme

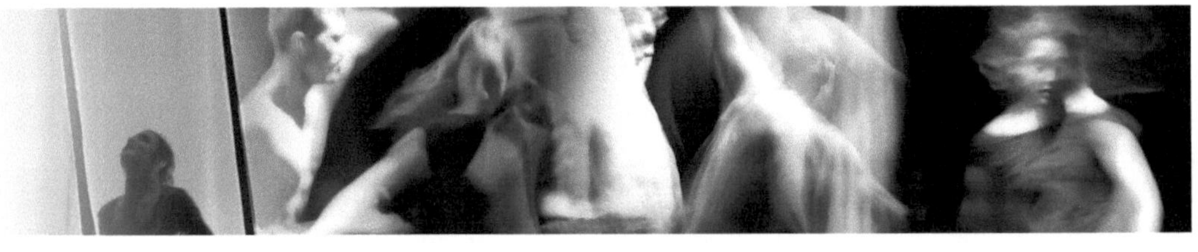

in relation to

the emotional journey
and the dramatic arc

The emotional intensity of a dance piece and its development over time

Do not insist on what you want to see on stage when you are working on a scene. Instead, focus on how you feel when you watch it for the first time in context, without any additional explanation. If it doesn't have the effect you are looking for, change the structure. The same scene might work really well somewhere else in the piece. If you are bound to a particular sequence of scenes, then you will have to consider altering the scene altogether.

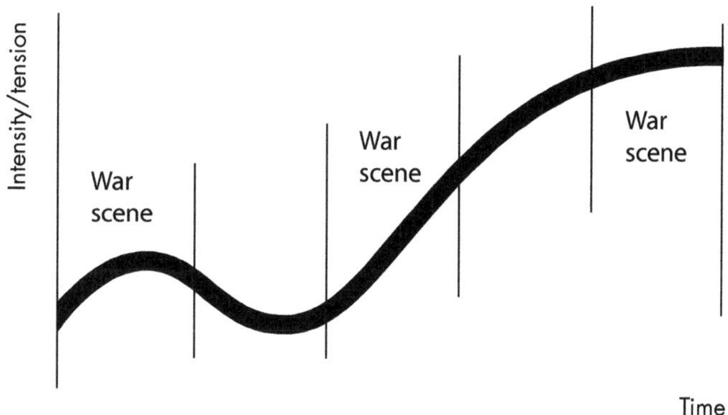

Referencing the same subject matter in several scenes will require you to find different ways of expressing it during the dance piece.

Embedding your content differently into the structure does not mean you are being overly accommodating to your audience; it means that you are engaging it. That is an important difference. Have you ever watched a film that was so scary or suspenseful that you wanted to look away, but found couldn't? Your eyes were glued to the screen, even though the content made you feel very uncomfortable? If you are sucked up into the slipstream regardless of content, be it pleasant or jarring, that means the structure of the piece flows, proof of the artist's attentiveness to detail and craftsmanship. If a piece is badly structured, it will work against any quality you want to achieve, because you lose the audience's attention. If you are afraid of being too accommodating to your audience, do not try to be jarring by employing a clumsy structure. Unleash all the emotional power of your dance vocabulary and its narrative possibilities by creating a structure that supports rather than hinders it.

Introduction

The audience want you to grab their attention. They arrive at the theatre with the whole world on their shoulders, and it takes a little time before they can prise themselves away from their thoughts and concentrate on your dance piece.
So, the first thing we need to consider is the introduction:

- How do you introduce the piece?

- How much time does the introduction need?

- 15 seconds? Ten minutes?

- Do you introduce the characters individually or in groups?

- How long should the introductory phase be?

- Are you making a statement, are you postulating a thesis?

- How will you bring your theme to the audience's attention?

Middle section

The introduction is followed by the middle section which usually progresses through a sequence of of different parts that complement and contrast each other. This is where the piece gathers momentum and reveals its core, so be careful to avoid overly predictable dynamics. In other words, don't fall into clichéd patterns.

Questions to ask about the middle section of the piece:

- How many elements make up the middle section?

- Do these elements have a common denominator on a deeper level?

- In terms of their dynamics, how do the elements contrast with each other?

- Does the middle section go through some kind of progression?

- Does it build towards a finale?

Finale

The finale needs careful planning, since it sets the mood in which your audience will leave the theatre. Make your conclusion clear and unambiguous. It strains the audience's nerves to be tricked into thinking they are seeing the finale, ready to applaud, and to then have to sit through yet another and another scene.

Questions to ask yourself about the finale:

- Do you want an open ending, a soft fading out, creating the illusion that the piece never really ends, or do you want a clear stop?
- Does the piece end with the climax?
- Can you identify aspects of the finale that set it apart from the rest of the piece?
- How do you want to leave your audience - having reached a conclusion, looking to the future, or feeling euphoric?

Structural considerations

Introduction	Middle section	Finale
Getting the audience's attention	Investigation of the theme	Resolution
Lead-in to the theme	Momentum	Outlook
Stating a thesis	Counterpoints	Conclusion
Introduction of the characters	Development	Escalation
Setting the scene	Stylistic focus	Apotheosis

Structuring a dance piece

Naturally, it is difficult to work on one particular section of your dance piece and keep an overview of the entire structure at the same time. You could compare it to walking through a forest – when you are in it, it is really hard to tell where exactly you are in relation to the forest as a whole. But it would be much easier if you first sketched a map of the entire forest from a bird's eye perspective. Now, while a forest is a physical thing you can see and divide into individual parts, a dance piece is an entirely different matter. The problem is that, at the start, it is not there yet, and so it is not at all clear how it should be divided or structured. A very experienced teacher of improvisation once said to me, 'I get on very well if I prepare in great detail beforehand, and then don't stick to it.' Were he not to prepare in advance, he would have no framework for his work. He knows he has something that he can fall back on, and that gives him freedom. He has a map of the terrain in the back of his head, which permits him to move unrestrictedly without losing his way. Structure is that map at the back of the choreographer's mind.

Don't imagine the structure of your dance piece as a finished, rigid thing. Rather, think of it as provisional, mutable, flexible, otherwise it will rob you of all the creative opportunities that may present themselves along the way. In the end, it doesn't matter exactly how you manage your framework, as long as it works for you. You may choose to plan ahead every detail in advance, or to arrange the final sequence of your scenes the day before the opening night. What matters is that there is a solid framework at the core of the piece, because structure is key to whether your audience takes an interest in your work or not. If your piece is well-structured, you will capture your viewers' attention, even if they are not particularly interested in the actual theme of you piece.

Two types of structure

Structuring in advance	Structuring as you go
The choreographer prepares a full structure for the entire piece and spends rehearsals developing the scenes.	The choreographer develops material for each scene during rehearsals based on his theme and its associations, and then structures the scenes to form the piece.

Structuring in advance

There is always some kind of material available to the choreographer before
rehearsals start. Sometimes it is a piece of music, sometimes a literary reference or a theme. It may be a series of movements or an aesthetic concept
or simply individual images in his mind's eye. The question is to what degree
you want to structure your material around a framework at this early stage. A
framework has the advantage that it gives you a sense of direction in your own
piece, which makes it easier to define goals connected to the dramatic arc of
your piece, its form or aesthetics. You will see the dynamics of the dance and
the scenes in front your mind's eye, and then on paper, and you will be able
to feel the necessary intensity of individual sequences or scenes in advance.
Structuring your dance piece prior to starting rehearsals allows for a dialogue
between the choreography and the subject matter. Also, having an idea of the
necessary intensity of each scene will help you work out a suitable approach
to developing scenes.

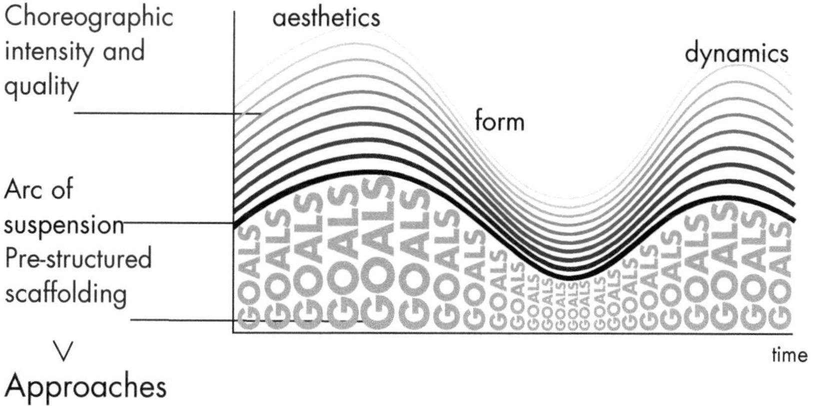

Creative goals in the dramatic arc suggest the choreographic
approach required.

Structuring as you go

Many choreographers and companies refuse to be restricted by structure, choosing a purely associative approach to create scenes, dances, pas de deux, films and music to go with their theme. If you work within a pre-defined structure, you will find it harder to access things that fall outside of its confines. You may have richer material resources and a broader range of scenes available to you if you choose to forgo a structural framework and allow yourself to be inspired by the theme in an completely open way. The material you develop from theses inspirations can then be structured and linked together in a dramatic arc.

It does not matter which of the two structuring types you choose – what is important is to be aware of which approach you are working with. Be clear about whether you are freely developing material in the moment, irrespective of any dramatic arc, or whether you need to develop a form, dynamic or aesthetic of the piece to fit into a certain place in your dramatic arc. Being fully conscious of the working method you choose gives you a better hold on your piece and leads more quickly to satisfying results.

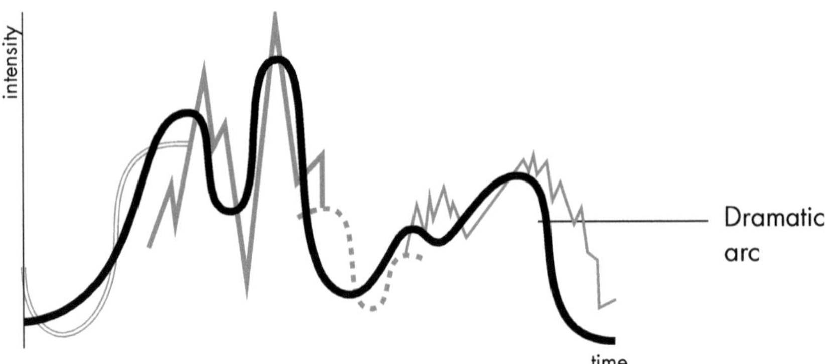

If you choose to structure your dance piece as you go, you will need to fit scenes and fragments within your dramatic arc.

The dramatic arc

Every piece, even if it is only a minute long, has a dramatic arc. During the dance, the audience's level of attention will change, depending on the individual sections of the piece and their dramatic arrangement.

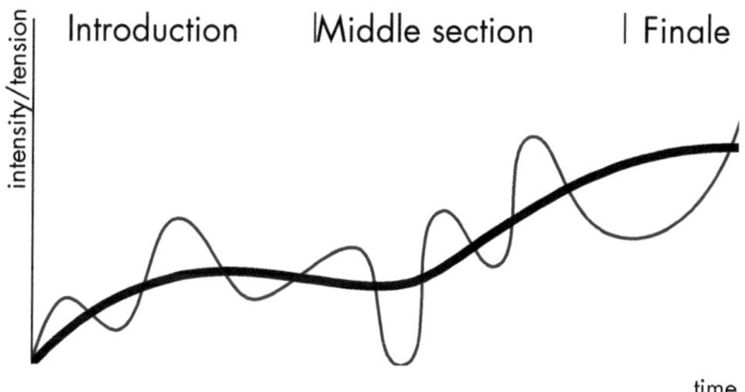

The effect of the sequencing of the scenes produces the piece's dramatic arc (thick line).

Now, remember that whatever the audience sees just before and after any given moment within a dance piece as important as the moment itself, it is essential that a choreographer develops a sense of the whole. In order to consider one moment in relationship to the whole piece and to be able to properly visualise the dramaturgic dynamics of a piece, many choreographers and directors will sketch the dramatic arc out on paper, referring back to the drawing when they are working on a particular scene. The dramatic arc is always part of a stage performance, even if you don't pay any attention to it. Over the course of the show, the audience will experience moments of tension and relaxation. These moments that build or ease intensity can be visualised in the shape of a curve.

Experiencing time within a dramatic composition

Time is always relative. Measuring it means to abstract it from our experience. What we experience and label as 'real time' is purely subjective. Our emotional state determines how quickly time runs for us - a day can feel like a year, and an hour may pass in the blink of an eye.

In a dance piece, I create time. Since there is no such thing as objective time,

I have to create the sense of time within the piece. Depending on the nature of the dance, the sense of time may be brief or it may be drawn out. One of the most difficult things is to 'expand' time without the dance becoming tedious. When you stretch time, it means that the great contrasts in spatial terms and the choreographic dynamics of the piece take a different form to that which they would in a dance with faster choreography. Fewer audience members will switch off during a fast piece than during a slow piece. Speed means they get caught up in the performance far more readily than they do when experiencing the apparent slowing down of time.

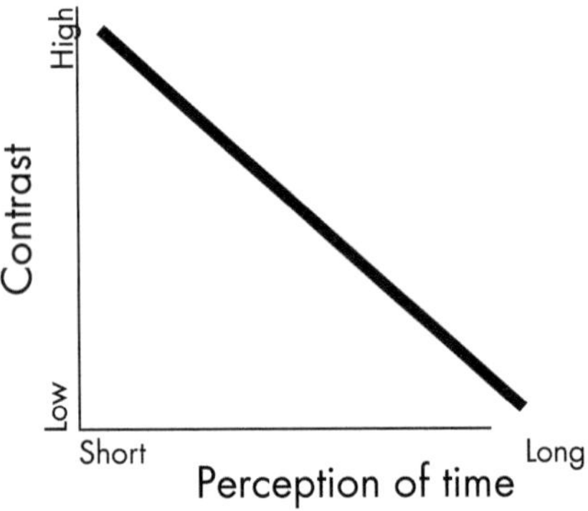

Link between contrasts and a subjective sense of time

Slowing down means that your audience has to be ready to stay with the dance through a moment that lacks stimulus or impulse. So before you start stretching time, consider in detail whether your piece is at a stage where it can take the audience with it into a decelerated passage of time. You will need to prepare the spectators by creating conditions in the preceding scenes that make them long for emptiness or calm.

Another way of stretching time is to slow down the piece so gradually that the spectators at first don't realise what is happening. Whatever option you choose to introduce slowness into your piece, bear in mind that you risk losing your audience if you keep it up for too long, because it is much easier to pay attention to dynamic action than to monotonous movement. It takes a lot of courage for a choreographer to create a dance piece that moves within slowness and silence, and it takes great skill to make such a piece anything less than excruciatingly boring for the audience. As choreographers, we may take great pleasure in seeking meaning in slowness, a depth that we miss in dynamic movement. We must, however, remember to take our audience with us on our journey. How can we delve deep without losing their attention?

Since people's attention tends towards the dynamic, you will need to teach your audience how to approach an increasing extension of time in the piece. If your piece works well, spectators will not feel the time passing, but will be present in each single moment of the piece. They will notice every change, no matter how big or small. As long as they perceive the constant changing of the dance, they will have a sense of progression that they can follow. Only if they start to feel that nothing is happening they will lose concentration. So what you need to ask yourself is whether the changes in your piece are visible and perceptible to your audience, or whether you see the changes because you choreographed the piece and know what you are looking for. You can stretch time as far as you like, but the development of the piece has to be evident to your audience.

Example 1

The ensemble on stage move very slowly or stand completely still. At random intervals, a jolt passes through the bodies of some dancers, like an existential shock. With each repetition, different dancers are affected. This setting creates tension because the jolts come arhythmically, randomly, and because we can't predict which dancers will be struck next. The dancers accept their fate, but their internal focus is on the question 'Who will be next?' (if the dancers don't feel the existential dread in this question, the audience will not perceive the jolts as existential either). If the dancers succeed in making the shocks feel significant to the spectators, the pauses between the shocks can be quite long. This is a way of extending time without losing the dramatic arc.

Example 2

If your piece features actors who just sit there reciting their lines, and dancers who stand still for long periods of time and then take up a new position just as significant as the last, then at some point your audience will lose interest. They will come to the conclusion that nothing is happening on stage that demands their attention. This is a dramaturgical catastrophe, and sadly not as rarely seen as you may think. It may have to do with a choreographer's desire to work against the tide, to do something fresh and different.

However, dynamic dramaturgy is not just a trend. It is in our very nature to react to dynamic processes. This is not some new-fangled myth, it has to do with the laws of perception. If you want to work against these natural laws, you have to be very certain about what you are doing and how you are doing it. You will also need a lot of stamina to find and test new principles of how to expand time without losing the dramaturgy.

Expansion of time works well as a means of manipulating the sequencing of movements. Watch a choreography and try to find moments when you could expand time. You may draw out only one movement or expand time over the whole piece. As a choreographer, you are in the fantastic position of being able to direct your audience's perception of time. Every audience member will perceive an hour at the theatre slightly differently, but there will something in your piece that will make it interesting regardless of whether that hour feels shorter or longer.

The principle that changes are only effective if they are visible to the audience not only applies to the stretching of time, but also to the tempo of a piece in general. Watching a continuous whirlwind of dance on stage will overwhelm me, and I won't be able to perceive individual movements and be touched by their meaning. Because the details are lost in the tumult, the piece will appear almost static, and just as boring as if nothing were happening at all. It is as if you were running through a field of corn - you will perceive the first leaf that touches your hand, but if hundreds of leaves are brushing against your skin at the same time, it is impossible to focus on the sensation of the touch of one single leaf.

Watch the dance swirl around the stage. At the moment you can no longer distinguish individual movements, play some really slow music. Like this, you can turn fast movement and the slow music into contrasting units. You are now creating tension through the opposition of music and dance, and not, as before, through visual changes. There is a variety of techniques to create tension, and each technique will bring out a different dramaturgic aspect of your piece. If you use none of these techniques, the only stimulus for the au-dience's sense of progression will come from the dance movements. When several stimuli overlap, time will appear to stand still.

If a visual stimulus speeds up, it will make the whole dance seem to move faster. At some point, the tempo becomes too high for our eyes to distinguish one impulse from another. Individual movements blur into one big mass of movement. The visual effect of this blurring is a sense of slowing down, even though the dancers are still moving fast. This illustrates that 'moving fast' and 'perceiving a movement as being fast' are two different things.

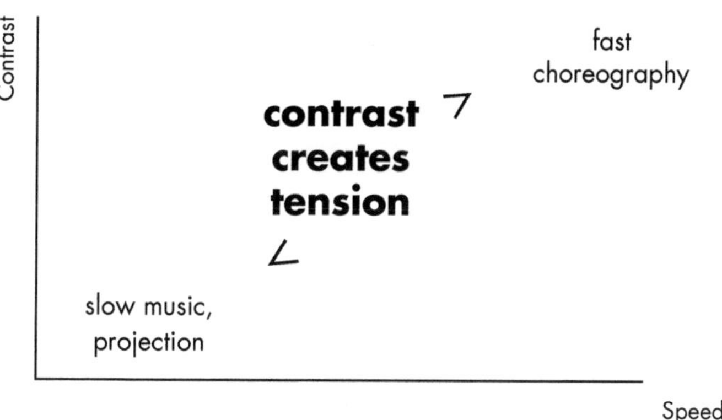

The tension between contrasting parallel media

Progression

How you fashion the dramatic arc for your show depends on how the theme is introduced within the piece. Some themes ask for a clear progression towards a finale, others will make you want to embed them in a mosaic of associative images.

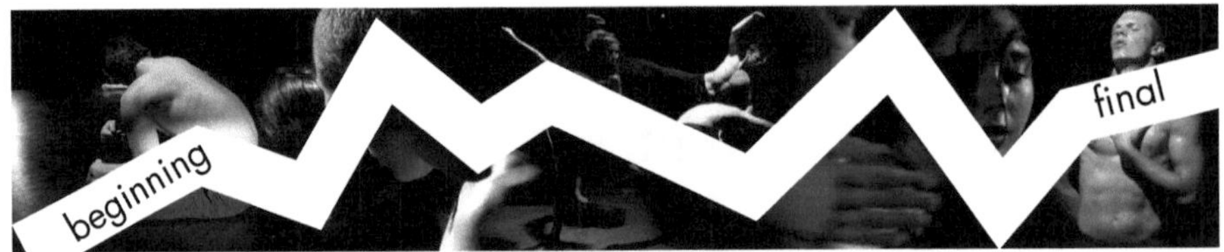

In a thematic progression, the development of the theme from scene to scene creates the arc of suspense.

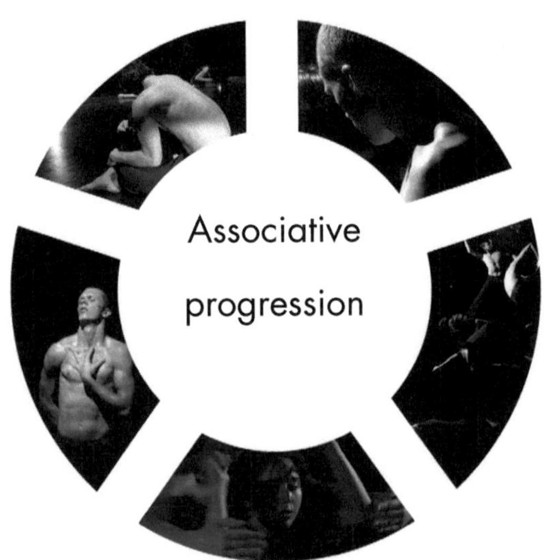

Scenes without a fixed order surrounding a theme in a so-called associative progression.

If you base your piece on source material such as images, biographies or stories, they often suggest a certain dramaturgical progression. By developing your own perspective on this progression, you create a relationship between the source material and your perspective.

The relationship with the story

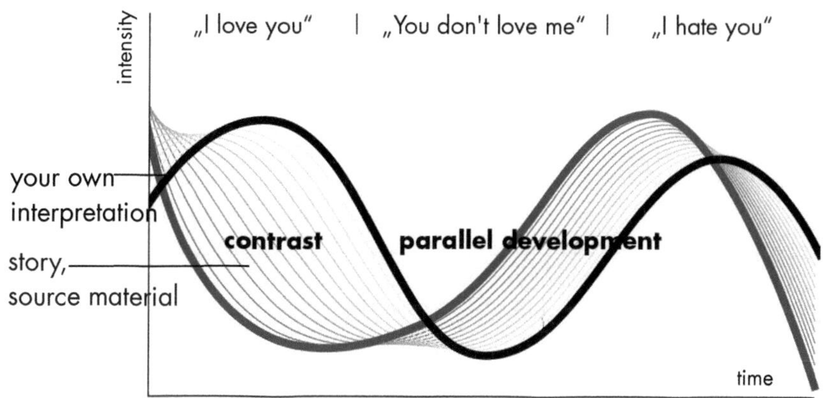

Your own interpretation may change the dramatic arc of the original plot.

Turning points

One key aspect of a narrative is how it introduces its protagonists and their circumstances. The turning points bring the narrative to a head, forcing the characters to react to their situation. The tension created by the turning points is then released in the solution, where matters are resolved for better or worse. Even if you don't tell your story chronologically, you will need to introduce your characters and their setting, and there will have to be some kind of turning point to set off a development. Likewise, in a dance that has no thematic content or storyline, there will be some kind of development – a dramatic arc with turning points that runs through the piece like a thread, shaped by the intensity of the different scenes.

Let us leave the bird's eye perspective from which we have been analysing the structure of our dance piece for a moment, and dive into movement to illustrate what I have explained above.
Every movement has a turning point. If you twist something into spiral and release it, it will untwist; extension is followed by contraction. A leap consists of a series of phases: preparation, initiation, climax, reversal, and landing. Each phase rises towards a turning point. So it is not only your scene or the sequence of scenes that follows this pattern, but even the movements themselves. The movements, the scenes, their progression, the whole piece, all

rise towards a turning point. Even if you just link a series of movements or place random scenes in a sequence, you will produce a progression which may have a condensing or relaxing effect. Also, the intensity of the effect – condensing or relaxing – will come and go in waves, just like our own emotional processes. Nobody just starts to cry out of the blue, for example. There is a build-up phase and then an outburst of tears. And once you are crying, you usually won't cry steadily for an hour. There are phases of catharsis, sobbing

So, we can say that the dramaturgy of storytelling in some sense also applies to an associative, abstract dance piece without a concrete plot:

- A turning point follows after tension has increased. Before the turning point, the audience are so involved with the fate of the protagonists that they will be touched, emotionally or intellectually, by the changes brought about by the turning point.

- Individual, self-contained scenes with their own arc of suspense may be placed alongside each other or set in contrast to one another. The audience will perceive the transitions between these scenes as turning points.

and then again new outbursts, interspersed with complete calm as the grief eases. The same is true for laughter. You may even forget what made you laugh in the first place, but your laughter will increase and decrease in a rising and falling, wave-like pattern.

Building up to a turning point

In order to create an effective turning point, the circumstances need to be sufficiently developed. Let's imagine a scene: You are painting a picture. At a certain point you become frustrated with what you have painted, so you cross it all out. For the audience, it doesn't matter what exactly you were painting. The important thing is that they can clearly distinguish the action of painting from the action of crossing out, otherwise, they will miss your point.

You cannot destroy what you have not built beforehand.

Before a scene can convey a feeling of constraint, of being trapped in a confined space, your audience first need to positively experience open space and
freedom, free from negative connotations such as fear of the unknown. To
be able to disturb the order of things, you have to create it first. This kind of
structure requires precise timing.

> For a turning point to be effective, the audience first needs to settle into
> the mood of a scene that can then be broken. Let's take a narrative ex-
> ample: A woman suffers because she suspects her husband of being
> unfaithful. She has no proof, but it becomes more and more evident over
> time. Her mental health is affected by the situation, until she finally breaks
> down and makes a huge scene. This break in the story will be effective
> because the audience is following the story, and the turning point occurs
> when they are identifying most with it. Setting the turning point too early,
> before the mood is established, will weaken its effect.
>
> A turning point will also lose its effectiveness if it is set too late in the plot.
> If the mood established within a scene is held for too long, the audience
> will lose interest and become indifferent to any turning point.

It is easy to understand the effect of an early or late turning point in a narrative
structure. The same principle applies to abstract pieces. Developing a movement idea requires the same care that a storyteller takes to weave his tale,
using introduction, identification and turning points.

Turning points create contrasts which can evoke feelings, build up or release
suspense. For effective turning points, you need to be sensitive to the timing
of the following components:

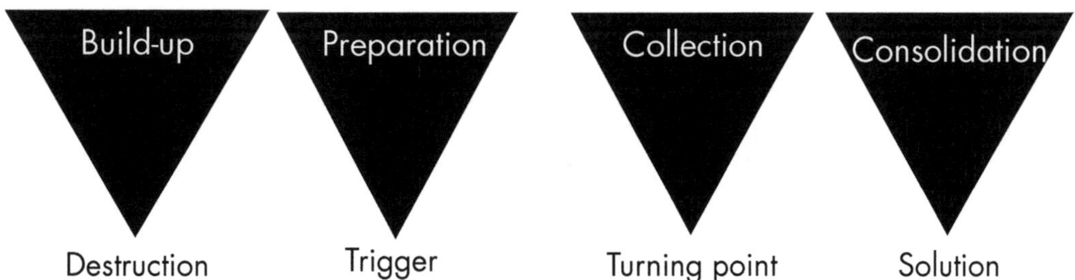

Dramatic components of the turning points

Arrangement and effectiveness of contrasts

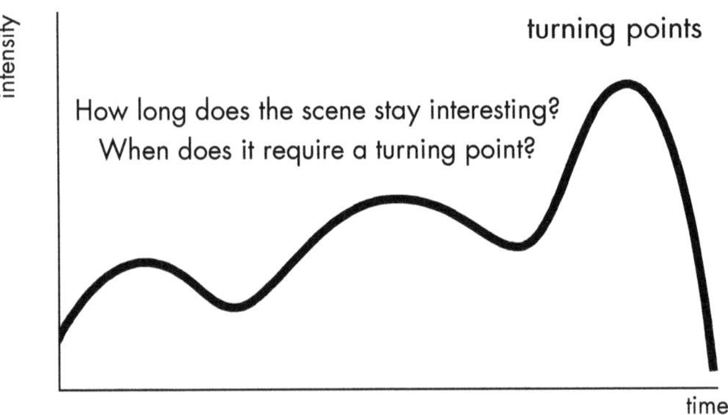

An arc of suspense including a turning point

Watching your own piece, you will feel at some point that a scene or an idea is no longer worth pursuing; but your audience's view on things will be different from yours. It is natural that you are much more interested in the subject of the piece, having chosen it yourself, and less likely to be bored than the average spectator. For this reason, it is advisable to be extra sensitive to boredom, so you feel where to build up tension or place a turning point. Simply imagine you are a spectator who is not particularly keen on the show, and take a cursory glance at it from time to time. You will soon find out whether a scene grabs your attention or not.

The triggers for turning points, however, are not determined by how much a scene captivates the audience. It is the rising intensity of a moment in the plot, the moment when nothing but a change is possible. In the example above, it is the protagonist's suffering, building up to breaking point. As choreographers, our challenging task is to tell the audience everything they need to know about the situation without wallowing in it. We can't be superficial, because we need the audience to care about the characters and the scene, otherwise they won't stay focused. At the same time, we need to be careful not to overextend the build-up to a turning point. If a situation stagnates and stops developing, the spectator's interest in the scene will stagnate as well. Once they have understood a situation, they want to know what happens next.

If I take a movement idea to the stage, I need to know when the audience has understood my idea, and how to proceed from there. Take as an example someone who wants to choreograph an opening sequence. The dancers are lying on the floor, all very relaxed. Out of this relaxation, they ease into a flow of organic movements across the floor. Because the choreographer really likes this image, he develops more material than he actually needs, and decides to extend the opening scene instead of developing it further. As a consequence, the piece becomes boring before it has really begun. The choreographer loses the audience in the first scene, and it takes quite some time before he is able to win back some of their attention. Diving into the depths of a scene, or exploring an idea, stands in opposition to the progression of the piece.

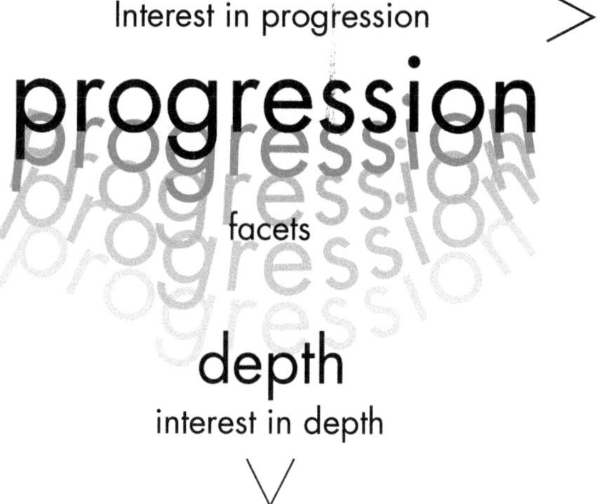

For the audience to be interested in a piece's development, you need plot progression and in-depth exploration.

On the other hand, by moving the piece onwards too fast you risk losing the audience because they are not given enough time to understand the scene. If the individual steps towards the point of climax are too big, the spectators are left behind with no chance to connect to the piece.

In order to create the necessary build-up needed before a dramatic change or fall, you must ask yourself again and again, 'Am I ready for a turning point at this stage of the composition?' Every time you watch the piece you will perceive it differently. As rehearsals progress, you know what comes next, you know the intended effects, you know the feelings you want to evoke with each image. Repeated watching may make you want to place the triggers for turning points earlier if you get impatient with your piece, or later if you find more and more depth in your scenes as your piece takes shape.

In the placement of turning points, these are the two most common mistakes:

The choreographer / director is nervous and worried about boring the audience. His scenes seem sketchy and ill-conceived. The whole piece lacks depth and contrast, and some of the scenes seem out of context.

The choreographer / director wants to give his scenes room and over-expands them. The whole piece becomes long-winded. Turning points don't read as dramatic, but instead as a welcome change, so that the audience's perception of the dramatic arc becomes distorted.
The intention behind emotional turning points becomes too evident and predictable.

It is only through practice and observation that you will be able to work out how much time you need to build up to an emotional turning point within a scene, and you are likely to be surprised over and again. The piece *Die sieben Ströme des Flusses Orta* [The seven currents of the Orta River] runs to eight hours. Seven hours into a performance, people began to cry in the stalls after a turning point. Tears then started flowing in the circle, the boxes and even up in the lighting box. People who had never cried at a film or at a book, let alone at a play, were crying in the auditorium. It was not that anything particularly exceptional had happened, but their tears had everything to do with the way the identification of the audience with the piece had been structured. For seven hours, the audience had been gripped by events on stage, and nobody was able to resist the carefully constructed climax once it came.

Regardless of how long your dance piece is, whether it lasts two minutes or seven hours, you will always have to ask yourself if a sequence can be sustained over the required length of time, or if it needs to be condensed. It may require an unexpected, sudden break in a scene to create contrast, or a consequent build on what has previously occurred.

Some tips for developing the skill to see the dramatic arc in a performance:

- – Watch the entire performance.
- – Take a moment to let the experience sink in.
- – Draw the piece's dramatic arc from memory.
- – Thinking harder about the piece, check which scenes you have left out.
- – What are likely reasons why you forgot these scenes?
- – What do your reasons have to do with the dramatic arc?
- – Where would you change, add, or leave out a turning point?
- – What would the optimal curve of the dramatic arc be?
- – Develop a dramatic arc – based on a theme or dance piece – that corresponds with your ideas, and draft some scenes that relate to your arc.

Retardation

Imagine a man standing in an enclosed courtyard. The ground first heats up and then begins to burn. The man discovers a ladder and tries to climb over the wall. The ladder catches fire, he only just escapes by tilting the ladder down into a pond which is already warming up. There is a metal ladder lying in the water. The man begins to climb again, but half-way up the rungs give way; meanwhile the fire comes ever nearer. He tries to pull himself up the uprights of the ladder, up to where the rungs are still intact, but they are slippery with algae from the pond. From now on, we could insert various other delays preventing the resolution of the story, or we could confront the audience with a new turn of fate at a later stage in the narrative. This sort of delay is known as retardation. It is used to create suspense not only in narrative contexts, but also in music. There are many examples of a postponing of the final resolution in music, for instance in the finale of the musical *Hair*. There, the plot is kept from plunging directly into the apotheosis of *Let the sun shine in* by the continuous inserting of new musical elements.

Using deceleration in a theme-based or narrative dramaturgical concept

In a narrative or theme-based dramaturgical concept, the storyline of a character or theme clearly seeks resolution. Deceleration hinders or postpones resolution, either by introducing an obstacle or a new plotline.
Examples: A woman and a man slowly move towards each other, the audience is almost longing for the moment they touch.

Possible decelerations:

> They keep missing each other, their paths never crossing, like in *The Sleeping Beauty* by Mats Eck, when the father enters at the beginning of the piece.

> A third person intervenes and separates the couple before they meet.

In an abstract dramaturgical concept

Example: A dancer moves as if bound in a straight-jacket, but then finds a way to escape. This is prevented by a particular form of music or the appearance of another figure. The music forces the dancer back into the straight-jacket.

There are numerous parameters on the level of movement with which you can influence intensity, the most significant being:

- force and release

- speed: fast – slow

- tension and ease

- on the vertical level:

- on the ground – mid-level – in the air

- spatial level: at the back – in front

- relationship to the audience

- energy and movement radius of the dancers

Parameters of intensity

In order to create suspense within your dance piece, you will at times need to increase or decrease the intensity of a scene. To be able to manipulate intensity, you have to know what parameters it comprises.

The internal tension of the scene increases or decreases, depending on how the parameters of intensity are combined.

Different forms of expression are inherent to different artistic media; and thus their qualities of intensity vary. For contemporary post-modern dance pieces, there is such a wide range of artistic devices available that choreographers often fall into the trap of using too many of them in one piece without giving enough thought to the effect the devices will have in combination with other elements.

Example
A particular scene is meant to convey a sense of ease to make it contrast with both the previous and ensuing scenes. The choreographer uses release, slowness and relaxation, with the dancers on ground level at the back of the stage. So far, so good. However, video footage with vivid colours and quick cuts accompanies the scene. The contrast this creates raises overall level of tension within the scene rises, and the desired dramatic arc suffers as a result. In other words, the lack of balance between the artistic devices destroys the desired mood of 'ease' the scene was meant to create, thus destroying the required contrast with the other scenes and throwing off the whole dramatic arc.
In productions where different artists are responsible for different elements of the show, such as projection, dance, performance, or staging, it will be necessary to find a way to balance the intensity of each separate art form. Whether you want to combine different media, such as film, sculpture, music or performance, or simply dance, music and light, it will benefit your production if you compile a score or storyboard to help you keep track of the media involved. The score can then serve as the primary basis of discussion with the other artists involved in the project. If you are in charge of all aspects of the performance, the score will help you to retain an overview and keep you aware of the dramatic arc, particularly where it is composed of a variety of media.

Example: Storyboard   Scene 1, duration 7 minutes

Text / music	Action
Noises, suspense.	The musicians and the dancers take positions in the corridors and in the auditorium. The musicians try to communicate with each other by knocking and making noises, as if they were miners trapped in a caved-in tunnel.
'My soul lives in a far-away place, trapped somewhere in this body. But my body is a labyrinth, and I have forgotten where I hid my soul. So I look for it in the labyrinths of other bodies, as if I could find it there, feeling my way through them, through you.'	The dancers / actors dance in the auditorium as if driven by demons, using all the space, tables, staircases, podests etc.; often dropping to the floor, temporarily becoming invisible to the majority of the spectators. The dancers touch the spectators as if trying to find out what their bodies are made of.
'I can only find myself by experiencing my boundaries. Am I not what I am because of them? '	6 Dancers: try to penetrate the invisible or visible walls. 1 in the lift 2 in the entrance area 3 behind the glass wall in the stairwell 4, 5, 6 in the auditorium, blindly groping for someone
The question is: what goes on what account? The drama of the others can hardly be booked at my expense.	Actor changes between the rooms Dancers gather in the middle. Confrontation. Slowly.

light	sound	stage	video projection
Flashlights from auditorium produce a restless light, supported by the flickering of the floor lights	Microphones A PA in the stairwell with 12 CH and echo.	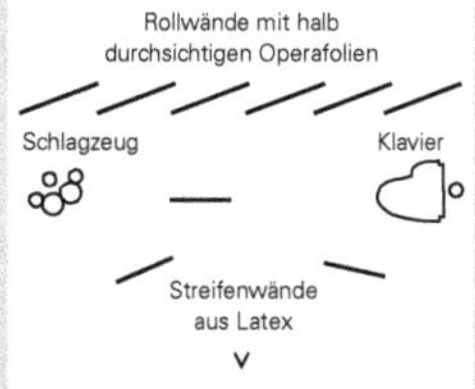	
Cold indirect light from floor spotlights creates the illusion of a floating floor.	Radio microphone 1 Cellomicro 2 Micro 3 - Unplugged		
The guide light changes from scene to scene. It jumps from position to position.	A ll PAs in use. Three sound engineers for mixing the different areas.	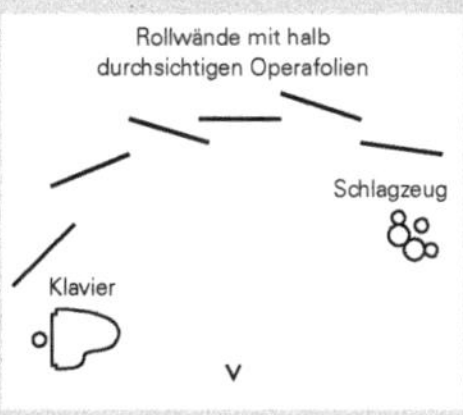	
Back light and floor spots.	As previously.		

How do the individual parameters influence the intensity of a movement?

Parameters of intensity within a movement:

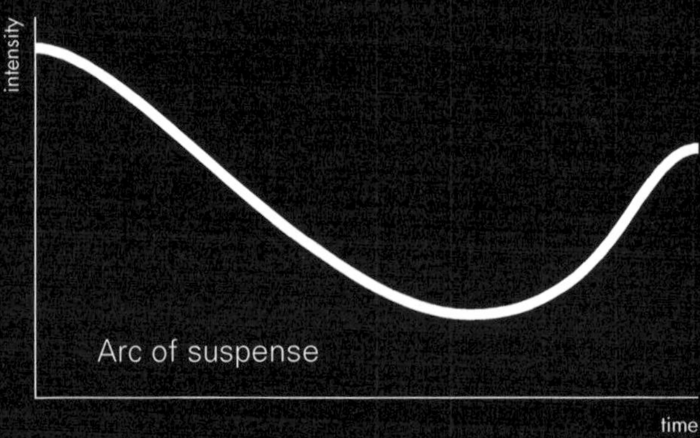

A draws an 'intensity diagram' that shows different levels of intensity on a time axis and an intensity level axis.

B translates A's diagram into movement, experimenting with parameters of movement that create tension or a sense of ease.

Which elements does B choose to increase and decrease tension?

B arranges movement sequences.

B tranfers these sequences to a group of dancers and develops the material.

What possibilities for modification emerge from the group work?

How does B's solo material need to be modified so it can be danced by a group and yet retain the same dramatic arc as the solo dance?

C, who has not seen the diagram, watches the dance and draws a diagram from what she has seen.

Amongst other things, she analyses the phrase using the following parameters:

- force and release

- speed: fast – slow

- tension and ease

- ground – mid-air – aerial

- at the back – in front

- relationship to the audience

- energy and action space of dancers

Where does C's diagram correspond with the original diagram, and which movement parameters are responsible for the correspondences?

This exercise demonstrates how the parameters can be employed to create suspense, which elements to use to increase tension, and how to build up to a climax.
Develop several phrases and experiment with integrating them into different dramaturgical structures.

Structuring source material

If you choreograph on source material, such as a piece of music, a biography, or a story, structuring the dynamic intensity of your piece is always a dialogue with the material. The material defines the dramatic arc, and you decide where you follow its dynamic and where you oppose it. The piece of music, biography or story is the measure, the constant you engage with as a choreographer (for more detail on the topic of music, see chapter *Music and Movement*).

Choreographing to a certain music or translating literary sources (or even a series of drawings) into dance means to react to an already defined structure. Because the source material has a structure with turning points and a climax, it also comes with its own dynamic intensity. Making choreography doesn't mean you just use dance to illustrate this pre-defined structure (although it is possible to do so), more than that, it means to negotiate the relationship between the choreography and the defined matrix of a story or a musical composition.

Relationship between source material and interpretation

Dialogue between choreographic intensity and a pre-defined structure from the source material

Choose a piece of music, a biography, a literary source or something else that provides you with the fixed matrix of a dramatic arc.

Draw an arc of suspense that corresponds with the changes of intensity in your source material. For example:

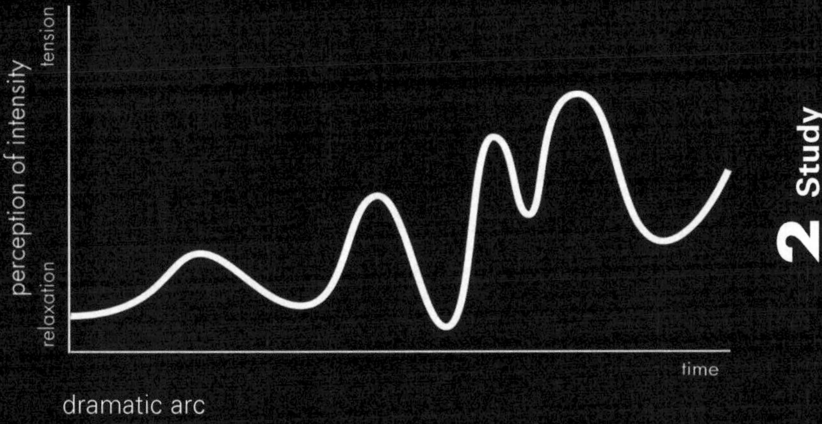

dramatic arc

Develop the arc of suspense of a choreographed piece as a dialogue - it sometimes follows the curve of your original dramatic arc and sometimes diverges from it.

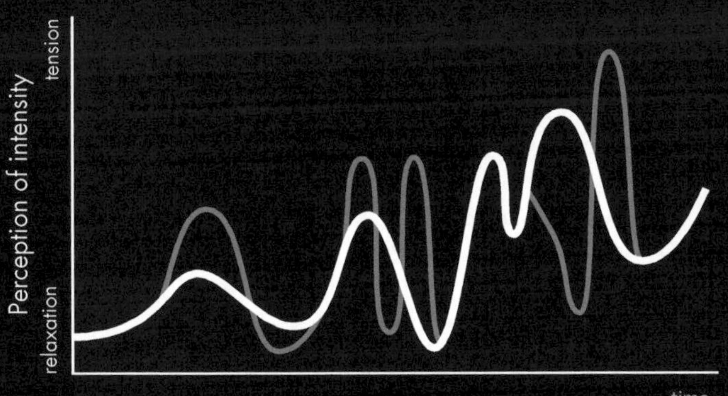

Scenes / dialogue within the arc of suspense time

Try to make your dialogue interesting, but don't lose sight of the original source.

The elements you add to the source (printed in bold in the diagram) should add their own dynamic to the whole without taking on a life of their own.

Reflect upon the work using these criteria:

- Does the arc of intensity, that is, the journey you want the audience to undergo, correspond with the theme?

- Does the dynamic of the arc of intensity correspond with the overall intention of the theme?

- At which height in your arc does the piece start? Once you have reached the peak, you might run out of steam. Can you then find a different kind of intensity through reduction?

- Consider different ways of increasing intensity. How can you condense a scene?

- Which change produces which effect?

- How can you create drama?

Spend some time reflecting on which performance elements, such as video footage, setting, special effects, etc., you could use to extend the arc of suspense, and then create your storyboard.

Transitional scenes

Dancers often develop individual scenes or movement sequences during rehearsals. The tricky bit is how to link these set pieces with one another in such a way as to create a coherent dramaturgy. Even if you decide to perform a series of scenes in the form of a collage, the whole will have a dramatic arc comprising the intensity and rhythm of the collected material. Its effect will be the result, for better or worse, of how the individual pieces are combined.

Let us assume that you have a small number of scenes which you would like to integrate into a structure. In order to retain an overview over the material, it is worth breaking it down visually. Draw the dramatic arcs of each scene. This will help you later to combine the individual scenes successfully.

Example

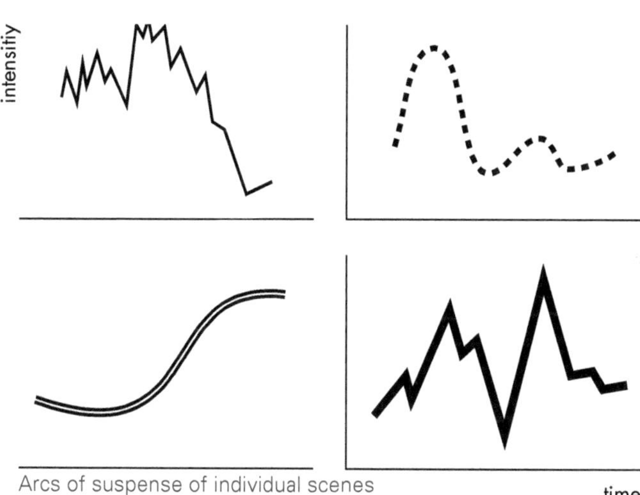

Arcs of suspense of individual scenes

If these scenes are to work together in a piece, they will need to be linked in a coherent dramaturgical form. In order to achieve this, you will have to develop new scenes to serve as transitions between your set scenes. If the transitions don't work, your collage will lack a convincing chronology, and will remain no more than a collection of random scenes.

Transitions

Start with the sequences you developed in Exercise 1: How do the individual parameters influence the intensity of a movement or use some other material.

With your dramatic arc in mind, place your scenes on a time line (see figure).

- Play around with the placement of the individual scenes and imagine the possible transitions between them.

- Check the dramatic arc for missing transitions between scenes.

- Look at the whole piece.

- Is the dramatic flow logically coherent?

- Do you find yourself emotionally involved when you think about the flow of the curve, or are there moments where you disengage?

- If you do feel yourself drifting off at any point, that is where you need to find a new transition.

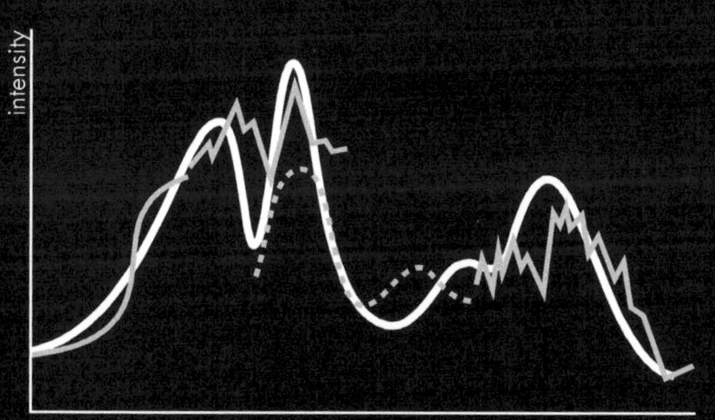

Individual sequences in the arc of suspense.

Direction

There are choreographers who limit their use of directional movement to forwards, sideways, and backwards. If we add diagonal movements into the mix, we double the options, arriving at eight directions.

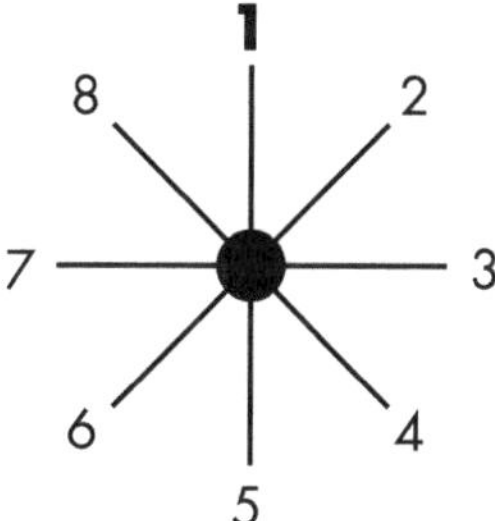

8 directions on horizontal level in bisectors and diagonals

This numbering system has the advantage that each dancer immediately knows which direction is called for in the choreography. Each dancer forms the central point of all directional movement wherever they are standing. It does not matter which direction they are facing; direction 1 is always upstage. Regardless of where they stand at any given moment, they can move in direction 5 or direction 2, and so on.

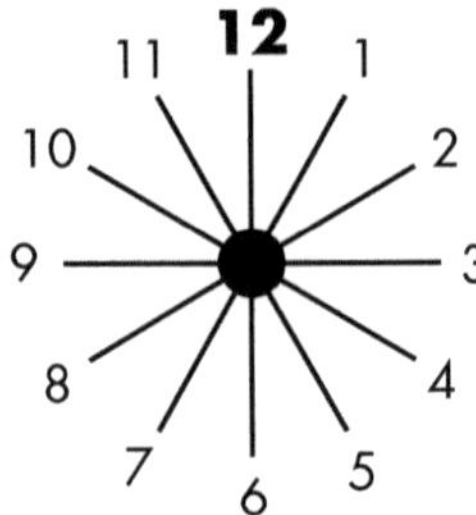

12 directions on horizontal level in the form of a clock face

Even easier than working with eight directions is using twelve directions. The advantage is that everyone can imagine a clock face sketched out around themselves on the ground, and it does not take long to remember where 7 o'clock is. In addition, there are more directions to choose from, so this system offers more options. On the downside, the diagonal directions between 1 and 2 are missing in a 12-point clock face system. If we add these directions, then we get a total 16.

16 directions on horizontal level in the form of a clock face with added diagonals

Whatever numbering system you choose in the end: note that each direction also has emotional meaning. If someone approaches you and then changes direction, turning diagonally away from you, it will not leave you unaffected. You will probably feel insecure and wonder whether there is something about you that made this person shy away from you, or whether they moved away for a different reason. But if somebody approaches you, then stops and changes their direction by 90 degrees, moving away from you at a right angle, anyone who watches you will read emotional meaning into that movement. This becomes even more obvious if whoever is approaching you not only stop in their tracks, but then even step backwards with their gaze fixed on you.

If this happened at a party and the person approaching you was a good friend of yours, then you would probably feel quite hurt by their change of direction. Of course, as the viewer of a dance piece, you are more anonymous. You won't burst into tears when all the dancers moving towards you suddenly change direction, but the emotional mechanism is similar. This turning or backing away elicits responses in us, based on our past experiences and visual patterning, similar to those we might have at a party; they are just weaker because the setting is different.

Direction in relation to the audience is an important dramaturgical tool to create strong effects. Especially in dance pieces for musicals, shows or video clips, the dancer's pathways and which directions they are facing plays a significant role. If you are working with several dancers, then orientation not only matters in relation to the audience, but also in relation to the other dancers. Depending on the storyline and situation, the dancers' positions will have meaning, and it will matter whether two dancers stand next to or behind each other. The key point is whether you, as choreographer, recognise the relationships based on such orientations in the piece, and how you acknowledge them in rehearsals.

Even if your choreography creates a self-contained world on stage, that does not seek a direct relationship with the audience and has its that does not seek a direct relationship with the audience and has its own inherent rules, with relationships to which the audience can only react as observers, you have to ask yourself what effect the directions of the dancers' movements will have.

It is extremely unlikely that the spectators will sit through a whole perfor-

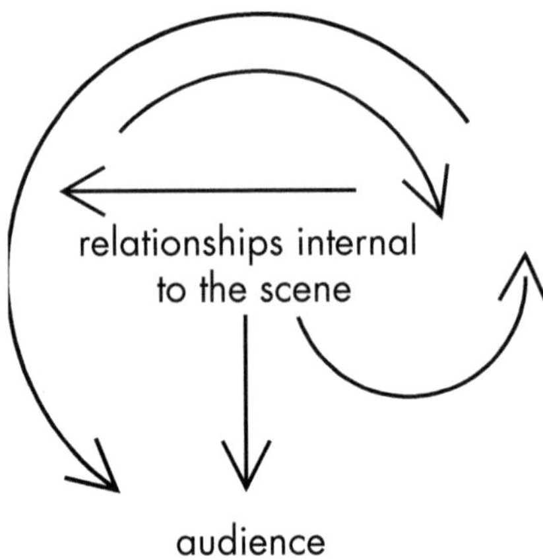

Relationships internal to the scene and to the audience

mance feeling like invisible voyeurs. It is far more probable that they will personally engage with what is happening on stage.

So if you plan to hide away to rehearse a dance piece focusing only on the relationships between the dancers, and then put the finished piece on stage as it is, do not forget the relationship between set, dancers, and audience. Think about directions in terms of their dynamics, because they will have an effect on your audience's feelings, regardless of what the dancers do or think as they perform.

Tension between audience and performance space

Divide the dance studio into two areas: 'Audience' and 'performance space'. Get some of the dancers to sit in the audience's half, and the others to stand in the performance space.
Let the dancers experiment with the directions in space. The viewers pay attention to the tension produced by the dancers' movements and the directions they are facing. See if you can work out which emotions are evoked by the different directions, depending on where the dancers are within the performance space, and notice the degree of tension produced in relation to the audience.

- How long does a direction stay interesting?
- When does the dancer need to change directions?
- What meanings are suggested by a direction, a pathway or a position?
- Now work only with walking and standing.
- Create a repeatable movement sequence for one dancer.
- Test the sequence by showing it to the audience group, and discuss the arc of suspense associated with the sequence. Compare the audience's perceptions with your own.
- Transfer your 'spatial concept' to several dancers and add in some supporting or contrasting movements for arms and legs.

Directions between dancers in relation to the audience

Develop an exercise which contains all twelve directions. Have your dancers move simultaneously, but in different directions. Use powerful rhythmic contrasts as well as changes in direction and rhythm. Pay particular attention to the relationship and dynamic effects between the audience and the dancers.

Focus

Direction in a performance space is only visible for an audience when there is a directional intention behind a dancer's movements. This intention is called focus. It is when dancers have a clear idea of the direction in which they are going to move, a sense of space. Focus is a physical feeling, a relationship to space that has to do with tension felt in response to the proposed direction and to the performance space as a whole.

Have you ever been in a room and suddenly felt you needed to get out of there immediately? When that happens, you don't stare fixedly at the door, but you anticipate the direction in which you will need to walk. Your focus is on the door. After you have focused on it, and you are on your way towards it, you will keep your focus on that door. Your pathway will be purposeful, and an observer will not have to ask where you are going. He will clearly see that you are heading for the door, and not, for instance, for the aquarium elsewhere in the room. If you relax before you get to the door, your impetus will diminish. You will no longer look as if you were being pulled out of the room by a magnet, but instead just like someone who is approaching a door. Your movement will look less urgent, the direction less important.

In dance, focus plays a key role in giving meaning to directional movement and thus to the performance space. Dancers feel the spatial context in which they find themselves, and let the audience participate in their sensation. However, dancers can only feel and transmit a spatial context if they have a focus.

Focus can be created using smaller movements within the kinesphere or large movements travelling across the stage. If a director avoids long walking sequences with an actor, it is usually because the scene loses intensity as soon as that actor crosses the stage.

Focus I

Walk towards a point in space. Imagine your chest is being pulled towards that point by a magnet. Staying with the magnet idea, reduce your tempo until you are almost standing still. Experiment with different magnetic forces, various tempi, and inserting obstacles to your forward momentum.

Add level changes. Clearly define your direction before physically focusing on it.

Work with as many directions as possible and create a sequence of movements.

Focus II

Imagine that the performance space has been reduced to a long, narrow alleyway.

There are two magnetic poles, one at the start and one at the end of the alleyway. When dancers walk towards one of the poles, some of their body parts are pulled in the opposite direction – a hand, their upper body, or even just their gaze. Try and find unusual ways of reversing the direction of the separate body parts, varying rhythm and tempo. Every movement should be held in tension between the forces pulling from the two opposing poles.

Focus III

Devise a piece of choreography without a focus. The movements have no continuous direction, changing constantly from circles, figures of 8, spirals, etc.

Then add directions and focus.

Work with a changing number of dancers at both ends of the spectrum between purposeful and not purposeful. If themes come to mind, take inspiration from them but do not let yourself be limited by them.

Focus IV

Different tempi and degrees of internal tension in relation to directions in space.

A takes the position of the audience. B approaches A and moves away again. Try coming from different directions and using changing degrees of internal tension.

Getting familiar with the dance space is like learning a language; the more you practise, the easier it will become to express yourself. Fathoming the nuances of emotion behind words or between the lines is a process you cannot consciously control or reconstruct. It is the same with the language of space. When you become more familiar with the directions and varying forms of focus, you will develop an intuitive sense of their links to emotion. You will be able to trust yourself to use the language of space as a means of expression.

Structuring pathways based on literary sources, plays, musicals or opera

It is possible to develop a piece of choreography for a musical, an opera or a play by translating the emotions and relationships of the characters into spatial motifs and pathways. You will need to familiarise yourself with the relationships between the characters and their emotions and be able to transfer your understanding of them to the performance space.

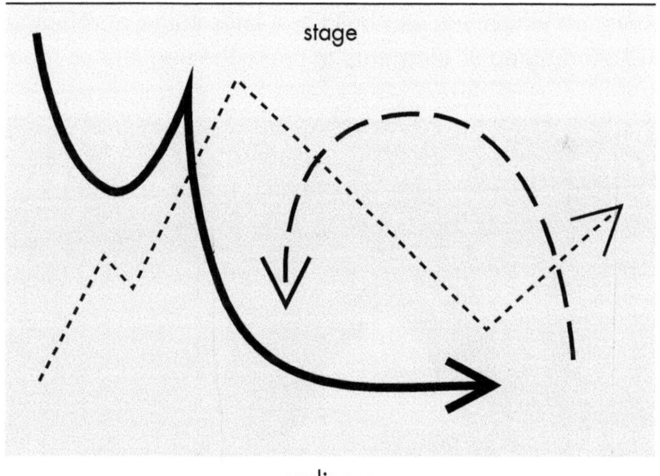

You can assign positions and pathways to the characters in a play or a musical according to their emotional journey.

When choreographing for musicals and opera, with their complex mix of dance, song, music and other artistic components, it is important to be able to break down complex movements step by step. Since the performers still have to sing and speak while moving, it is advisable to initially just map out their pathways in space, so that they can get an overview of the scene and concentrate on singing and speaking instead of worrying about their movements. In mapping out their pathways, you provide the performers with a safe structure which will keep them from feeling overwhelmed. Within this framework, the performers can find new stimuli and may offer you suggestions for additional movement material. Watching the scene, you can see your half-finished design unfold, and envision more elements to add to your basic framework.

What sounds easy, however, often isn't easy at all. When you are working with a half-finished, complex movement sequence with several performers, and then add in equally half-finished stage sets, projection designs, music and lighting, there are so many factors that may distract you and keep you from visualising new movement sequences. It is hard work to imagine movements for a particular moment in the piece inside an incomplete construct – and that is the job of the choreographer. If you find yourself stuck, then you may have to turn to your team of performers to assist you and offer you ideas for their pathways, on which you can build at a later stage of rehearsals, adding gestures and choreographic elements to make the sequences more complex.

Mapping a literary source

Choose a literary source that offers several protagonists with different motives and relationships with each other. Draw a diagram showing the relationships between the characters.

Add directions for each character, translating the characters' motivations and their emotions into directions in space.

Add elements of movement and gestures to the directions that either illustrate or contradict the plot.

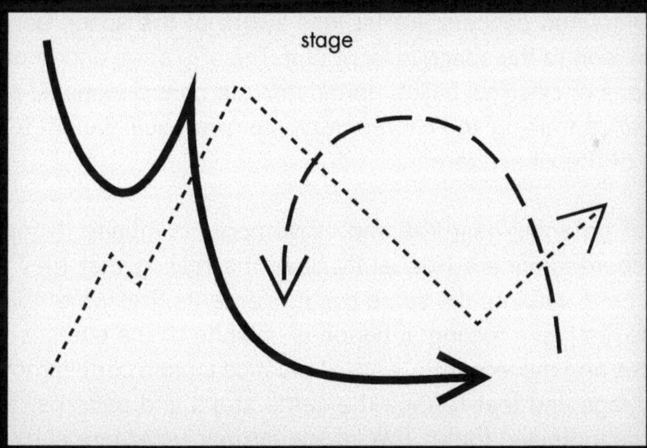

Personal space

The space we are most aware of lies in front of our bodies, between our hips and our heads. This spatial consciousness drops away to either side and disappears almost entirely behind our backs and below the navel. This has to do with the position of our eyes and their range of sight, which is concentrated on the radius of action of our arms. This radius of action represents the space around our bodies which we know well, our personal space.

Primary active space of a dancer: personal space

Although the dancer's active space extends through the whole kinesphere, even very well-trained dancers are far less aware of the space behind their body in comparison to the space in front of it. The arm area, encompassed by the five positions of classical ballet, dominates our consciousness, and it is a challenge to dance training and choreography to give equal weight to the less present areas of the kinesphere.

The number of potential gestures and movements is infinite. Nonetheless, dancers and choreographers frequently have the feeling that they keep repeating, or, at best, varying, the same five movements. The worst thing about this is that it is not just a feeling: it happens, in spite of the endless possibilities for gestures and movements. Years of practice ingrain certain movements in our bodies, legs and feet retrace the same steps and patterns, arms and torso repeat gestures and forms. We let the familiar repertoire curb our freedom, and the infinite options we could choose to express ourselves through dance within our personal space slumber unnoticed. Personal space is no longer seen as a blank slate on which one can write using the language of the body, but as a space of daily repetition.

Under the heading *Manipulation* in the chapter *Designing movement,* you will find techniques which can help you bring variety to such repetitions. Also, you are less likely to repeat yourself if you are aware of your actual range of movements. Another option is to consciously limit that range, and let the reduced number of available movements inspire you to play with them. By doing so, I have here reduced the limitless number of directions possible within the kinesphere to around 114 as a useful number with which to work.

A technical break-down of personal space

As described 16 directions can be demarcated on the horizontal level. If we draw seven similar circles around the body, we then have 112 directions. Add to those the vertical directions of 'straight up' and 'straight down' and we arrive at 114 directions.

The seven levels of a dancer's personal space

You can also imagine two clock faces, one on the horizontal
plane, one in the vertical plane. The vertical clock face can now rotate on the
horizontal clock face from 12 to 5 to produce different directions (once you hit
6, the directions will repeat)

Directions using a system in the form of clock faces in two planes

This system offers 128 directions in space. Whichever system you choose
to divide up the dancer's kinesphere into diagonals and straight lines – 114
directions, 128 directions, or a different system altogether – what is crucial
is that you develop an understanding of, and sensibility for, the entire range
of choreographical expression available to you, using spatial directions within
the dancer's kinesphere.

20 different directions

Devise a movement exercise with the aim of working with at least a quarter of the directions from the systems outlined above. Look for organic and unusual links between them. Work with as many body parts as possible.

Dancer standing in clock face system featuring two planes

14-7

7-1

4-2

7-3

...

..

Understanding the 128 directions on a technical level is one thing. It is another to be able to express yourself using your perception of the subtext intrinsic to the directions. A subtext is the text or meaning behind a word. Take as an example the word, 'come'. You can say this word in countless different ways, that is, you can infer a variety of subtexts. A 'come' spoken tenderly is very different to saying it forcefully, but the letters form the same word. If you embed it within a beckoning gesture, you have the choice of its meaning being either tender or forceful. It depends on the quality with which you carry out the movement. Then, if you want to interpret the word in spatial terms, you might extend your hand in a diagonal movement forwards into space and then let it sink, or you may choose to bow your head, or lean back into a diagonal, and so on.

Assuming you are not dancing along to sentences in your dance pieces, or, for that matter, plays, but are exploring themes, then your perception of the dancer's personal space will be a key methodology for you. Virginia Woolf said that all of her books were inspired on those shores where words cannot reach. In such a place, books are complete and perfect in and of themselves. The difficult thing is to fetch material from that place without shipwrecking yourself. If you wish to dance material without merely illustrating the written word, then you will need to use space as your language, and you will need to train yourself to perceive its diverse and vital nature.

If you choose to stay mainly within the movements associated with the dance canon, then the range of movements you will have at your disposal to express the nature of space will be bound to those of that repertoire, and will thus often be more limited. There will always be exceptional dancers who are able to interpret space well by using conventional movement, but you can't count on exceptions. Very often, working in this way means that the sensitivity for emotion dwindles, movements become mechanically precise, and their spatial references are not understood by the dancers, and thus, as a consequence, cannot be conveyed to the audience.

The limits of internal and external space

There are dancers whose movements fill the entire stage and project out into the auditorium, while other dancers barely seem to fill their own skin. Successful projection is not a question of dance technique or a well-trained body. It has to do with the degree to which dancers can extend their internal space and share it with the audience.

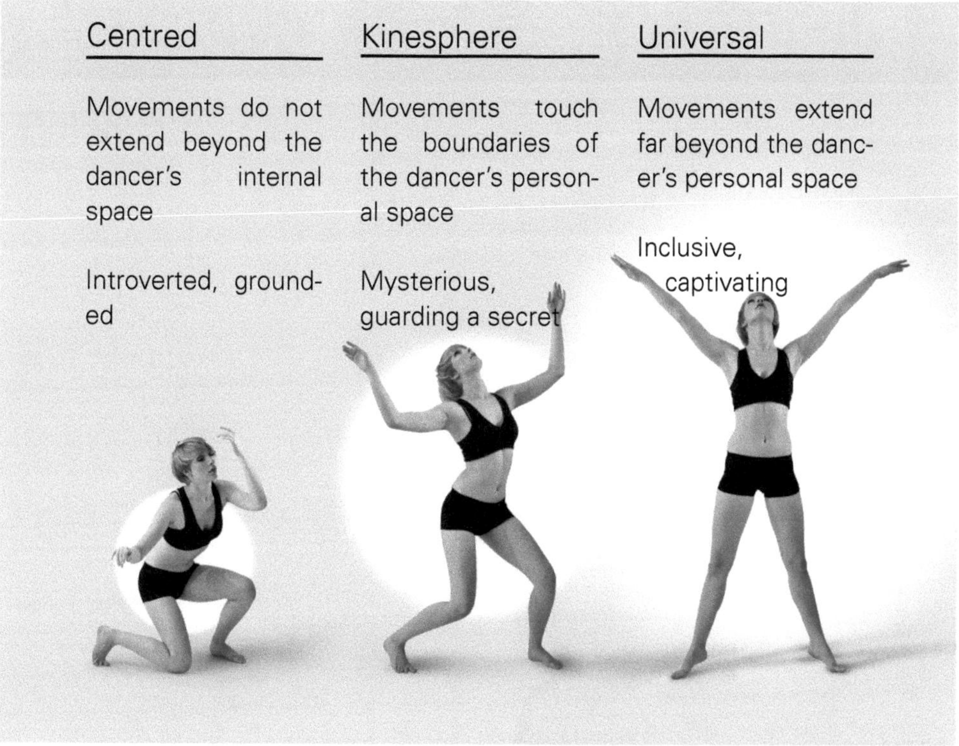

The boundaries of a dancer's space only seem to be limited.

If you know how to extend and diminish you personal space, you can influence and vary how you claim your space and how much attention you draw to yourself. A dancer who extends her awareness beyond her personal space will be much more visible than one whose intention never projects beyond her kinesphere.

As a choreographer, you have to connect with people all the time. You need to be sensitive and able to put yourself in someone else's shoes, so your own personal space must be be thin and permeable. If the connection between your inner self and the outside world functions well, you allow yourself to be touched by the world, and this will inspire more ideas and material than you could ever choreograph.

Music and movement

Metre

Music is a mystery. It cannot be properly explained. When we feel uncertain about how to face a mystery, we tend to simplify it in order to grasp it. So when choreographers analyse music, they usually choose the metre or beat as the main feature to refer to. The result are amateur choreographies stuck in two-bar-cages, with accents on 1 and 5, regardless of what else the music has to offer. And why not stick with 4/4 rhythms only, if counting from one to eight makes life so easy?

1 2 3 4 **5** 6 7 8

The division of music for dance by eight beats is often phrased so that the stress is on the first and fifth beat.

If you prefer to go with the beat, or if it works better for your dance group if they do, try to leave the door open to the possibility of placing movement accents on other beats than the first and fifth.

1 2 **3** 4 **5** 6 **7** 8

1 **2** 3 4 5 6 **7** 8

1 2 3 **4** 5 **6** 7 8

Example of accents on other beats

Shifting the first beat of the dance creates a dynamic relationship between the dance and the music. The audience will experience this relationship not just in conjunction with the metre of the music, but also in tandem with all other elements within the score, such as song, phrases played by individual instruments, and so on. In this way, dance becomes a dialogue with the music. There are correspondences between the metre and the individual elements of the music, which the audience will feel.

Metre

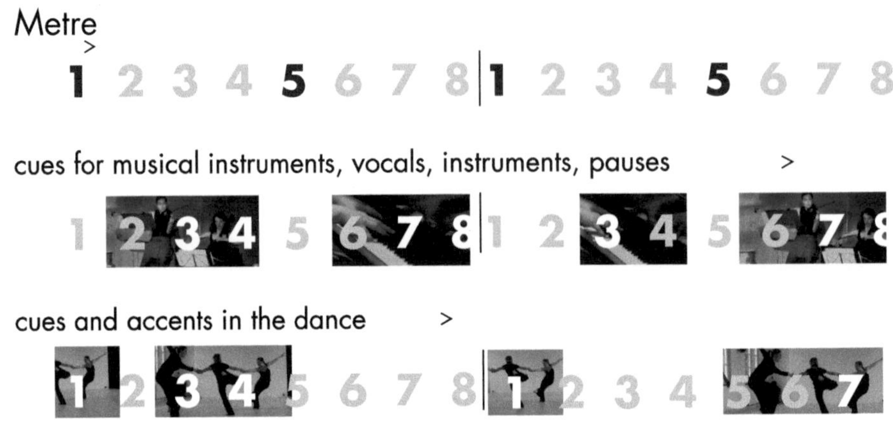

An example of how various choreographic elements can be brought into relationship with the metre and other components of the music.

When we work with set pieces of music, we are constantly questioning the relationship between the dance and the music. There are many ways of combining dance with the beat or melodic elements. If your music is clearly accentuated, you can work with accents in your dance as well. You could do that literally, so to speak, synchronising dance accents with musical ones, but there are also other possibilities. You could off-set the elements chronologically, so that the dance either anticipates or echoes the musical element; or you could let the dance move in opposition to the music, pausing on a musical accent and moving into the silence of a musical pause.

Density of music
Relationship
Number of dancers
Density of dance
Quality of movement
Direction
Space level
Metre - Accent - Speed
1 2 3 4 5 6 7 8 1 2 3 4 5 6 7 8

Counts and accents in music

This exercise is based on a 4/4 beat, but it applies to other metres as well.
Place the stress in your choreography on the first and fifth beat. Perform the piece with all your dancers as a group.

Divide the group into 3: A, B and C. Group A dances to the beat, group B to the vocals, C to an instrumental phrase. The dynamics of the three groups will be very different from each other.

Choreography A

1 2 3 4 5 6 7 8 | 1 2 3 4 5 6 7 8

Choreography B

1 2 3 4 5 6 7 8 | 1 2 3 4 5 6 7 8

Choreography C

1 2 3 4 5 6 7 8 | 1 2 3 4 5 6 7 8

Transfer each piece of choreography to the performance space and have it performed by different groups:
Choose a moment somewhere half-way into the piece at which all three groups return to moving in unison.

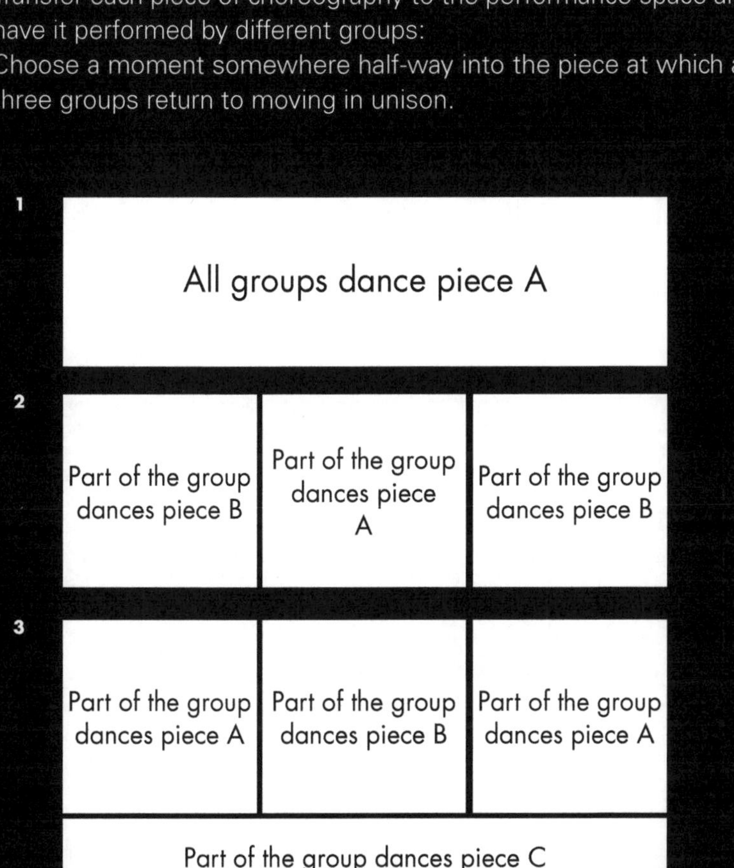

Group A – beat

1 2 3 4 5 6 7 8 | 1 2 3 4 5 6 7 8

Group B – singer

1 2 3 4 5 6 7 8 | 1 2 3 4 5 6 7 8

Group C - instrument

1 2 3 4 5 6 7 8 | 1 2 3 4 5 6 7 8

From counts 1 to 5, each group dances their own sequence: A follows the beat, B the vocals, C an instrumental phrase. On count 5, all three groups switch to follow group A and the beat. On the next 1, all groups follow group B's sequence.

How you mix the groups will depend on the piece of music and on the movement material. This exercise is about experiencing the dynamic of movements in relation to the beat, and the relationship between the individual musical components of a piece.

Watch the often copied and seldom paralleled choreography by Jerome Robbins for the number 'Cool' from *West Side Story* for a masterclass in dancing with and against the beat, making use of accents in the music, and creating accents in the dance independent of the score. It really illustrates how to enter a dialogue between dance and music.

To develop a more creative way of using metre and break away from the time-worn pattern of 'one, two, three, four, five, six, seven, eight', try structuring your class using the above exercises, with a focus on developing a dialogue with the music, instead of staying with a lazy 4/4 or 3/4 beat. You need to train your dancers to understand the importance of, and to think and act in relationship with, the metre and other components of the music. Often, it is just about allowing them to feel instead of counting the music.

When I first took up dancing, I could not keep time. I was a bit like a drummer who keeps dropping his drumsticks – not a great outlook, if you are looking forward to applause rather than pity. The reason I could not count to four along with the beat of the music was that I was distracted by every instrumental line, the vocals, the dynamics of the music, everything that made up the piece as a whole. There was so much to hear, and I was interested in just about everything that I heard in the music, so focusing on one single element like the beat was simply impossible for me. I felt that if I did, I would miss key aspects of the music. I was more concerned with the question, 'What is this music saying, and how does it make me feel?' than 'How can I define this music metrically?' Only after I had heard a piece countless times, when it stopped taking me by surprise again and again, and lost its seductive power, was I able to consider the beat in relation to the music, alongside all the emotions it elicited in me. But even today I can still lose myself in a musical passage, and abandon the lowest common denominator, the metre, as I surrender to the sounds.

If your dancers cannot keep time, please do not immediately dismiss them as unmusical. People who believe that they understand music as a whole, when, in fact, all they grasp is the metre, have as much of a problem. Choreography as a means of expression is more than just movement in time to music. Music is born from emotions, and before you start working with music, it helps to think about the following issues:

What role does music play in choreography?

Is the music at the heart of your dance?

In other words, is the whole point of your dance to express the emotion of the music, or to make the composition visible in your dance? This type of work will aim at translating music into movement and at developing a physical expression of the feelings evoked by the music.

Do you combine dance and music as a means to work on a theme?

Are the music and dance completely equal in the piece, attuned to each other, inspiring one another and representing a unity? Working in this way offers great creative potential, since the two elements, dance and music, stimulate each other. Whether you succeed with this approach or not depends on the ability to tune in with music and dance and respond to both. This works very well with live musicians, but you can also use this approach with recorded music.

Is the choreography the centre piece of your work?

In other words, are you focusing only on the choreography because you want to explore a particular theme through dance, and you just need a piece of music to accompany the process of exploration or the final results? Are you looking for an atmospheric effect from the music with the dance being the prime focus for your audience? Or do you want to add a piece of music which turns the dance into something entirely new? If the music you choose has enough expressive power, it will shine its light on your dance, and they will merge to create a whole new unity.

There are two options for this approach:

> You can experiment by playing different pieces of music to the same choreography and observe the different effects. In this option, the dance is still work in progress, and allowed to respond to the music. It will change and look different each time you play a new tune.

> Your choreography is finished, a composition polished to the last detail, ready to be performed. All you need is music to accompany your composition.

> I remember showing a composer one of my choreographies because I wanted him to write music to go with it. He watched the piece and said 'What do you want music for? It is perfect as it is.' It is always worth considering that your piece might work just as well without any music at all.

> If you work with a musician, choose carefully when to first take him to your rehearsals. It is very likely that he will find it harder to complete a half-finished piece of choreography in his mind than a dancer or a choreographer would. A musician can only respond to the dance when it really has something to say. Sometimes, a piece of music only supports parts of a choreography, and goes its own way in other parts because there was not enough in the dance that the composer could draw from. It is wonderful when a musician profoundly engages with the dance and, like a choreographer exploring a piece music, creates a musical composition that enters into a dialogue with the dance.

Choosing musical accompaniment for a dance piece has to be done very carefully, with a great deal of thought and sensitivity. Studies on film scores have shown that the emotional effect of a scene is determined far more by the music than by the images. Remembering a scene in retrospect, the visual component becomes more significant, but when it comes to the emotion that a scene evokes in the moment it is watched, sound is what predominates.

Music, in and of itself, is far superior to dance. Beethoven said that music is able to convey the moods of a composer's soul to the soul of the listener. As a choreographer, I believe in movement. My movement is my breath and it runs in my blood. It is absolutely, truly the stuff of humanity, but despite all that, it is probably harder for dance to transmit the moods of the choreographer's soul to its audience than it is for music.

As a dancer, you can feel the music and allow your response to flow from your soul throughout your body. You can make music visible without becoming a slave to it. Your dance gives a voice to the emotions the music evokes in you, so your performance becomes a symbiosis of the music and your movement, and your audience will hear in the music what they see expressed in your dance.

This means that as a choreographer, you can actually force your interpretation, your vision of the music on the audience.
In other words, the audience will hear what they see in the dance, so you decide what they hear. You hold the magnifying glass, so to speak, and can focus on particular passages within the music that the audience might never have perceived just by listening to the piece. Whenever you choreograph, you have the opportunity to let your audience see things through your eyes and listen through your ears, even if its just a dance around a maypole in an operetta you choreographed because you needed the money.

What you make of this opportunity depends mainly on what you perceive in the music, and that, in turn, depends on how you listen to the music, how often, to what depth and with what kind of attitude. Hearing a piece for the first time, you will get an impression of the associations it evokes in you. There may be two or three main associations that you can identify. In simple compositions, these associations will get stronger over time and only change very little. If you listen to the piece frequently, the effect of the initial impression will wear off – the piece has nothing more to say to you.

When you listen to a complex, multi-layered piece of music, however, your perceptions of the music are likely to intensify. The music will reveal different, ever more subtle aspects of itself to you. The more you listen, the more the piece has to say to you. However you choose to define the composition, you will be excluding some of the countless other possible interpretations of the music. Try to immerse yourself in the essence of the music, just by listening and waiting. Allow yourself to dive into the depths of the music without expecting or forcing any outcome. Of course, the problem is that we, as choreographers, tend to listen to music under a certain amount of pressure. It is in the nature of our work, we are expected to be inspired and come up with an idea. As long as that idea has not yet seen the light of day, we have to bear uncertainty and doubt. Any structure that supports our process minimises these fears, and our work takes on a familiar face, but, at the same time, we forfeit other potential interpretations of the piece.

For as long as you do not stick with any associations in the music, you stay with your authentic emotional response, and the more you experience in this way, the easier it will be for you once you have started working on a more rational level. Your work, the choreographer's craft, is to translate your emotional response to the music into the dancer's personal space and the performance space.

Choreographic aspects of the relationship between dance and music

- The relationship between the density of the music and that of the dance.

- The relationship between the density of the music and the number of dancers.

- The relationship of the beat of the music and the accentuation and tempo of the dance.

- Correspondences between dance and musical composition: movement quality, directions, and correlations to the various levels of space.

Musical interpretation

Choose a complex piece of music. Close your eyes and listen to it using headphones. Try to assign spatial correlations to the elements that speak to you in the music. Imagine that you are floating weightlessly at the centre of a large room, watching the music move three-dimensionally within the space around you.

- See if you can find spatial correlations for the music and sketch them on a piece of paper.

- Listen to the piece again and do the same with directions.

- Try to find movements in the music to which you can assign a direction. Sketch them on your paper, too.

- Listen to the music in the dance studio and see if you can find a quality of movement for a few selected passages.

- Do not fix them in terms of form yet. Concentrate on quality for now.

- Experiment with the density of the music and that of the dance. Transfer the things you have discovered into an improvisational sketch. Run a rehearsal with your dancers in which you work on a group piece using the spatial correlations, the directions you have assigned to them and the quality of movement you have chosen. Let the dancers improvise within that structure.

- Now experiment with the density of the music and the number of dancers in your performance space.

Musical notes are the letters musicians read and interpret when they play. There is no point in working with musical notes as a choreographer, since they don't tell you all about the sound of the music. If you are working with a conductor or a musician, however, you could use the score as the basis for discussion. Perhaps you will find it necessary or helpful to be able to read scores as a choreographer. But your ability to develop a vision for your choreography will certainly not depend on it.

What I would suggest is that you make a graphic representation of the music. Sketch out what you hear in dots, wiggles, curves, straight lines and dashes, running upwards and downwards as you see fit. Select individual passages from the music and listen to them again and again, until you are able to filter out different instrumental lines, moods and impressions. Sketching these elements allows you to create a structure without having to verbalise what you do. There is room for a whole dance piece on a large sheet of paper. I divide the sheet into small squares, to each of which I assign a unit of time. When I am working, a single glance at my sketch tells me where I am in the music.

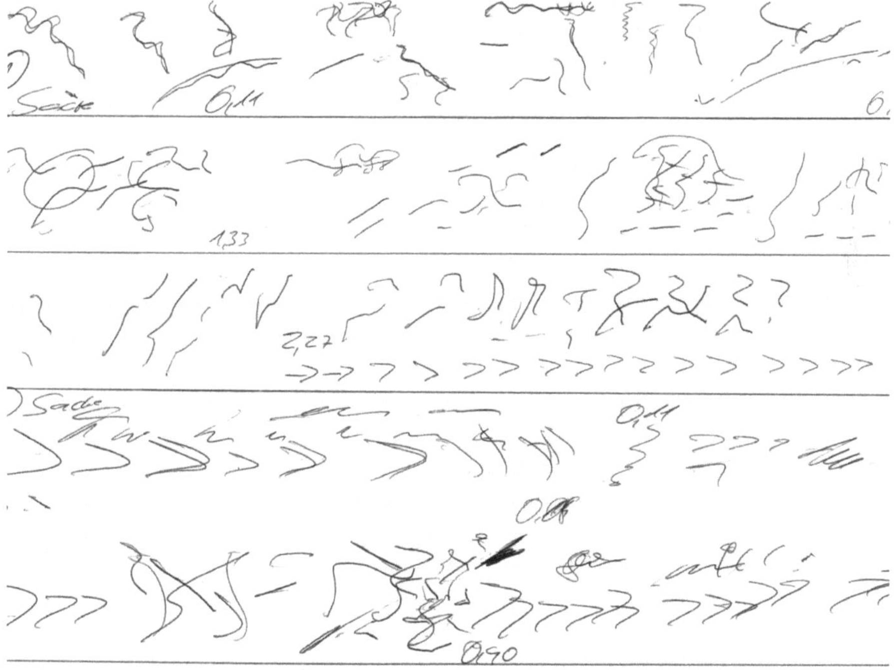

An example of a sketch of a piece of music.

Example of a sketch of a piece of music with other notations, including summarising 'feeling words'.

These wild drawings already are evocative of spatial movement. They give an indication of directions, a rhythm and other elements inherent in dance. The most important effect of sketching, however, is that I have to immerse myself in the music to do it. What I draw is a reflection of the music which goes beyond mere illustration. And even if all I do achieve is an illustration, then that is my first step toward the translation into dance.

Another way of approaching the translation of music into dance is to listen to a piece as often and as thoroughly as possible, reflect on the theme you perceive in it, and then condense your impression into one single word or sentence. This word or sentence is the essence of the musical piece and the starting point for your dance. Once you have extracted the essence, you can ignore the music - the dancers don't even have to know the piece, they just work with that word or sentence. On this basis, they can develop individual sequences and soli, work on the techniques necessary to perform them, and then film the sequences. You can then set the sequences to different passages in the music and observe how the relationship between dance and music changes. The dance can flow with the music or oppose it. As described in the previous chapters, you now have the opportunity to arrange individual sequences with several groups of dancers to produce a spatial composition.

Next time you listen to a piece of music that you know well, try if you can find its essential characteristic, something you can express in a word or a phrase. You may need to dig deep to do this, to immerse yourself in the music, in order to find the correlation between the music and your personality.

Dance and music often enter into a dialogue and, in doing so, produce a symbiosis. You will achieve the best results if the two art forms are allowed to deeply connect with each other. There is little point in hiring good musicians who don't care about dance and just want to make their own mark. Equally, it is pointless to take on a dancer to interpret a brilliant composition unless he is prepared to explore its mystery.

For additional exercises on the theme of music and movement, see 'Exercises' in Chapter 12.

4 Thematic development

4

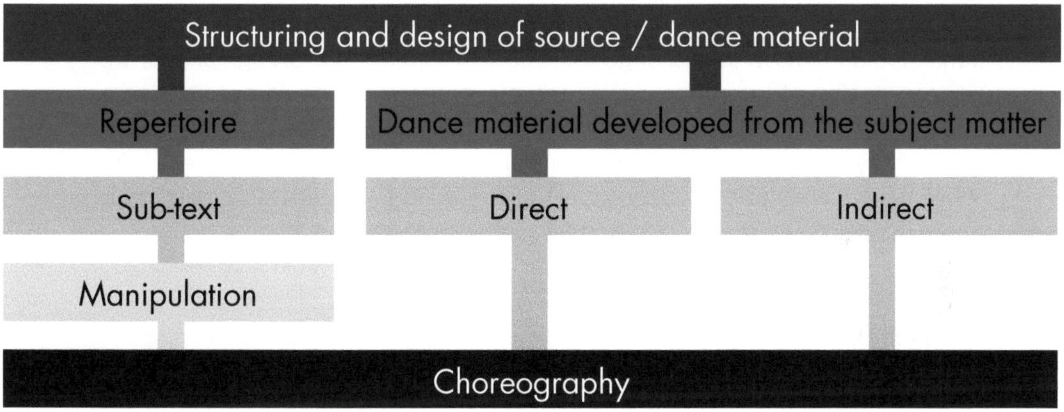

Structuring and design of source / dance material

Repertoire

Dance material developed from the subject matter

Sub-text

Direct

Indirect

Manipulation

Choreography

Connections between theme and dancer

When Vaslav Nijinsky choreographed the legendary *L'après–midi d'un faune* in 1912, he transcended the repertoire he had worked so hard to achieve. The great acrobatic movements of the classical ballet, drilled hour after hour at the barre, were free of thematic context. But Nijinsky let himself be guided into movement research by his theme, and from this research his dance emerged.

Taking a risk like this was incomprehensible to many of Nijinsky's contemporaries. Wasn't it the 'Ballets Russes' repertoire that had secured unimagined fame for the company, and for Nijinsky himself? Why did he take such a risk with the success of his dance piece and his reputation as a choreographer? He could just as easily have captivated audiences by merely showcasing his skill and talent in the classical repertoire. One can only conclude that, however well a choreo- grapher masters his repertoire, it may not give him the depth of personal satisfaction that he desires. Depending on how skilful you are at implementing the repertoire in the particular context of your piece, how successful your dancers are at interpreting it individually, and how precise you wish to be with the material, you may not have to generate your own movement material. You don't have to exchange the safety of repertoire choreography for the slippery terrain of improvisation. All the movements one could possibly learn, drawn from any of the dance techniques in the world, can be increased exponentially by manipulating them and placing them within a specific context. With all of these riches at your disposal, you have enough material to create more more dance pieces than you can possibly stage within your lifetime.

Repertoire

The wider the range of dance styles, forms and movement qualities, the more likely it is that you have access to the kind of movement you need in order to express your theme. The narrower your spectrum of available repertoire movements, the harder it will be to convey the depth of your ideas in the non-verbal language of dance. But even if you can draw on a large variety of styles and techniques, you are still approaching your theme from an intellectual perspective. When you leave the sphere of the tangible, you exchange intellectual reflection for the intangible. Since this is not to everybody's taste, and not everybody wants to approach choreography through thematic research, I would now like to discuss some technical and conceptual ways of working with existing material and steps, and scoring them within a dance piece.

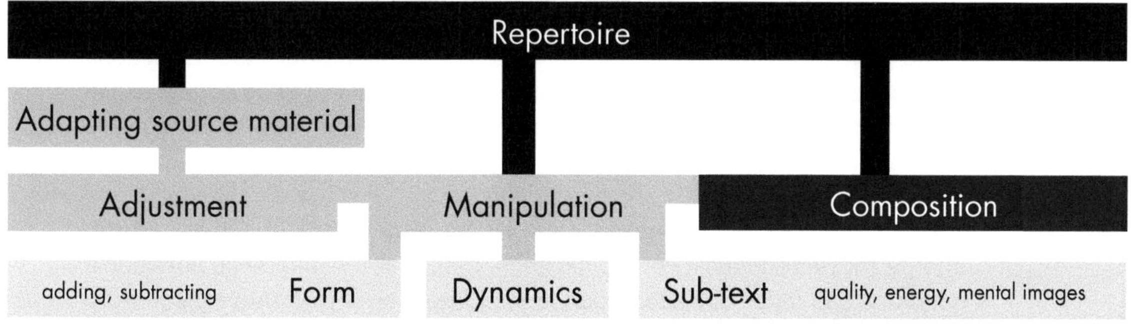

Adapting source material

Once you start working with source material, be it a story or a piece of music, it won't be long before you are confronted with the question of how you can integrate it with your dance repertoire. On the one hand, you want to do justice to the material, but the other hand, you don't want to degrade your choreography to a mere illustration of a source. In order to build a relationship with the material, you will need to familiarise yourself with it. Get an overview of your source first, and then consider different options of how to bring the source and your repertoire into a dialogue with each other.

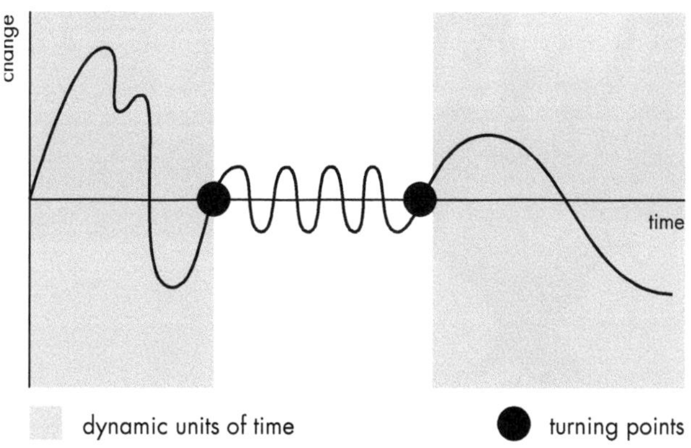

Example of source material analysis in relation to turning points

If you visualise an idea or a piece of music as a very simple graph, you will notice greater or smaller changes along its time axis. These variations might relate to volume, quality of nuance, expressiveness, plot or other deviations from the previous moment's state; aspects, incidentally, that do not necessarily need verbalisation. Approaching your material and your repertoire from this perspective may or may not lend spirit to your work.

How you work with your source material, be it by means of sub-text, form, energy, movement quality or composition, makes all the difference between a good or a bad repertoire adaptation. If your intention is to create a piece from your own and your dancers' repertoire, the first step should be an in-depth research of your movement options. You should also spend time considering the material from the perspective of the sub-text; developing the skill to change movement qualities in your dance; acquiring a good sense for dynamic movements, and familiarising yourself with the compositional principles of space. You will find inspiration and exercises for this in the chapters 'Arrangement and Composition' and 'Creating Movement'.

Implementing turning points and dynamic units of time

Without referring to any source material, sketch a graph with turning points and dynamic units of time that can later be filled with repertoire movements and steps.

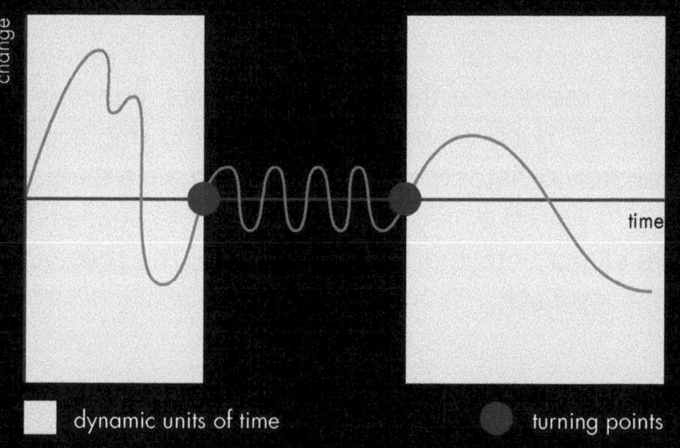

Pay particular attention to the turning points. Try slotting various elements of repertoire into the windows, keeping the dynamics of each window in mind. Choose movements that match the mood of the window, but avoid predictability within the movement phrase.

Working with the third dimension

Translating your source with its qualities, variations and content into a two-dimensional diagram provides you with a structure that gives you a sense of direction whilst also leaving enough free space for your creativity to unfold. Should you wish to further differentiate the matrix you have created for working with the source material, you can take the next step and add the third dimension to your turning points and dynamic units of time.

Because many of us spend a lot of time in front of a screen, exposed to two-dimensionality and mere fake three-dimensionality, thinking and feeling in the third dimension is much more difficult than you might expect. It requires a disproportionately greater mental effort to visualise things in three dimensions than in two. It will take practice and patience to successfully extend your source material sketch into the third dimension. The following exercise explains one possible approach.

Turning points and dynamic units of time in the third dimension

Choose a song that offers a diversity of changes (mood, rhythm, tempo, volume, melody etc.). Listen to it with headphones in an empty room.

Assign a spatial direction to each musical change. Try to perceive the music three-dimensionally. Don't be intellectual about it, remain on the non-verbal level: hearing, perceiving, space. Nothing else. Keep replaying passages of your song until you can assign spatial directions to distinctive moments in the music. Make a note of them. Please refer to the section, 'A technical break down of personal space' on page 85 and work with one of the notational methods described there. Alternately, choose another method for assigning windows of time to the musical passages and turning points.

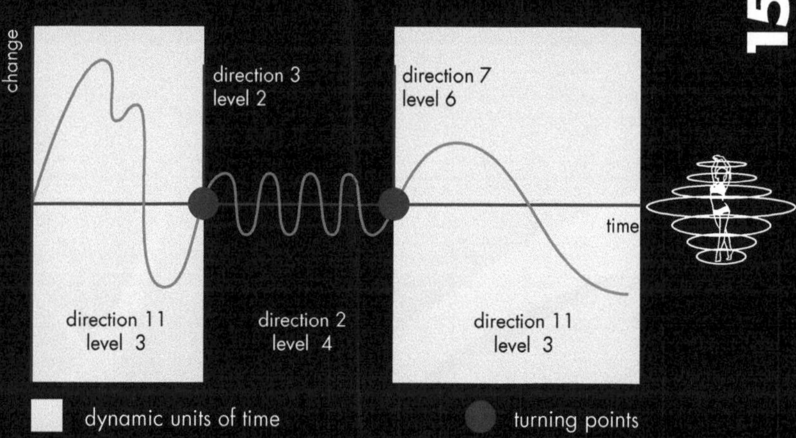

Turning points developed from source material each with assigned spatial direction

Now see if you can refine your sense of the music and add further directions to the direction you have defined within each given window of time.

Decide how far out into the surrounding space each of your chosen directions should reach.

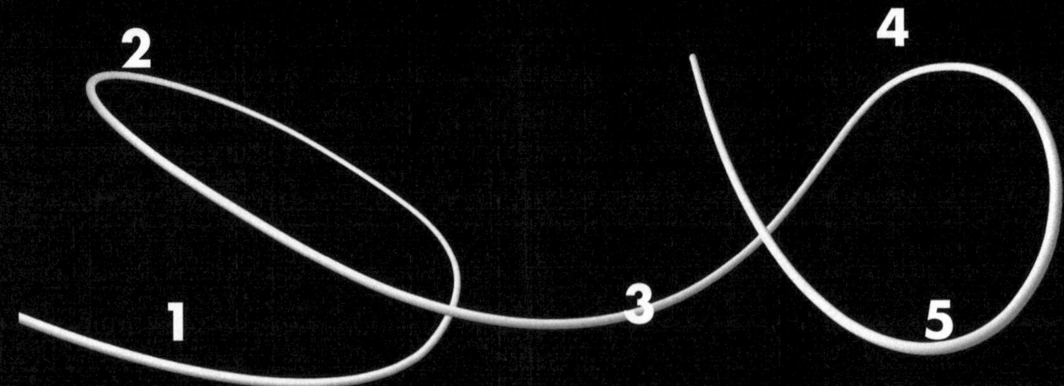

Design movements which hint at the directions you have chosen by using the guiding points of different body parts (knees, elbows, hands, head).

Analyse the traces each movement leaves in space. Sketch them out.

15 Study

Now visualise the traces expanding in three dimensions, like a kind of elastic hosepipe. To define the size and form of each 'movement pipe', imagine space as a solid substance instead of thin air. Depending on how much of the body is used to move through space, whether it is just a hand, an arm or the whole body, the dimension and form of the curve will change.

Space scalpel: Take your diagram of the piece of music from 2) and compare it with your 'movement pipes'.

Now decide where you want to alter the tube. Imagine you are using a scalpel to cut away areas that you will then place elsewhere.

Experiment with translating the changes you have made with the scalpel back into the dancers' movements.

This approach can be modified, further developed and conceptualised in many ways. It works with any kind of source material that you would like to use as a starting point for adapting your dance repertoire to your choreography, and then develop it further within your piece.

Manipulating available movements

When we work with repertoire movements in a piece, we face two major problems: endless repetition on the one hand and, on the other hand, the wish to be able to modify movement material, either to suit a particular theme or simply to expand our range of possible movements.

Framework

The results of your movement manipulations will vary depending on the framework you are using. You can choose a window of time, a so-called temporal frame, to be a whole movement sequence or just one single movement. Even if the manipulation parameters stay the same, the results of the two frames will be very different. For this reason, it can be of advantage to repeat the same parameter of manipulation within different windows of time. You could also use the principle of the frame to work with space, creating windows of space that define a section of the stage. You can vary this window of space by choosing between a format that fills the entire stage, or relates only to a small group of performers, a single dancer or a part of the body. You will thus achieve different results and create variety. In the following exercises, I will present options for manipulation that can be used within all the different types of framework to produce a variety of outcomes.

Frames

in space and time

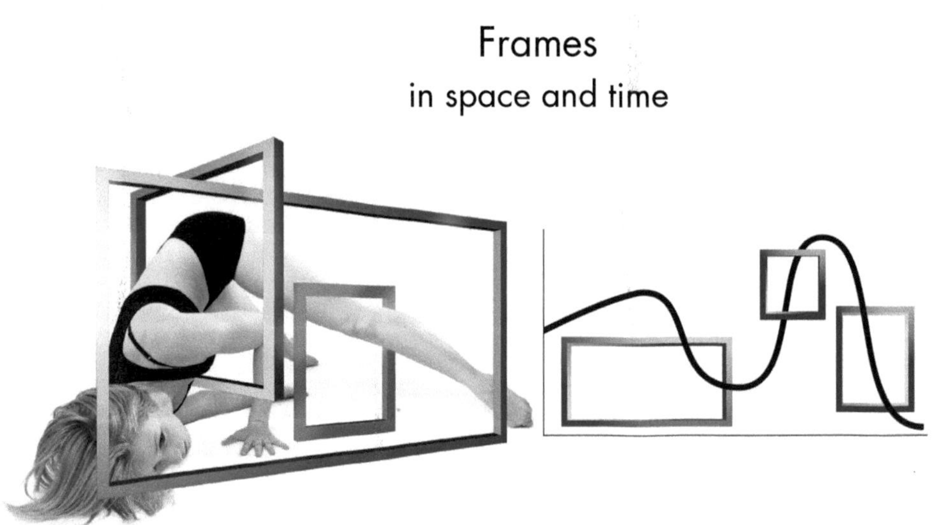

Manipulation parameters

You can use several manipulation parameters at the same time on a single movement phrase, regardless of whether the phrase stands on its own or is part of a framework setting. Below, I have compiled a list of manipulation parameters, which could of course be extended ad infinitum - I have limited myself to a small selection here.

Developing manipulation parameters by transferring the essence of a movement onto a group or body parts

Pinpoint the essence of a movement, in other words, what the movement represents to you as a dancer or choreographer. Give the movement a name, such as rotating and tearing apart or 'reaching and melting'. Then try to use the concept in different parts of your body.
If you started your 'rotating and tearing apart' in your arms and ribcage, you could now do it in your back and legs. In a group, you can experiment with making several dancers work together to represent , as if the group were one body. Try to avoid just dancing the same movement in sync, aim at adapting the concept 'rotating and tearing apart' for one 'organism ' made up of several bodies. Ask yourself: 'How can I express 'rotating and tearing apart' with a group of dancers?'

Manipulation parameters can be developed from:

Spatial transformation
levels

Sub-text
quality of movement:
lightness - heaviness

Shifts
temporal and spatial

Stimuli
external
with or without contact

Transitions

Shifts in accents and development

Breakdown

Limitation of
spatial and physical scope

Dynamic impact

Complementary aspects

Transformation
of individual segments of movement from one part of the body
to another or from a single dancer to a group of dancers

Changes in dimension

Rhythm and tempo

When you apply the examples listed in the diagram above to temporal and spatial frames it is very likely that the interaction between parameters will spark ideas for new parameters or manipulation ideas. However, developing projects in this way requires practice and time to broaden your horizons and expand the scope of your work. So let us have a closer look at the different manipulation parameters with the following exercises and examples.

External, relational manipulation parameters, with or without physical contact

One dancer dances the same sequence several times, a second dancer, the 'catalyst', interferes in as many different ways as possible. The catalyst can alter the sequence by briefly touching the first dancer, by redirecting the original motion in large swoops, by using their voice to change the movements through sounds, by breathing on the dancer, by a counter-movement, or by putting their body in the first dancer's way. The first dancer is free to react to some impulses and ignore others.

Developing manipulation parameters from transitional sequences

Divide a complex movement into several parts. This will leave you with a series of very short individual sequences. Rearrange them in different patterns. This will give you new transitional sequences, which can now be expanded and made the focus of your work, so the frame is now superimposed on your transitional sequences.

18 Study Reverse phrasing

For each phrase danced in a forward motion, develop a reverse version. Try using different temporal frames with a movement phrase and developing the reverse phrasing of those movements within the constraints of the frame. Now add the reverse phrases to the original phrases, offset against each other both temporally and spatially.

19 Study Transforming individual sequences

Divide a complex movement into several parts. This will result in very short individual sequences of varying lengths.
Try transforming the parts by altering the constituent movements. Place the parts in a new sequence using varying repeating patterns.

20 Study Manipulation parameters from the essence of a movement

Identify the essential aspects of five different movements. Explore different ways of expressing them with different body parts and with a group of dancers.

21 Study Manipulation parameters from dimension

Take an everyday routine, such as 'getting ready in the morning', and develop movement material for a choreography using extreme enlargement and changes in space.

Manipulation parameters from extreme changes in dimension

The title says it all. Let me give you an example to explain what I mean.

As part of our training at the Laban Centre in London, we had to mime our morning routine on getting up. Then we had to manipulate our movements by drastically changing the dimensions. I was a bit annoyed by this, because it seemed to have nothing to do with what fascinated me about dance. I was looking for some kind of secret or higher state; I did not want to mime getting up in the morning. Instead of working on the exercise, I wandered around the dance studio to have a look around. One dancer was crawling across the floor on her knees, her arms in front of her body forming a large circle. 'That's a strange way of getting up,' I said to her. 'I am already up', she replied, 'At the moment, I'm striking a match on the sandpaper so I can light the stove.'

Sometimes there is creative potential in a simple idea like this, something one only sees at second glance. You can only find out by being open to unusual approaches and challenges. I was not able to be open in this situation, because my mind was focused on something else. Later, a theatre group commissioned me to choreograph the morning routine of four astronauts in a spaceship on just three square metres, and so I eventually got around to doing the exercise.

Manipulation parameters from movement quality

Any thought, any visual or abstract idea, and any emotion, felt or captured in the mind's eye, can alter the quality of a dance movement. Quality in this sense is not about some movements being better than others, not about 'higher' or 'lesser' quality of movement. It is about the nuances of a movement that tell us something about the source of the moment, the dancer's or choreographer's inner world. If you alter that inner world by engaging with an image and the emotions associated with it, the quality of any movement you then make will be affected, and the shift in the quality of your movement will eventually alter the movement itself.

Controlling internal effort

It is easy to say, 'I will put more or less effort into this or that movement.' Effort as such is physical, and we understand it to mean muscular, bodily exertion. You could call it 'surface effort', since it is immediately visible on the surface of the body when the dancer applies it.

'Surface effort' translates easily and directly into movement – for example the difference between pushing over a cardboard wall and pushing an omnibus. There is, however, a different kind of effort in dance. It is a kind of inner effort that lies somewhere under our muscles, whose measure is determined by our mental and emotional engagement, and is accompanied by the energetic impetus that we find in Eastern bodywork, such as Tai-Chi, Qigong, Kung-Fu, etc. Using energy in different ways may not necessarily change the tension in our muscles, but a movement may become more intense, or develop a different quality. We don't need to judge whether it becomes better or worse, all we are interested in is a creative approach to the dimensions of a movement.

We can train how to use our energy just as we can train our strength or reactions, it just isn't as obvious. The energetic aspect of movement is practically invisible, and thus much harder to grasp. Many dancers are unable to actively use it or understand its scope, and it is no use talking to them about it. Then there are dancers who have a lot of energy and know what to do when they are directed to 'Leave everything as it is, but take some of the energy out of it.' On the other hand, it is very rare that dancers whose energy is low manage to change their energy if directed to do so. They will probably just move more quickly, excitedly, or more powerfully. However, working with energy operates on another, more immaterial level. In many Asian practices, such as Tai-Chi, dealing with energy is central to movement. A dance company that knows how to manage its energy in an intelligent and conscious manner will always be one step ahead of troupes that rely on artistry alone. Energy is produced in the mind and finds its correspondence in the body. It has to do with concentration and breathing. When the breath flows freely, chances are that the energy is also circulating unhindered through the body. The problem is that we often fail to notice how shallow our breath is when we move, because our physical actions take up so much of our attention.

Without actively changing your breathing, focus on your breath while you are reading these lines. Does it flow freely? Are you breathing deeply and regularly, or does your breathing become shallower as you concentrate on reading? Are you able to read on and at the same time deepen your breathing, so that it becomes regular, gentle and free? Can you take your breath deeper down into your body than you would normally do? Give your breath more space, let your lungs extend further out into your torso without forcing it. Let any inner tension go, widening your ribs each time you inhale. At the end of this sentence, close your eyes, and concentrate on the inner expansion of your breath, visualising your breathing space widening further and your breath transforming into something visible, flowing through your body.

How did you get on? Did it work? Or did you fall asleep? It only works if you stay present and curious throughout the exercise. You will feel how your energy expands with your breathing. The more you practice, the quicker you will achieve a deep, regular breath, and the easier you will find it to sense the level of energy present in your body. You will notice that your energy flow varies significantly from day to day.

Apart from the potential manipulations this type of energy work might inspire, a choreographer must decide what kind of energy the different parts of his choreography need, and the audience will notice whether the energetic aspect has been addressed in rehearsals or not. Sometimes the shift in energy within a dance is very slight and nuanced, but you will definitely see it if you pay close attention. It will be visible the very moment the dancer shifts from one energy level to another.

Dancers often don't know when to shift energies in a choreography, even though being aware of energy levels is crucial if you are aiming for synchronous movements. It is not enough for the dancers to just 'do the same step' if you want your ensemble to move as one. At the same time, knowing when you are supposed to shift your energy and actually doing it are two different things, and not all dancers will find it easy to learn. The more you focus on shifting energy during rehearsals, the more practice the dancers get, the better the chance that they will be able to use different energy levels on stage.

When improvising, dancers often stay on the same energy level for a long time. That is quite natural because we usually associate a particular kind of energy with a specific theme. While it is fine to go with your natural reaction to a theme, dance always benefits from contrasts, so try if you can find different types of energy for your theme and use them to add contrast and surprise to your improvisation.

Most people find it easier to imagine objects or materials than to visualise abstract, nebulous energies, but material work always entails the risk of straying from the essence of the dance. Every time you define a specific movement quality by saying, 'It is like glue', just to clarify what you are doing, you take a step further away from dance. It is better to notice a particular energy within the movement and to go after it directly. However, if you want to manipulate the movement, using material associations works really well, simply because you are immediately able to name the specific quality you are looking for.

Effort defined by material

Compile a list of materials with very different characteristics, for example:

– air	– rubber
– fire	– lead
– foam rubber	– water
– stone	– metal
– ice cream	– paper

One dancer picks a material and dances an improvisation in which she adapts her movement quality to the characteristics of the material. A second dancer picks an entirely different material as the basis of his dance, and joins with the first dancer on stage. Then dancer A and dancer B try to exchange movement qualities for a moment and then switch back again.
Pay attention to irregular rhythms as the dancers exchange movement qualities.
The dancers have to represent their material as exactly and clearly as possible.

Work with a dance combination you know well. Assign a quality to it that is asssociated it with a specific material. So instead of saying 'Move lightly', use images that include the material you chose, for example, 'Move as if you were a feather moving in a breeze' or 'Move like ice cream melting on a hot plate'.

Use these images to manipulate your original dance combination until it becomes a different, new creation.

Changing the flow

When we watch a dance composition, we may perceive it either as one whole piece, as a piece made up of different parts, or a series of random scenes following one after the other, depending on how smoothly the individual parts of the piece connect with each other.

As choreographers, we can interrupt the flow of the piece at any point. If we interrupt it, we can choose to develop a new pathway to return to the initial position. This route to realignment with the original trajectory of the piece can even be put at the centre of attention, so the original material is not only changed, but actually also enriched by the development of moments of re-entry.

As a category, flow can be divided into two directions on the level of quality:

Free or constrained

In some dance techniques, such as the Graham technique or classical ballet, a constrained quality of movement dominates, whilst post-modern techniques favour a free movement quality known as 'release'. It is relatively easy to switch movement qualities from free to constrained, since constraint is associated with control, and control is a matter of training. Release, on the other hand, is harder to achieve, because many dancers find it is easier to control than to let go. I often direct dancers to carry out movements without constraint, and I watch them inch cautiously towards freedom, whereas a constrained quality can be swiftly developed in a choreography. If you want to develop freedom of movement, you have to work on your control of letting go. It is only when you can let go consciously that you can modify movements and press forward into the creative details of choreography. It can be challenging to find your way along the border between over-controlling and losing yourself in release. Working with the moment of release is about recognising the predominant energy in a movement, and fine-tuning it.

Manipulations using separate elements

Step1: Pick one movement from a sequence and insert a stop into a flowing movement. Example: Perform a rond de jambe en l'air, but stop at the diagonal.

Select a new starting point and find different ways to proceed from it back to the stop. Example: After having stopped the rond de jambe en l'air at the diagonal, I find a new starting point somewhere in the room, on the floor or in the air, and find a way back to the diagonal.

Look for links between the movements and positions, and start again at step 1.

Transferring movements within the body

Transfer the movement of an arm into a hip movement, or an accent given by an elbow to a heel, or a leg movement to a head movement. Look for other possibilities to transfer movements. Pique your curiosity for modification and change.

Free and constrained manipulations

Develop an improvisation on the theme of 'free and constrained' using as many different nuances as possible. See what other nuances in quality you associate with the theme. What effect does a lightness of touch or a heaviness have on the quality of free-flowing movements? What are their effects on constrained movement?

Alter a fixed sequence of movement by trying out different kinds of flow.

Manipulations with energetic changes through sounds and breath

Focus on your breath and your awareness. Find a soft, regular breathing pattern, so that energy can flow freely throughout your body.

Link the breath with movements that support its flow.

Fill your abdomen with air, and then expel it all in one go by saying 'HA!'.

Look for movements that support this sudden exhale.

Work with different letters of the alphabet and different sounds. Experiment with different breathing patterns until you have developed a repertoire of moods made up of sound, breath and movement components.

Take a sequence from a choreographed piece or choose a sequence of movements from your own repertoire.

Use the repertoire of moods you developed in point 5 above, and start to alter the sequence and elements of your choreographed piece, bringing it to bear on the differing energies of the original movements, so that they clash with, or complement, each other.

Experiment with exaggerating the different moods. Can you transform your original sequence beyond recognition?

Spatial aspects as manipulation parameters

The audience will often not recognise a dance sequence they have seen before if the dancers face another direction. If the sequence is shifted temporally or spatially, or danced by several dancers at the same time, even trained dancers will not recognise that they are being presented with exactly the same thing. This means that I am able to produce a contrast in the material without radically altering it. Many choreographers worry about not finding enough movement material to create such contrasting elements. Sometimes all that is needed is a change of direction.

If we treat space like a three-dimensional screen onto which we project our choreography, various angles of vision become available to us. Depending on the angle we choose we have different options for manipulations. If we want to develop manipulations of movement material within a dancer's kinesphere, we first need to observe how that dancer uses space, and how she moves within her kinesphere. In order to illustrate a dancer's use of the kinesphere, I will use an example of an everyday stereotype. I hope this will provide you with a more concrete idea of what I am talking about, rather than describing it in abstract dance terms.

Imagine two people of a Mediterranean temperament in a heated conversation, and observe:

- How much space do their movements take up?

- What part of their kinesphere are they using?

- Are their movements direct or indirect, focused or flexible?

- How efficient are their movements?

Observe different stereotypes and compare your results: A police officer, a prostitute, a shy child, and so on. Try to limit your observations to their use of space, and train your perception to notice the way in which each figure uses space within their kinespheres.

Choose movements from a sequence that moves directly from A to B. Experiment with making the movements more indirect by adding a detour.

Choose elements from a sequence in which movements are kept close to the body. Experiment with expanding the movements to the greatest extent possible within the kinesphere.

Choose movements from a sequence with a wide range of motion. Limit the range of movement of an arm or a leg using a tape measure or string. Experiment with the possibilities within this limitation.

Translating movements from one spatial level into another

Develop a movement sequence that includes travelling steps and makes use of all spatial levels. Then transform your sequence by changing directions and translating the individual movements to a different level.

27 Study

28 Study

Transferring movement segments from one point in space to another

Every movement element can be transferred to any position and any level in your dance space. This spatial transfer links a transformation within the body of the dancer (as described in Exercise 24: Transferring movements within the body) with a change of direction and level.

Let's say you want to transfer a spinning jump that moves diagonally up and down again into a floor-level movement. The space you are confining yourself to – i.e. the floor – changes the movement and how you get into it. Several solutions are possible using just one single transfer idea, and you could even join them all up in a movement sequence.

A back flip in the air will probably translate into a backwards roll on the floor. A turn with arm movements, combined with a large jump, is rather more complex to transfer to the floor. If I then flip the movement by 180 degrees, at least two new movements result, that is, how I start the jump, which now probably looks rather more like a handstand, and how I come out of it.

Changing the dance space changes the performance

Have you ever rehearsed a piece in a place that was completely different from the stage it was to be performed on? If you have, you may have noticed how the choreography's effect changed with the change of space.

This effect can make it tricky if you are choreographing for a performance in a particular place where you can't rehearse until the last moment before the opening night. So you hold rehearsals at the studio, even though you will have to perform in a church, thinking you know what the effect of your choreography will be on the day. When you can finally try it all out in the church, you realise the dance has an entirely different effect than you had planned, and you overthrow everything and start again from scratch.

In a small, narrow space, movements have a different effect than they do out in nature, and certain spaces call for a dynamic that would not work in others. The tension between the space and the choreography changes. You can use this effect as a tool for manipulation: rehearse your dance in different places, staying open to the possibilities of the different settings and allowing them to influence your piece. I once danced a piece on an escalator to the underground during rush hour – you wouldn't have recognised the original choreography even if you tried.

On one hand, the dance space physically influences our movements simply through its properties; on the other hand, it also has an effect on our psyche. As a dancer, I emotionally open to the situation in which I am dancing. If I dance in a public space, this means a confrontation with completely unprepared passers-by. Depending on their reactions, I will adapt my dance. I may feel intimidated or encouraged; some settings may make me angry, and some may touch me with a sudden tenderness that melts every sharp accent from my dance. Each situation will change my inner attitude, which in turn alters the quality of my movements.

I once surprised myself when dancing a sequence on a traffic island by suddenly launching into a series of pirouettes. It really didn't fit with what I had originally choreographed, and I asked myself later, 'Why pirouettes?' I found the answer when I realised that I had been trying to assert myself as a dancer by choosing movements that the drivers in the passing cars would recognise as dance, unconsciously attempting to meet what I thought would be their expectations. However, it is not all that important why I decided to make my choreography more showy in the end. What is important is being able to exploit all possibilities of manipulation and use them – I am, after all, aiming at performance, not psychotherapy.

Film a solo piece in the dance studio. Then send the dancer and the film-maker off to explore the city and the surrounding region. Have the dancer perform the solo piece everywhere she can, and the film-maker record it on video.

Notice how the effect of the choreography changes. What was the relationship between the movements and the dance space? Which combinations produced suspension, and which diminished it? How could the choreography be adapted to the different places?

Look for spaces that provoke changes in the choreography, and be open to new influences coming from these spaces.

Manipulation using temporal aspects: Rhythm and tempo

When we change the tempo of a movement, we also change its quality. As a result, the emotional content of the movement also shifts, and with it the need to express it through the body.

Example

A very fast movement of the arm, such as that of a karate fighter, permits little incidental motion, and demands the dancer's full attention. If the tempo is slowed down drastically, it may take on different qualities, such as 'soft' or 'powerful'. The experience of movement quality will echo through the dancers' bodies: although they are just moving their arms, their shoulders, ribcage, back and legs will adapt to the required movement quality, finding a stance to support them. Like this, a karate chop becomes a complex, full-body dance movement.

Speeding up and slowing down a movement does not just have an effect on a dancer's emotional state, but also transforms it in physiologically. Speed can, for instance, induce a centrifugal effect, requiring the dancer to counter-balance; slowing down a leap produces an entirely different situation with other physiological constraints.

Rhythmic changes do not modify the form of a dance, but they can radically alter the emotional effect of movements. If, for instance, you interrupt a series of fluid movements at irregular intervals, the sequence will appear rhythmically distorted.

Manipulation using tempo and rhythm

Create a sequence of movements that switches between isolated movements and full-body movements, staying in place, travelling, and changing levels.

Experiment with slowing down and speeding up your sequence.

Explore the use of stops and their rhythmic phrasing.

Devising complementary elements from a choreographic concept

Give your dancers some time to try out different movement concepts. Then ask them to decide on one concept and to develop a movement sequence that expresses the essence of that concept.

In pairs: One dancer dances his choreography without naming the concept; the second dancer is asked to develop complementary elements that can be integrated into the dance sequence.

Accumulation

The Trisha Brown principle: 'Add an arm'. Assign a gesture from the original choreography to a particular part of the body or remove it from that body part.

Manipulation using complementary elements

In the section entitled 'Composition', I set out a number of ways of perceiving choreography. We can focus on the space a dancer takes and forms within his kinesphere and on stage, we can concentrate on movement quality, etc. Alternatively, you could ignore all these suggestions, and just watch the choreography to grasp the idea behind it. There are many ways of achieving this, and every single spectator may understand the choreography differently. Based on this idea, it is possible to develop the notion of complementary elements that have more to do with interpretation and individual sensations than they do with a technical analysis of the dance. These complementary elements can then be woven into the choreography as interpolations, altering its original nature and form.

What your choreographic idea means to you, and how you formulate it, is ultimately your decision. The main thing is that you are clear about the concept behind it, because it is only then that you will be able to develop complementary elements from it. If, for instance, your concept is about 'letting go of energy', then you could develop complementary elements around the theme of 'increasing and retaining energy'.

Developing movements for a theme

Although I have only briefly touched upon repertoire choreography on the last few pages, it is an aspect of dance that offers the choreographer a wide spectrum of options. Differentiated repertoire work proves a veritable treasure trove in which all our choreographic wishes come true, and so, at first glance, there does not seem to be any need for thematic research when it comes to developing moment. Whatever you want to express, you can express through the repertoire and its variations. But if you dare to leavebehind all you have learned, if you dare to stray from the beaten path, you will step into entirely new worlds. If you decide to develop dances afresh by researching a theme, there are direct and indirect methods that will lead you from conception to dance piece:

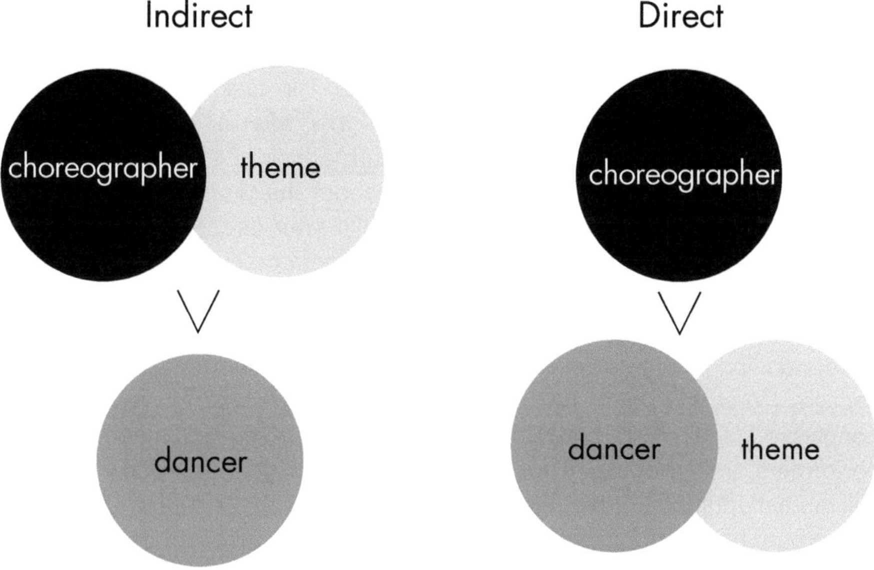

The theme inspires the choreographer to choose of specific movements and images. It is 'just' a matter of transferring them to the dancers.

The choreographer does not provide the dancers with prescribed movements, but simply encourages them to develop their own way of expressing the theme.

Let us analyse these approaches in more detail, and consider their advantages and disadvantages.

The indirect approach

Developing a piece of choreography in an indirect approach seems, at first glance, to be the most efficient and simplest way of doing it: after a period of intense research and preparation on my (the choreographer's) part, I can easily convey the result of my work to a group of dancers in a few rehearsals. This approach is particularly suited to those occasions when there is no ostensible need to examine the theme of the dance. But even in productions where you favour the direct approach, you will need to give the dancers a few movement inputs to experiment with. If you make the dancers do all the developing work by themselves, they will soon feel empty and burnt out.

The indirect approach skirts the risk of being confronted with dancers who are not willing to fully engage with the theme. The task is clear, and I can chuck out any dancer who doesn't comply – it is, after all, my idea and my piece, and a chance for the dancer to make something of it. Remember, however, that your dancers only know as much about the theme as you are prepared to share or develop during rehearsals. If your directing becomes too prescriptive, the indirect method turns into a dictatorship. If you choose to work in this way, dancers may simply not be able to make the link between the theme and the movement. Even if you explain it perfectly, your personal understanding of the subject matter may be entirely different to that of your dancers. What you deem organic movements and transitions may earn you nonplussed faces. Also, because a dictatorship reduces the dancers to mere performers, their motivation will not be particularly high. The group's potential will remain untapped. If the dancers can't identifiy with the theme, it will take a long time before the piece elicits an emotional response in them. With one solo dancer it will happen much more quickly, but the larger the group, the harder the task.

If you work imitatively, make sure you seek a dialogue with your dancers from time to time. Describe the ideas that lie behind the movements and the message you want to convey with the piece. You can let the dancers make suggestions for improvements by only marking a few movements that they can then shape according to the theme. If you feel that the theme is slipping away from you, begin again from the start. I have frequently seen dance pieces that start with a theme, and lose it as the choreography progresses. Everything looks great, and then you ask yourself, 'What happened to the theme?' 'Where is this leading us?' 'Are we still on the right way?' Ask yourself these questions before your audience does.

The direct approach

The direct approach presents the choreographer with the challenge of finding a way to pique the interest of the dancers, that is, to introduce them to the material in such a way that they can engage with it using the language of movement. The introduction of the theme has to take place on both an intellectual and a physical level. It is not enough to say to the dancers, 'Right, now let's dance an abstraction of the Middle Ages,' or 'Let me see you do the 1920s'. These examples may sound absurd to you, but I actually heard them during rehearsals, coming from directors who were educated, talented people. The results of such instructions ranged from cliché to confused silence and embarrassment.

There is no 'one size fits all' method of establishing the direct approach between the theme and the dancers, but if we know what individual steps we need to take in a direct approach, we can develop different approaches from there. The dancers 'inner space' plays a major role in the direct approach because all depends on the dancers engaging with the theme. When they do, they can develop their own movements and also justify them. Depending on whether you are working on a piece with a theme based purely on movement, such as, for example, 'isolation and space', or whether you choose an intellectual theme, for instance, 'the inner justification of violence', different methods of working will be necessary to encourage your dancers to start creating suitable movement material.

As a choreographer, you need to develop a strategy for directing your dancers in a fashion that will allow them to create internal material. Or you find a link between the theme and an idea for movement that will lead your dancers to improvise such material. The following examples illustrate different ways of familiarising your dancers with a theme in more or less depth. All of them - from working with synonyms to establishing a setting that elicits the subject matter to visualisation – can be adapted and used when working with actors, dancers, or even groups of children.

Synonyms as bridges between subject matter and movement

Working with synonyms is particularly useful for approaching material with which you are not particularly familiar, for example when you are commissioned to choreograph a piece.

Example
In a piece on 'The four seasons', I'm assigned 'Spring' as my theme. If I had to express the essence of spring in one single movement, it would definitely be anything that 'opens'. I improvise, looking for 'opening' movements so that I can compare the feeling of the movement with my idea of spring, and it works really well. Later, during a technique class, I review all kinds of ways to open up the body. I seamlessly move into an improvisation on the theme of 'opening' .With 'opening' being the common denominator between theme and approach to movement, the exercise is a success.

I then select elements from the improvisation, decide on their running order, and provisionally link them with repertoire movements to form a sequence. The more the dancers engage with the theme of spring, the more varied their range of movements becomes. Some dancers choose to open with explosive movements, so I ask others to try to open as gently and carefully as possible. This results in different dance solos. As I look at the material, it occurs to me how strong and confident the solos are, and I realise that spring as I imagined it would have to be far less forceful. In my mind, it would tread unsteadily, haltingly. The following day, I give my dancers key-words such as 'caution', 'unsteady', 'collapsing and starting over again.' I let the dancers play with balance, trying out extreme balancing positions, and looking for a feeling of caution. This continues until I achieve a wide variety of material that comes from each dancer personally, all stemming from the common theme of spring.

One pleasant side-effect of this work is that the dancers are able to demonstrate their own particular strengths during the improvisation. In training classes, it is important to also work on the exact opposites of these strengths to encourage dancers to develop different facets of their dance. When working with a dance troupe, however, you will want to explore your dancers' strengths, in order to bring the level of the troupe up to its highest potential.

As I look at the sequence's structure from a compositional point of view, combining small sequences of movements over and again, I am struck by the dramaturgical depth and densitiy of the choreography we have produced. It is great, but now I need an introduction that will prepare us for our 'Spring'. Since the music starts directly with the theme of spring, I develop a silent tableau to put before the rest of the choreography.

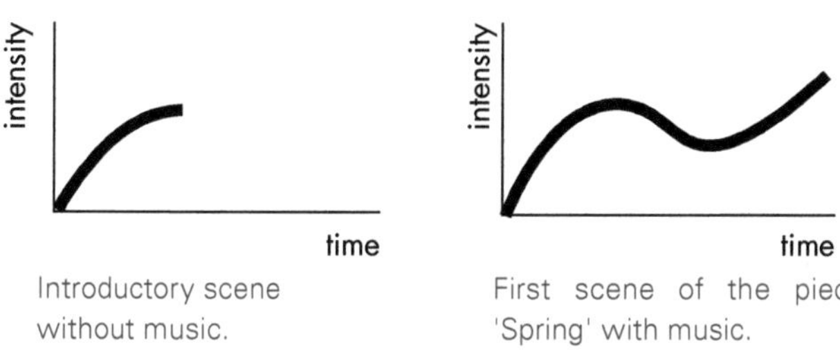

Introductory scene without music.

First scene of the piece. 'Spring' with music.

Movements that denote 'opening' are used as a first synonym for spring. Later other synonyms are added, such as collapsing and starting over again, unsteady movements, and aspects such as 'caution' that have come to light as important nuances of the movements or as a subtext.

Constructing a setting based on synonyms

1   In simple words, define the mood or expression of the scene, i.e. the things that you wish to convey. Do not construct a mini-drama; be concise. Simple and clear! Let's practise with the opening scene of the musical *Hair* - the keywords that spring to my mind are freedom, happiness, individuality, love, tolerance, attentiveness, joy ... (that is my version of it; for someone else, the words might be anger, drugs, rebellion, fornication, and so on).

2   It is generally a good idea to involve your dancers in the process, because then they will identify more with the material. You could brainstorm the keywords with your performers, and perhaps even discuss them in a group setting. If you opt for the latter, check in with yourself to see if you just want the group to back up your own opinions, or if you are genuinely curious about what they feel and think.

It is well-defined, select the synonyms that best translate into movement what you want to convey.

Synonyms on movement level

Freedom	Broad, expansive, flowing movements
Happiness	Extensive paths through space, jumps
Individuality	Individual, personal solos
Love	Contact
Tolerance	Moving as a group, not necessarily synchronous
Caution	If synchronous, then only in brief 'sparks'

3 Define the quality of the movements. Some synonyms include choreographic directions – 'moving as a group, not necessarily synchronous', whilst others define the nature of the movements: 'broad, expansive, flowing movements'. Divide each bullet point into choreographic directions and movement quality. Concentrate on the latter, and think about what its opposite would be, in order to filter out what you do not want. Examples: On the spot, small gestures, heavy, on the floor, staccato movements, isolation, and so on.

4 Develop an improvised way of addressing the key features of bullet point 3. Depending on your dancers' improvisational skills, it may be sufficient to specify the definitions and then directly dance them in an improvisation without any special introduction. The trick then lies in using the intellectually construed common denominator as a springboard rather than a restriction. Improvise in response to each bullet point, so that you examine all its possibilities. Put together sequences of movement created during the improvisation.

and movements.

Look for synonyms for the movements.

Set the synonyms and common denominators as your goals, and develop various ways to approach your goals in an improvised session.

Develop an improvisation from this.

Combine short sequences from the improvised material, and transfer them onto a tension chart.

Combine the sequences spontaneously, and build a structure from them.

Non-verbal and emotional links between theme and movement

Working with synonyms touches upon the verbal, that which can be named, to such a degree that some of the non-verbal aspects, the intuitive part of choreography, may fail to be considered altogether. To enable to stay on the level of intuition, I would like to suggest developing non-verbal links to, and synonyms for, a theme. This is about going into greater depth with the subject matter, and developing a vision on the emotional and imaginative levels. Let me illustrate this with a few examples.

Gestures

Using some kind of template, such as a story or a film, I try to intensify my emotional experience of it in retrospect, without falling back on verbal descriptions. I let the story, or the film, play in my mind's eye, placing my focus on the moments that mean the most to me, or impress me the most. As Lee Strasberg would say, I gently push my emotions and intensify them. I concentrate hard on my inner images and the feelings associated with them, expanding the effects of my soul and mind on my body. This expansion may initially take the form of being in the present, and then in tensing and relaxing various body parts. As I tense and relax my body, I sense the need to move in particular directions, make small movements, feel slight adjustments in my muscles and my whole body, such as changes in temperature, numbness, compression, attempts to break free, or collapse. These sensations produce gestures, and from gestures come movements and nuances, and with them the raw material for my dance created intuitively from the template.

Image

I look at a drawing or a painting, only focusing on my perception of light and dark. At the same time, I try to feel 'light' and 'dark' in my breathing. As I look and breathe, I try to intensify my breathing to such an extent that the contrasts become stronger and the grey shades between light and dark grow more distinctive. As I distinguish between these shades, I get a sense of concentration of energies, of density at certain points in the image. I work with my breath, allowing myself to experience points and larger areas of concentration and expansion both within the image and the sensations of my body. As I let these experiences in, I associate feelings of ease and depth with the terms 'light' and 'dark'. Then I concentrate on the available directions in the drawing or painting. My next step is to expand the directional structure I have perceived in the image into three-dimensional space. You could say I allow the directions to expand into and out of the image. Concentrating alternately on light and dark, wide and narrow, deep and high, and on the directions hinted at in the image, I work on movements and positions, employing tension and nuances of movement. I merge my working process with the image, developing choreography whilst avoiding entering the verbal, tangible world as much as possible.

Poem

Friedrich Hölderlin's poetry encompasses with language what might be described as a speechless consciousness. His language attempts to verbally express things we cannot grasp. Thus, a poem experiments with capturing something of the soul that we otherwise could not capture. If I want to find that something within dance, I have to approach it through the poem, in order to develop from it the movements I need. For this approach to work, I have to be prepared to enter into a process that takes me to the other side of consciousness. I listen repeatedly to the poem, and try to intensify my willingness to enter into the core, without validating or judging. I trust the movements of my soul, as I listen to the poem, in order to approach its mystery, as it weaves its fine threads around my work. Here is an extract from the poem:

Mnemosyne
[Third version]

The fruits are ripe, dipped in fire,
Cooked and sampled on earth. And there's a law,
That things crawl off in the manner of snakes,
Prophetically, dreaming on the hills of heaven.
And there is much that needs to be retained,
Like a load of wood on the shoulders.
But the pathways are dangerous.
The captured elements and ancient laws of earth
Run astray like horses. There is a constant yearning
For all that is unconfined. But much needs
To be retained. And loyalty is required.

Yet we mustn't look forwards or backwards.
We should let ourselves be cradled
As if on a boat rocking on a lake.

...

Working with a such a poem requires great concentration and exceptional commitment. It teaches us to feel that wordless consciousness, and it illustrates how language is just another attempt at expressing the workings of the soul.

Colours

A: Coloured foils are placed in front of spotlights in the studio, so that the room is lit by one particular colour at a time. I walk around the room, entering the mood of the colour, looking for shapes and movement qualities that reflect this mood.

B: I put together a repeatable sequence of movements that is neutral in terms of content, working with various body parts and different directions. Now I 'colour' the sequence with the ideas that came to me during the exercise from section A above. How do the movements and their quality change?

Music

I choose an excerpt from a concert or a short piece of music and listen to it again and again, letting it evoke images and sensations from my mind. I focus on these images and from there develop movements and nuances without listening to the music. Then I experiment with setting the choreography to different parts of the music.

Sculpture

With their eyes closed, two dancers form a three-dimensional shape from clay. Two others analyse the sculpture's lines, curves, tensions and dynamics. What basic mood can you elicit by its characteristics as a whole? With the sculpture in mind, develop a solo.

Theme and structure

The primary focus of this exercise is to connect the development of movement with working on movement within the context of a given theme. As source material, I use a series of images by the painter Roland Peter Litzenburger; the images were put together in a video for projection. Alternatively, you can choose your own sequence of images. Working with a video clip has the advantage that it serves as a template with a defined duration, rhythm and dramatic arc.

Have a look at the image series by Roland Peter Litzenburger on the theme of 'The defeated man' or 'Love and eroticism' and choose one of them as the theme of your choreography. Notice that there are videos of both series at:

https://vimeo.com/427310293
https://vimeo.com/412462746

Part 1: Thematic superstructure

Define a general structure within which you would like to respond to the sequence of images.

Look for a gesture that corresponds with this structure or style.

Give this gesture a position in space.

Use the following parameters on the gesture, and develop it further to create a thematic vocabulary of movement:

-   force and release

-   transferring the movement and the position
    within the body and in space

-   high speed and low speed

-   tension and relaxation

-   floor – mid-level – aerial

-   at the back - in front

-   relationship to the audience

-   number of dancers

Look for another gesture and take it through the same process.

Working this way will help you define the theme.
What kind of introduction, main part, and finale can you imagine for your theme?

Part 2: Thematic consolidation, sub-themes

Now look for sub-themes in the individual images. Pay attention to the dynamics of the video.

For each sub-theme, choose a main focus from the following parameters, and use it to develop movement material:

- force	- fast
- release	- slow
- placement of a body part	- tension
- placement on the stage	- relaxation
- level: floor - mid-level - aerial	- relationship to the audience
- number of dancers	

Within the sub-theme, try out the different parameters that you used in the exercise before, and vary the level of suspense.

Take stock of the material that you have created so far. Notice the structure of the piece, its progression, flow, and how it relates to the video at this stage.

Part 3: Theme and contrast

Decide on a contrast you want to set against your theme, and consider which parameter best to use to express it.

Where and how can you work the contrast into your piece?

Part 4: ABA-structure or canon

Create a dance combination in an ABA-structure by opposing theme and contrast.

Let a group of dancers perform the combination.

OR

Develop a movement loop. Vary:

time
space
number of dancers

As a second step, add the contrast into the piece.

Part 5: Examine your piece again, especially paying attention to:

dramatic arc
progression
structure and emotional journey

Inner substance and evocative setting

When we define movement with synonyms to achieve a thematic resolution of material in movement, there is a certain point at which we limit the possibilities open to us. After all, the mood of a scene or what we seek to express through it may, in certain circumstances, be expressed more broadly than is possible via synonyms. The expression of a theme in movement – the common denominator between dance and subject matter – does not necessarily need to be defined in advance, you can also develop it during rehearsals. To achieve that, the choreographer has to elicit emotional responses to the material from the dancers. These responses will then act as catalysts for improvisation.

Example
Let us say you want to develop a piece about loneliness – about its causes, forms and effects. You ask yourself where loneliness comes from, and which mechanisms cause it. You probably also think about your own reasons for choosing exactly this material. Your theme is the filter through which you look at yourself and at the world. Then you decide not to outline the theme for your dancers, but to try an experimental choreographic study with them. Your aim is to elicit in your dancers an authentic feeling of loneliness, so that they can then produce creative material from it. If you were to speak to your dancers about loneliness before they move, they would aim to address the subject matter, and in the worst case end up dramatically miming loneliness in the improvisation. So instead of talking about loneliness, you outline an 'evocative setting', that is, an environment that elicits a feeling of loneliness. How you achieve that solely depends on the elements with which you fill your loneliness-provoking space.

Here is one possibility how to give your dancers an experience of 'isolation'.

Let them improvise, but limit their movement options to:

- fast actions on the spot

- throwing themselves on the ground

- mechanical arm movements whilst moving forwards.

Set the improvisation within a in a limited spacestructure of changing directions and tempi, so that the dancers are forced to repeatedly cross each other's path.

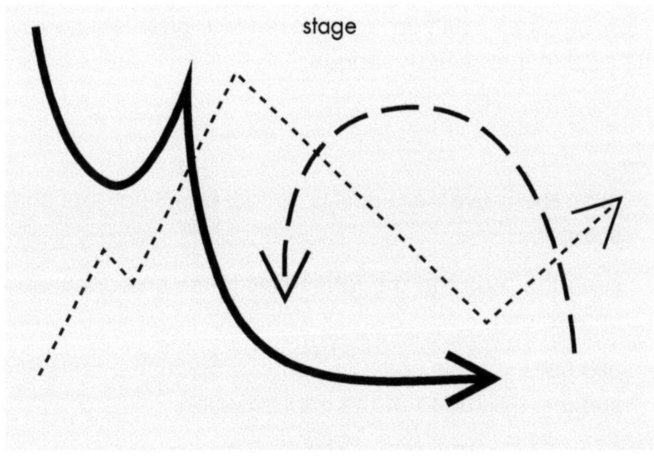

Individual movements in a limited space

Assign different directions and changes of direction to each dancer.

Each dancer works with their directions, varying the starting point of their movements.

Add another level of constraint by introducing time pressure into the improvisation. The dancers are to move as if they were late, constantly running behind by several movements. Don't make the dancers rush their movements, but have them give their attention both to the moment and the things to come. Any contact between the dancers – eye contact, physical contact, speaking - is strictly forbidden. So the dancers are all racing through the room, throwing themselves on the floor, preoccupied with their arm movements and obsessed with the thought of lagging behind. Their eyes are open, that is, they are connected to space 'outside' of themselves, but not to the other dancers, having been forbidden to communicate with each other. They have to focus both on themselves and their environment at the same time: 'What is happening around me? What do I have to do to avoid contact? What is going on inside me? How can I fulfil my task in this improvisation on the levels of emotion and dance?' Watch the scene. Notice the effects the dancers create.

Do the figures seem isolated enough, or could their isolation be increased by some kind of quantifiable condition?

You talk to the dancers and let them describe what they felt as the danced the scene. Still, you do not bring up the concept of loneliness, but you do speak about isolation, because isolation is supposed to trigger feelings of loneliness. How can the setting intensify this trigger?

You can

- push the movement quality to make movements sharper and sharper

- keep the music at the rehearsals harsh and dominating, unrelenting

- use setting tools, such as lights, projections, texts and so on, to support the mood of the improvisation.

After you have established the basic mood of isolation in your scene, let it run for a while. Then ask the dancers to start looking for physical contact with their fellow performers. The task is to try to cling to another dancer while at the same time shaking off any dancer that tries to hold on to them. Somewhere in this process, dancers will find the 'raw material', the emotional resource for the feeling of loneliness. If the setting works, it will evoke feelings of isolation both in the spectators and the dancers. Some of the dancers will react emotionally to finding themselves in a scene of constant rushing, shaking each other off, and seeking and denying contact. When this happens, they need the freedom to explore the movements born from this reaction. By allowing them to diverge from the setting, you open a way for them to develop authentic movement material for solo dances. The dancers experience isolation, and get a glimpse of what it means to feel lonely. Depending on their personal history and their involvement with the theme, they will integrate this experience in their dance, and develop it further. They will be able grow out of 'acting lonely' into actually feeling some of that loneliness when they perform. They may also draw on personal experience and use a memory of loneliness to help them find the right mood for the scene. Keep in mind, however that the initial trigger for that feeling of loneliness was the setting. Make sure you stay with that setting, and use it again later in your work when you want to provoke these emotional responses again.

Next, lift the strict constraints of the setting, and let the dancers improvise freely. By now, the dancers have become so involved with the theme that they will have stopped thinking about what kind of movement material to choose. Because dancers are used to expressing themselves with their bodies, they will intuitively develop a physical response to the theme. In this process, the boundaries between dancer and choreographer dissolve. It is the choreographer's task to relieve the dancers of the burden of responsibility for the piece at some point, and re-define the boundaries. In such moments, it is as if the dancers were sitting in a drifting boat, and they need to know that someone is steering for them.

The setting defines the exterior world of the dancer, creating an environment that provokes a response.

The environment opens the door to the interior world of the dancer: experience, emotion and imagination.

The interior world of the dancer creates movement.

In this method, we move from the exterior world of the dancers to the interior world that is the source of movement. This means that if the dancers change a movement, they can compare the new movement with their interior world. They can adapt the new material to the emotion. This means that their material will not become vague when it is defined and refined in dance technique classes, because its starting point, the dancer's attitude, will remain.

The dancer's attitude is created by a setting.

Don't worry if you temporarily lose the emotion when you start defining and choosing movements, decide on rhythmic patterns, try to feel in which muscle a movement starts, and think about how to disperse solo dances in space and transfer the solo movements onto smaller groups. Your dancers will find it easy to return to the emotional inner space that yielded the material in the first place.

The dancers draw fragments of material from out of their inner being, and the choreographer can work with that material to a certain degree without losing its essence in the process. Scenes created from these fragments may either shake the foundations of the dance piece, or, conversely, form a supporting framework for the rest of the material – it all depends on the choreographer's feeling for the placement of the fragments within the context of a scene, and for the placement of the scene within the piece. The choreographer must be mindful to preserve the power of the valuable material born from the dancers' inner selves. It is very easy, both for dancers and choreographers, to lose direction when working on these bits of material, generally because they want to take them somewhere far too fast. Let's say, for example, you have an idea for a scene based on association with your established movement material. The new movements of that scene actually do not have much in common with the original material, rather, they evolved from it and develop it further. This means you start working on a scene that requires new movement material that has little to do with the material you developed during the improvisation sessions, and that might take you to a completely different direction. Chances are that the rehearsals now veer off into randomness, because the intention of the piece becomes muddled with all the possibilities of association. The original topic gets lost – which is not a bad thing per se, as long as those involved are aware of it.

What you should be aiming at is the development of scenes from the material you have created, in such a way that it supports the direction of the piece, reinforces, consolidates and concentrates the original material. It is a question of the choreographer's awareness of whether things are going in the direction of the theme or not. It is about distilling the integral essence of the theme from the movement material. Is the scene you are working on conducive to the subject matter; will it provide extra substance within the full context of the choreographed piece? If not, there will be little justification for its continued presence within the context of the piece.

How to work with an evocative setting

The question is not just whether you are can become the kind of teacher that inspires the group to trust you enough to follow you into unknown waters and work together towards a common goal. More importantly, you need to find out whether the dancers have the potential to plunge into this kind of exploration. There are many dancers who enjoy in-depth analysis and wish to develop their movements from inside out, expressing their own, authentic emotions, but they have never been trained in an approach that allows them to do that. In the end, however, it depends on the personality of your dancers. With the 'Four Seasons', the example I have mentioned previously, I took it to the extreme. I used an approach that would even elicit good results from children without any effort. How far you choose to go with which theme has less to do with your ambition, but more with the people with whom you work. I have experienced groups of amateurs with whom I was able to reach for the stars, and professional dancers who just wanted to know what they were meant to be performing without having to go through an introductory seminar during rehearsals. If you want to take the performance to another level, because you enjoy investigating things in depth, you will need to find people who are happy to engage in this kind of dialogue, and who find it exciting to immerse themselves in an uncertain process.

An inner approach does not necessarily have to be about emotions, themes vary greatly after all, but has to be about experiencing the core ideas of the theme. Anything that goes beyond a simple illustration of clichés is in some way associated with this kind of approach, regardless of what is being choreographed. Even if you end up choreographing something entirely different, such as an evening of cowboy songs – it is the experience of the characters that makes a scene convincing. In the previous example, we elicited a feeling of loneliness in the dancers through a setting that isolated them from each other. In the case of types (cowboys, for example) or animals, you will have to look at their typical environments or habitats. From the type's environment you then choose so-called 'suppliers', evocative aspects that will help you create a setting to approach your theme.

Exercise

Choose a theme

Look for words that, for you, reflect the chief characteristics of the theme.
You may add emotions.

Look for interesting suppliers around the emotion.

Select some of the suppliers to build a setting for an improvisation. Remember, the setting is only about movement. You are creating a world of movement according to the laws of movement.

Give the improvisation a direction to make the key idea visible to a spectator.

Precisely explain the intention behind the approach.
One part of the group keeps strictly to thr specified improvisation; other dancers open things up and improvise freely, albeit with reference to the subject matter.

Set small sequences from the improvised material.

Loneliness

Ostracism, burn-out.

Isolation through overwork, stress, rushing, everyday life, lack of receptivity, exhaustion.

Fast actions on the spot, collapse, mechanical arm movements, prohibition of touch, and so on.

Define the movement qualities. Alter the music and the lighting.
Introduce permission for contact in the form of clinging to, and shaking off, one another.
Key impression: Separation of the group, isolation.

Conversation.
One part of the group creates the setting; the other dancers reflect it in dance. Improvisation on the theme of loneliness. Switch roles.

Work on solo dances.

35 Study

Conclusion:

Links between theme and movement, movement synonyms, such as 'opening' in 'spring', as used in the above
example.

Non-verbal links between theme and movement.

With the help of suppliers, you can create setting for an improvisation in which the link between theme and movement
will naturally fall in place.

The goal is to approach the theme from the other side of
language.

Using visualisation to develop movements specific to a theme

Visualisation is a process in which an image held in the mind's eye is intensified and transferred onto the physical level of the dance.

Example

You choose 'lightness' as a theme. You visualise gas, air, and so on. Transferring your visualisation to the dance could mean dancers moving as if their arms were filling with air and lifting up from inside, giving the impression that their whole bodies will eventually fill with air, and lift, and that individual body parts will start to soar. This may sound very simplistic and superficial at first glance, but the outcome depends ultimately on how you work with it. If the dancers' inner experience of the image translates into their movements and overrides mere illustration, it will be fascinating to watch. You can always spot the dancers who have access to inner images and are able to let them show in their movements. If the dancers are open to trying visualisation, and if they are trained well to use it, this method will produce an intensity in choreography that is seldom reached with other methods when it comes to transferring a theme into movement.

This may have to do with the fact that visualisation intensifies the image without verbalising it. This process is closer to the essential nature of dance than to intellectual approaches. If you wish to elicit thematic associations with movement alone, the visualisation technique can support you in your work. There are hardly any themes that cannot be transferred from visualisation into dance. In almost every dance style, teachers use images to describe the quality of a movement, such as 'Move as if against the resistance of a rubber band …', or 'Draw your foot across the floor as if it were a match striking a match box …' ; and for some movement schools, such as Body-Mind Centering (BMC) or the Skinner Release technique (SRT), the visual imagining of a movement is a key principle. Both methods train the dancer in visualisation and are often used to approach choreography work. It would beyond the remit of this publication to try and integrate techniques like BMC or SRT, but there are a few principles worth mentioning here to show how visualisation functions in respect to choreography.

In principle, there are two ways to create a space for visualisation work:

– An inner, emotional image that elicits movement, such as the above example of lightness.

– An external image that determines the environment in which the dancers moves. The dancer creates the movement by reacting to the external image.

Emptying body and soul
through relaxation techniques

Verbally approaching visualisation
sharpening the mental image

Transfer – expanding the image.
Building a connection between the image and your body. Stationary, no movement.

Expansion – mental image

The identification with the image provokes poses, tension, movements.

Focus?

Expansion – outward image

The image creates the environment, the conditions to which the dancer responds physically.

Composition
Using compositional parameters on the material created through visualisation.

Using visualisation to develop a choreographical approach to a theme

Create a space for your visualisation and structure it, that is, think in detail about what steps you need to follow to create the image. Try to be as precise as possible, and focus on either an inner, emotional image or an external one that determines the environment. Follow the steps on page 162. Finish the study with your composition.

In the exercise section, you will find a fully structured case study. It deals with an attempt at bringing out the animal aspect in human beings through dance. Try the exercise described in the study to get a better feel for visualisation techniques.

36 Study

Working with elusive themes – abstraction and focus

Often, the themes treated in choreography are far too abstract to evoke any images or associations from which movements can be developed. Such themes, to use a term we used earlier, lack suppliers. Sometimes it is not even possible to clearly name the theme. Still, there seems to be some kind of essential core that can only be defined by zeroing in on it, because the focal point is not tangible and cannot be accessed as such.

Example
You are working with a video artist on a commission for a music clip. The aesthetic concept for the clip consists of intersecting and parallel lines in a three-dimensional space. There are absolutely no images associated with the theme, no suppliers at all. Let us imagine that you have no idea what you are supposed to do with these lines, how you or anyone else can make use of them, or would even feel inspired by seeing them. But you need this job. As the choreographer, you are now faced with the task of matching your discipline, dance, to the aesthetics of a customer. How do you do that?

You experiment. You begin by placing your dancers at different positions in space. Like in a randomised computer program, the dancers start to improvise along straight lines and diagonals. You try out various linear movements.

Some constellations of lines will appeal to you and others won't. You develop a standard measure, and eventually you find a logic within it, its own complex grammar, so to speak. Now, the lines begin to relate to each other, building connections that hold tension. This is the point where randomly ordered lines are no longer arbitrary units, but do finally relate to one another. They become elements of an overarching system.

If the material is considered from this perspective, an observer will know immediately whether you have reached the point where the relationships between the lines become visible. If you stop just before you hit that point, it will be impossible to distinguish in what relation the lines are to one another, and you will have your work cut out as a choreographer. You will find that you need to allow the lines to become part of a system with hidden rules. You will have to develop a system with its own logic and aesthetics. The relationship between the lines will become the focus of your work, and the core of the choreography.

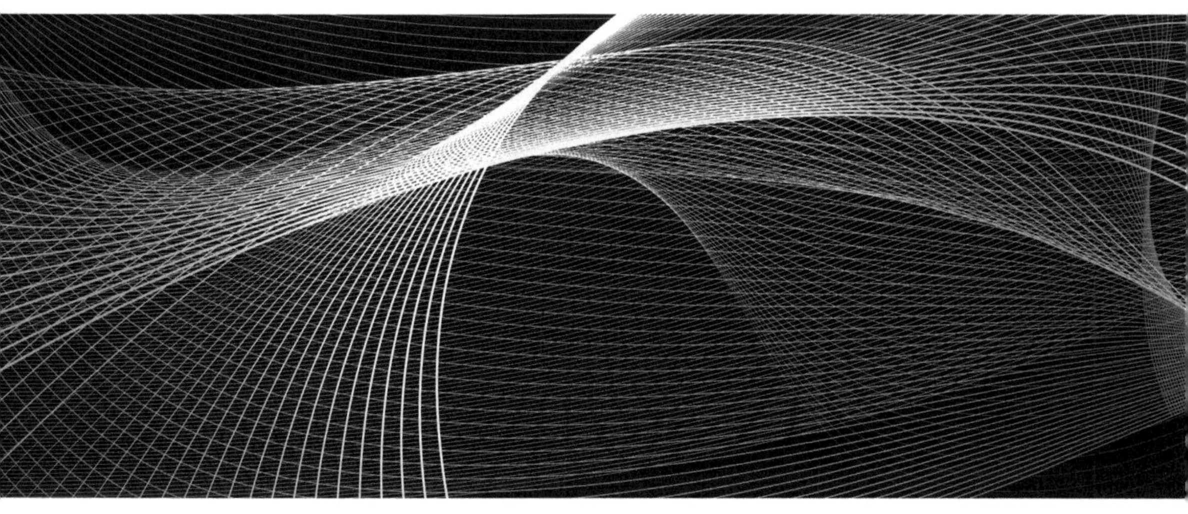

Sample image from a video installation

In the above example, 'spatial relations' became the central theme of the choreography. Abstract approaches always offer several possibilities for setting a focal point within the choreography, around which a codex can be developed, giving you a measure to work with. If you choose an abstract theme for your choreography, consider the following elements that can serve as central focus for the piece:

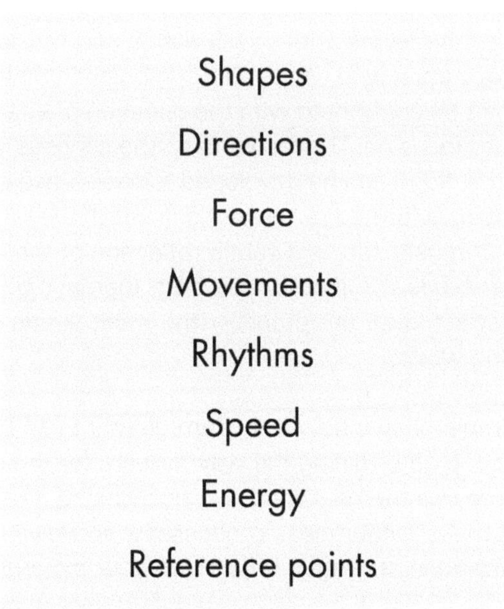

Compositions of these elements are what we encounter in nature, and that is reflected in all kinds of art forms. Everything can be viewed from the perspective of these relationships. When we observe natural structures, we tend to assign boundaries to them because that is what we are used to, and we frame the structures as cohesive images, as complete entities - the wood, the tree, the leaf, the fibre, the atom. Within each of these frames we find shapes, directions, forces, movements, rhythms, speeds and energies in different relationships with each other. The intensity of colours and shapes, and the relationships between them, determines the way we perceive things, and the way in which they evoke memories and feelings in us. When we observe things, we give some of the elements mentioned above more attention than others. Visual artists can inspire us to look at things afresh, because they are used to shifting focal points and perspective, bringing unusual elements into the foreground, or overthrowing the labels that we habitually assign to things - a forest, a tree, a leaf.

One of the key characteristics of abstraction is to avoid any kind of realism. Abstract artists work only with the relationships between elements and their key features. Complex social processes or a person's contradicting thoughts can be transferred to the relationships between such elements, and be divided up into their key features.

Working with these relationships between elements and their key features, we are able to wrestle something organic from abstraction. Thus, we gain access to one of the levers with which dance and music touch the intuitive and unknown. Any artist who works on a composition that is not theme-based will at some point be confronted with the question of arranging elements and choosing what to focus on. The focus he or she chooses will give the piece a structure within which it can be developed further. Since our entire visual and musical perception is formed by the world in which we live, any artistic reflection of images or music, too, is a subtle reflection of the world we are facing every day. Approaches completely free from thematic boundaries, operating on a purely abstract level, are probably the most subtle mirrors of our own perception of the world.

The above example shows how a random element can become a necessity that creates a code determining the way forward for the choreography, without any reference to a theme. When you are working on an abstract choreography, you can make randomness a necessity, and give depth to the superficial if you succeed in staying in touch with your experience of the world in relationship to shape, direction, forces, movement, rhythm, speed and energy. You will counter the interchangeability of movement with the reflection of your emotional and spiritual experience of mind and soul, and thus you will be able to breathe meaning into abstraction. This may well mirror a deep aspect of your inner personality, and yet also give your piece an elevated, timeless form.

The proportionality of elements, as described above, occurs in music in exactly the same way as in dance. Experiences and visions are reflected on an abstract level, touching the listener very deeply. Some compositions reach a wide audience, whilst others only touch people of a particular perception or experience. As in dance, some composers are better at using elements for artistic reflection than others. Charles Mingus once said, 'For me, jazz is about what I experience, and that is what I play.' After his solo, he often thought, 'Now I've told them; I hope they heard me!"

Summary of approaches to choreographic material

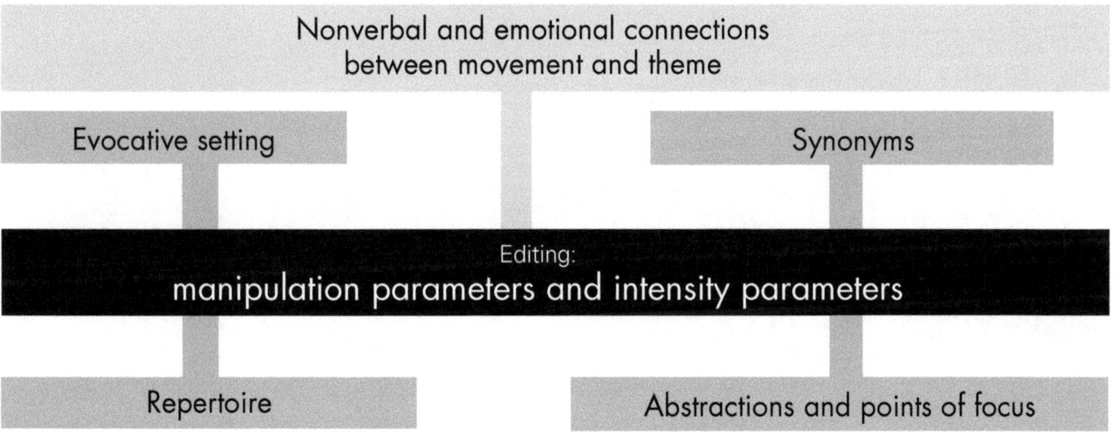

Abstraction and basic components

1 Consider the basic components of a piece of music.

- form — rhythms
- directions — speed
- force — energy
- movements — reference points

2 Find a way to note your observations. You can use a mixture of key words, sketches, or other things. Decide when to focus on which components, and which relationships occur within an element. For instance, in the element 'shape', how will large and small, diagonal and straight shapes relate to each another, etc. Take inspiration from spontaneous ideas that come to you while listening to the music. Look for something beyond the typical approach.

3 Look for relationships between the elementary components in other environments:

- landscapes
- buildings
- sculpture
- dialogues
- monuments

Use this to train your perception.

Use this approach to analyse choreographies that you see in the theatre or in a video.

4 Develop a movement exercise involving three people, starting with the focus on one of the factors mentioned in point **1**, and then moving it to another.

5 Arrangement and composition

Internal components

Seeking the whole and the sum of its parts

At first glance, it may seem overly analytic to break down choreographies and movements into their single parts. It feels almost like a dissection, taking apart a complex organism in an attempt at understanding what makes it tick. We can grasp – literally and metaphorically – what we see, and are able to link each single explanation logically to the next. In the end, we are convinced that this is the only way any organism can be understood. At the same time, however, we get this feeling that there must be something more, that the whole can't just be the sum of its parts. There is something that eludes us, something that can't measured by our much vaunted analytic methods.

5

Of course it is tempting to limit oneself to trying to comprehend only that which offers itself to analysis. If you are trying to invent a really good bread dough recipe, you will say that the quality of your bread depends on the ingredients and how they are processed. You will work on perfecting your ingredients and the bread-making process, which is hard enough work. Chances are slim that you will consider the moon phases, the amount of love that went into the dough, or what kind of energetic environment your dough needs to rise.

When we yield to the temptation of simply measuring that which lends itself to being measured, we deny all the invisible, hidden dimensions, we lose the secret, the part we feel must be there but evades proof. We may claim to have unveiled it by running tests and analysing its single parts, but we are just deceiving ourselves. This does not necessarily have to be a bad thing, as long as we are happy deceiving ourselves. The problem, however, is that it is the secret, the mystery, that made us wonder in the first place. The secret is what sparked our interest, made us embark on our quest, and by denying that there is a secret, we belittle the very thing we so desperately sought.

The naked explanation narrows our range of possibilities. In a way, it kills the mystery, even though we may realise that no explanation can throw light on every single factor of a given problem.

Whenever we deal with a mystery, we face the danger of mistaking the visible, understandable part for the whole. Dance, like music, is such a mystery. In academical studies of dance, it is reduced to facts, terms, and numbers, and you can feel how it loses its secret, its magic. We need to appreciate science and the insights it gives us, but we must remember that all numbers and terminologies are only the tip of the iceberg, with manifold secrets hidden below the dark surface of the ocean. Let academic research enrich dance, not diminish it.

Internal and superordinate form

You probably know the kind of mosaic pictures where many small photographs make up a new, big picture as soon as you take one step away from the frame. If you stand close, you can see every detail. One photograph will contain more black, another more red, and so on. The further you step away, the more the small pictures will blur. You may see a black or a red dot, but no details. If you move away even further, the dots will merge with the others around it to make up a whole new picture, which can be completely different from all the tiny pictures it contains. Dance works the same way, if you replace spatial distance with the passing of time. Like a mosaic, a dance piece is made up of many individual scenes merging into one big picture that can only be seen from a distance.

In rehearsal, you will mainly work on the details. The deeper you go, the more complex your piece will be. To perceive the superordinate form, however, you need a distance that feels almost superficial, which is far from your daily in-depth work as a choreographer. Experiencing this distance is very easy if you are watching a piece that is not your own, but much, much harder when working on your own piece. However, it is essential you provoke this feeling from time to time during rehearsals, because only distance will allow you to compare your inner image of the piece with the effect of its superordinate form. If you catch yourself defending your piece while you are watching 'from a distance', you know the piece is not quite where it should be. In a mosaic, this would be the moment to step closer and check your colours. Maybe your overall picture seems too dark, so you need to lighten up some parts. You might need to step even closer until you can see the individual scenes, and the individual characters in the scenes, which finally create the general impression of the whole picture.

This change of perspective, from the work on fine detail to the big picture, is necessary if you work on a composition. It is easy to get captured by in-depth work, and neglect the checking-in on the superordinate form, so we need to make sure to remind ourselves every now and then to step back from the picture.

Finding the balance between detail and overall picture can be daunting. Not only is it easy to lose yourself in details, the superordinate form can sometimes get in our way, too. Imagine working on a scene, and up pops this thought, the superordinate form's voice, saying, 'This is quite nice, but how does it fit into the overall picture? I can't see where to put this at all!' Uncertainty raises its ugly head, and we may feel tempted to drop the scene altogether. If we give in to this feeling too quickly and drop every scene that doesn't fit one hundred percent with our superordinate form, we may lose the diversity in our piece. Restricting ourselves to only one language or expression for intensity's sake will make the piece one-dimensional. We need both: intensity and diversity. Try to keep your overall picture in mind while also staying open for things that might not fit into that picture at first glance. If you create a piece about 'light' without using its contrasting element, darkness, it will be very hard to make your performance shine. On the contrary, a piece on light could be almost entirely made up of dark scenes and still its message or expression could be 'light'. In terms of our photo poster analogy, 'light' in this case is the overall picture, whereas the details are mainly dark. To see whether your details come together to the expression you want, you'll need to step back.

The possibilities of losing your intended direction are endless. They have to be, because we are artists working associatively, and we love it. It flows. It feels like flying. Opening night is still months away, and trying out different ideas is so inspiring. However, at a certain point, there you are, stuck with a collection of colourful dots (to stay to with our poster analogy) and no overall picture in sight. Suddenly, you need to pull it all together and jump from working in-depth on single scenes to working on the overall picture. You might need to change the 'colour' of a particular scene to make it work, or re-arrange all the scenes in order to make it work.

With opening night looming ahead and your creation still in bits and pieces, pressure increases. All performative artists know this feeling: the conflict between art and time (or lack of the same). Like everybody else, they have to earn their keep. They may try out a new approach or a different idea, but they should deliver a finished product on time. Often, this results in artists under pressure abandoning promising ideas and resorting to well-known, safe structures just to make things work out in the end. How many chances of immersion into a new idea have been lost to the need of a quick and safe overall structure? As a dancer, I have worked in productions in which touching ideas couldn't be articulated because there was not enough time left to explore them in depth, leaving the product – the piece – superficial when it could have been deeply meaningful.

Structures

In all the arts, music, poetry, film etc., there are compositional rules and patterns. If, for example, you arrange motif (A) and contrast (B) in an AB pattern, it will have a different effect than in an ABA pattern. Pay attention to the rules and patterns of other art forms, and see how you can translate them into patterns for dance. This usually works beautifully if you use all the expressive potential dance has to offer: time and space. If you are trying out an AB form, also use it as a spatial structure. If you want to use repetitions, you can experiment with looping movements, arranging them in a canon, varying the number of dancers and their placement in space, and so on. Make sure, however, to include an element of surprise as well – if your piece's structure becomes too obvious after the third repetition, it will become predictable and tedious for the audience.

Be aware that strict rules may also inhibit your creative process. If that is the case for you, it might be enough to start by just sketching out a rough 'introduction – dynamic – resolution' structure and start rehearsing according to this sketch. The material gathered in this fashion can then later be pulled together into a tighter structure.

ABA structure and canon

ABA

Create an AB structure in which you oppose motif and contrast. Sketch an introduction to the motif, a middle or main part, and its resolution in the finale. Notice how, when, and where you set turning points. Turn to the illustration on page 47 for a reminder how to create a dramatic arc.

Example: 'Motif and contrast' in movement

open	close
full-body active	isolated
wide	tight
round	sharp-edged
big	small

Try your creation with a group of dancers.

Canon

Create a movement loop of three times eight beats.

Vary your loop in

- time

- space

- number of dancers.

The language of space

Whenever we dance, we move through space. It is always there, making itself an integral part of every motif in dance. So far, I have discussed the different aspects of the dancer's space: internal space, kinesphere, and universal space. When you are working with a group of dancers, yet another important aspect of space emerges: the space between the individual dancers.

In the following chapter, we shall explore the possibilities space offers us, starting with the three levels 'high', 'middle', and 'low' and proceeding to the concepts of symmetry and asymmetry. All these ideas can be applied to different aspects of space, be it the dancer's kinesphere, the whole stage, or just a detail in the whole arrangement.

We cannot grasp or measure empty space with our eyes. Dancers, however, can make it visible by moving through it, sharing their experience of space with the audience. The way the dancers move their intention will shape the spectator's perception of space.

You can try it – put down your book for a moment, and move your arm through the air in a cutting motion. You can do this with two different intentions:

> Focusing on the path your arm makes in the air, or
> focusing on the shapes your hand would cut if the air were solid.

Depending on which focus you choose, space will feel different to you. A spectator will either see the movement path, the shapes created by the movement and around the movement, or how you experience space. Usually, we don't just see one of these elements, but a combination of them, including the dancer's emotional focus.

In the next study, let us work on shifting our focus between shape and experience.

The potential of space

Create a solo, shifting your focus between

the shape the dancer's movement creates in space,

the dancer's experience.

For both approaches, specify an intention or feeling to the dancer's movement, for example cutting, bathing, stroking, devouring etc.

Any topic you choose to address and express in choreography has its own subtexts. If you learn to identify and name the subtexts, and then project them into space, your dance language will become more articulate.

The first impression of your piece will be how you use your space, and the first thing we notice is your set-up is stationary or dynamic. If the choreography is stationary, then the audience will focus more on the individual figures on stage. Imagine the curtains opening and showing several dancers positioned on the stage, motionless. This set-up is more likely spark your interest in the individual dancers than a scene showing the ensemble moving dynamically around the stage. In a group of motionless dancers, each dancer's personal space is given more meaning, and with it the portrayed character's story, emotions and expression.

A stationary set-up explains itself through the individual figures placed in it.

A dynamic set-up rather explains itself through the composition of movements in space than through the individual figures.

There are many possibilities to create a dramaturgy. If a piece depends on characters and their personalities, a typical approach is to start by introducing them first. The audience will identify with the characters, and can follow them on their journey through the piece.

If you choose to work with this approach, the introduction will be the most critical phase. To emotionally connect with the characters, the audience need the opportunity to focus on each individual dancer separately, as if looking through a cameralens, zooming in on each character. If your piece starts with a lot of action and expansive movements through space, then you will need to allow for 'islands' of stillness to which the figures may retreat to be introduced. The audience's focus will be on those islands, and all the other moving figures on stage will fade into the background for a moment. If you want to show how a certain character develops throughout the piece, using islands of stillness works particularly well. You won't need them, however, if the dancers in your piece are not representing characters with different or evolving personalities. Here, the question of how to use your space and when to use stillness or movement depends entirely on the compositional aspects of dramaturgy.

Implied emotion in an empty space

When I start choreographing in a place I am not familiar with, I take a moment to just sit in the auditorium and feel the space. I imagine people in different places throughout the room to check what it does to me as a spectator. How I experience the place has a strong impact on the mental images I see when I start choreographing, and also on where I place the dancers. It is an emotional way of scanning a space for its possibilities. In some places, the atmosphere is so obvious that I immediately feel where I want to put a certain image in a piece. At a later stage in the creation of the piece, I can come back to this feeling of the space to check if it corresponds with my compositional motifs.

In her book 'The art of making dances', Doris Humphrey describes a study that was set up to show how the emotional impact of a dancer on the audience changes according to where on the stage the dancer is placed. The range varies from 'familiar' to 'neutral' to 'uncanny'. You can use the results of this study for your own choreography work, and / or you can do your own. Ideally, you do it twice on two very different stages. In my experience, every stage has different properties, especially if you dance in unusual places such as a forest or inside some labyrinth-like architecture.

Certain moods correlate with certain positions in space. If you look at a stage with only one person on it, the position of this person – far away, close, centred, or off to one side – will affect how you feel. The importance of a dancer's position in space is at the core of the question where to let dancers enter and exit, and along what floor pattern they should move. The floor pattern is the pattern that the dancers' feet would create on the floor if they had dipped their feet in paint before dancing.

In our next study, let's explore how the audience experience the different positions on stage.

Divide your space in squares.

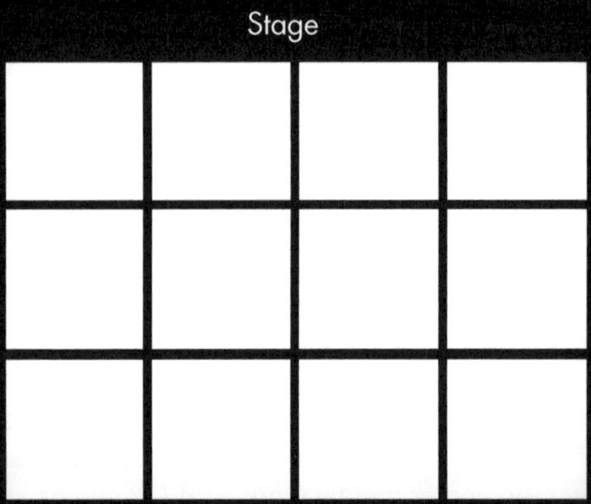

Stage seen from above

40 Study

In the dark, a dancer takes a position, and the lights come on. The lights black out while the dancers choose a new position. The spectators note how the different positions affect them. At the end, the participants compare and discuss their results.

Balance points in space

Take a look at the arrangement in your choreography and imagine the whole stage as a platform balanced on a ball.

- How would the platform move with your arrangement?
- How big would the platform's amplitude be?

The mental image of the balanced platform will help you answer these questions:

- How do I use the space in my arrangements?
- Does my arrangement 'shift its weight' on the stage, or am I using the same arrangement principles throughout the whole piece?

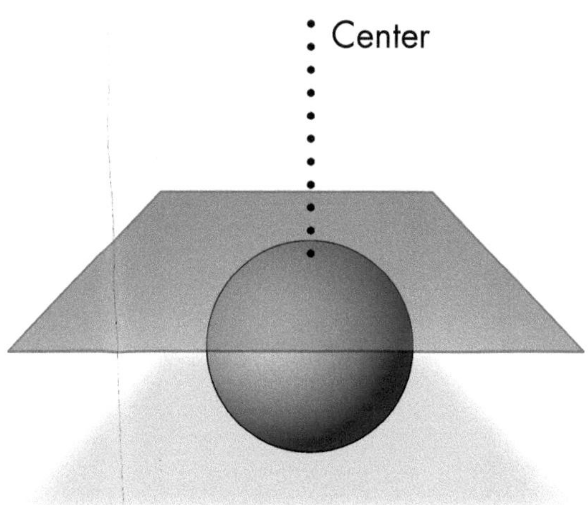

The stage as a platform balancing on a ball

Different arrangements of balance points in space

Work with at least five dancers. Use tape to create a square dance space on the floor.

Imagine that dance space balancing on a spire.

Create a structure for a choreography with the goal of moving the square into different positions.

Mobile stage, supported at the centre

The dancers have the following options:

to support the spatial structure by movement, focus, or subtext

to oppose the spatial structure

Watch any choreography. Imagine how the dance floor would move under the dancers if it was balanced on a spire. Note where the dancers put their weight, where they direct their movements, and what relationships result from these weight shifts and directions.

Places and spaces

Some locations seem to have a particular spirit or energy. There are places where houses have been destroyed and people killed, and still, after complete destruction, out of their ruins, the old spirit or feeling develops again.

Maybe places keep their energy over time, an energy that asks for certain things and hinders others. In East Germany before World War II, there were many buildings that were homes to art and artists. During the DDR era, some of these buildings became army barracks, while others fell into ruin. When the political situation relaxed, however, the artists came back to the same places to make their art, to connect with their time, their past and their identity.

Time will change the spirit of a place at some point, leaving only traces of the original idea. A good example are the Roman ruins on the coast of Libya. There is nothing left but ruins, but there is no judgement in this change. On the contrary: the loss of the original meaning can invite a new dialogue and give fresh impulses. The interesting question is where this new input will lead the artist – to the past, which will inevitably be distorted by our present-world point of view; to the here and now, perceiving the old place with new eyes and ignoring all context; or to visions of the future. The power of the past, the incomprehensibility of the present and the fear of the future unravel the contemporary artist's concentration and make developing a vision difficult. But each era has its spirit and schools of thinking, and artists are children of their time like everybody else. The era you live in will always influence your work, regardless of whether your piece is about the past or about the future.

Just as the time period you live in influences your work, so will the place where you live. If you don't believe that time and place have an impact your work, you might just not notice that it does, or it doesn't bother you that it does. What you will notice, however, is the change in atmosphere when you choreograph in different locations.

Go and take a closer look at the city you live in. Let unusual locations challenge you to use them for your next dance performance. They will always add something to your existing repertoire, because a place offers images and atmospheres that can inspire and expand your dances. You will see not see the same images standing under a motorway bridge that you see standing in an open field.

These days, most art takes place in hermetically sealed, conserved spaces. Atmospheres are created artificially. As long as we can imagine our performance only in our familiar theatres, we won't be open to the message another space might have to convey. A performance, however, could take place anywhere. It will become harder to classify the piece because it will be out of the ordinary. Thinking outside of the box takes courage and flexibility, and the will to let go of the need to feel safe. If you don't want to leave the theatre with your production, that is fine, but it doesn't necessarily mean you can't be inspired by new places and spaces.

By staging a piece in an unusual location, you create new and unexpected perspectives. The place you set your piece in is authentic – it is not an artificial backdrop, but a real place with its own atmosphere and history, which will add to the atmosphere of your piece.

A classical theatre stage, on the other hand, offers different possibilities of arrangement and expression. Choreographers and stage designers can work together on an idea to create a seamless production without being limited by the location.

Just because there aren't any theatres available, however, it doesn't follow you can't create your own pieces. As soon as you let go of the notion that the performing arts necessarily need a conventional stage, you'll be amazed at how many locations can be turned into stages. I have once seen a dance performance in a furniture shop. The ceiling of this shop is a metal grid, and the dancers performed on this grid with the audience beneath them. This perspective was new and fascinating in its effect. The majority of the audience, however, complained about not being able to see properly, or that the perspective didn't bring out the dance's nuances very well. This reaction made me realise how we are all enslaved to theatrical conventions – we all struggle to let go of our expectations, dancers, choreographers, and audience alike.

Settings in landscapes

Collect different details of landscapes or architectural structures.

Create an 'image' with one or several dancers for each detail. An 'image' is one single moment. Examples: Dancers' arms rise out of a meadow full of flowers. Eight dancers step up a staircase in perfect unison. Ten dancers glide down a window pane.

Develop your image into a short piece.

Compare the choreographies from the different images to find differences and similarities. You may even be able to arrange them into one dramatic composition.

42 Study

If you choreograph a piece in an unusual location, you should also rehearse in that location. You'll need to at least have a rough idea of the scope of your production, just because space and time will work differently for you in such a location. Sequences that grow boring after 30 seconds on a conventional stage may stay interesting for 3 minutes in a different location. While a dance combination may look full of mesmerising contrasts at the studio, the stage setting might not support these contrasts and make them disappear to the audience's eye, so that even the most interesting piece ends up looking flat and dull.

Example:
Setting our piece in a former assembly hangar where tanks used to be re-paired, we planned to let our dancers perform three metres above the floor, suspended from a crane moving towards the audience. We tested the crane and saw that it took seven minutes for the crane to reach its designed place on stage. Back at the studio, we simulated the seven minute crane drive by just walking the necessary distance, which struck us as tremendously boring. So the dancers and I developed different combinations that could be danced dangling from a rope, and we set the combinations in interesting time frames, making the choreography denser to fill these seven long minutes. When we finally rehearsed the choreography in the hangar, with the crane, music and lights, we realised that too much movement destroyed the picture. The actual set did not need all the action we had packed into our seven minutes, and we decided to cut back our rope choreography to a minimum.

Change of perspective and 'black holes'

It is hard work for the audience to take in everything that is going on on stage if you don't structure your space. Avoid using the whole of your stage over a longer period of time; instead, try to use lights and movement to visually expand and diminish your space.

The light structures the space.

The dancers need to know which part of the stage they have to fill with their movement and energy. If the stage is evenly lit, with dancers evenly positioned, the space will have no power and no depth, the stage positions will be rendered less effective than if you were using your space dynamically. Even if you manage to maintain an arc of suspense on an evenly filled stage, your audience will tire eventually because they have to make up for the lack of depth in your setting that renders your piece two-dimensional. They will have to structure the space they are watching, and they will usually do that by focusing on details.

Imagine you are looking at a crowd, maybe a demonstration of some kind. You will probably first take in the whole picture, and then your eyes will focus on individuals in the crowd. It is natural for us to first want an overview and then be curious about details. As choreographers, we need to bear this in mind when we arrange a piece. We need to be able to gauge how long an audience's eye will stay with the overview before switching the focus on details, and we have to decide whether we want to influence this switch or not. You may want to leave it to chance where the spectator's gaze wanders because you find it exciting if every individual sees a different piece. Most of the time, however, this is not what choreographers want. In my choreography coaching sessions, most choreographers want to direct their audience's focus, they want them to see one particular action, and then the next. Frustratingly, though, this often doesn't work, especially in performances without movable stage lights. But even if you have stage lights zooming all over the place, you will have to think about where you want points of focus on stage for your structure to come alive.

Directing attention in overlapping actions

Change and standstill

How can we direct the spectator's eye, his 'camera lens', from one action to the next? First, we need to understand the principles of how to direct attention.

If something catches our attention, there will be little room for anything else.

Consequently, if we want to introduce a new element and we want the audience to notice it, the element that first caught their attention has to fade out slightly to allow the audience's focus to shift.

As long as something keeps changing, it will hold our attention.

If we want to make an element less interesting, the first thing to do is to stop it from changing. Ideally, we will cease to change movements in a sequence and let the activity subside at the end of the arc of suspense before the spectator loses interest.

If nothing changes, nothing new will follow.

The most radical way to stop change is a standstill. Even though a standstill right after movement will at first read like a powerful change, it will settle after a moment and give space for new things to happen. The other way of withholding new information is the establishment of a movement loop. It moves, but it does not show new movements or accents that might increase suspense.

Let me give you an example for these two possibilities. Imagine two dancers moving and suddenly stopping. One of them stays immobile, the other starts moving again. Your attention will automatically be drawn to the moving dancer. Now imagine the two dancers walking in a circle. After the second repetition, you will get the feeling that nothing new will be coming from these two dancers, and you will direct your gaze to where things are changing on stage.

I've watched many performances in which an element on one side of the stage caught my eye while a new element was being introduced on the other side, making me miss half of the new element. It was a frustrating experience, because I kept missing parts of the dance and eventually lost the plot, trying to follow the constantly overlapping elements. There was simply too much going on at the same time. Often, this happens when the choreographer is worried that there isn't enough action on stage, and tries to compensate for this feeling by piling on more movement. But 'more' doesn't necessarily mean 'better', even though there are pieces that work fine with a multitude of things happening simultaneously. The question is how these actions connect with each other, and whether you are setting a focus or not. If you don't want to direct the audience's attention, that is an artistic decision which can be interesting as it leaves the spectator to choose his own points of focus in the piece. At the same time, there is a certain danger that this openness will read as arbitrariness.

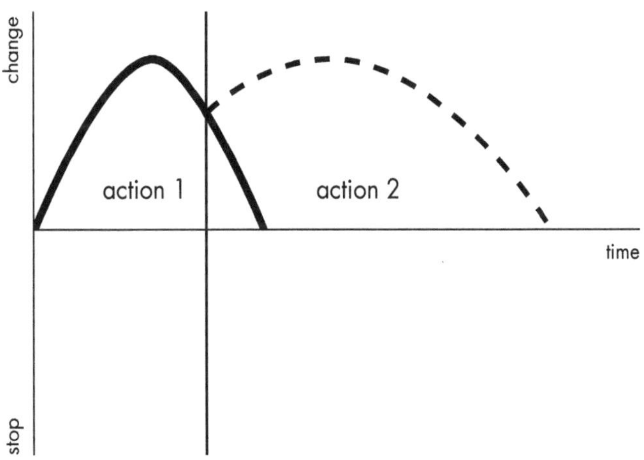

Action Nr. 2 starts when action Nr. 1 decreases and makes space for 2. How the introduction of 2 is perceived depends on the timing of the takeover from 1 to 2.

Directional accents

If two people stand in the street looking up at the sky, a third person joining them is very likely to look up as well out of sheer curiosity. The same will happen in a dance performance: if the majority of spectators suddenly turns their heads to one side, you will automatically do the same. If something 'draws our eye', it catches our attention. The most powerful tool to direct the audience's attention is the dancers' gaze, but there are also more subtle possibilities. When ten dancers throw their hands to one side, they also create an impulse towards that direction. By starting the next action in the same direction, we can build a smooth transition from one element of our dance to the next. Starting the next action in the opposite direction will make the transition less fluid, which is useful if you are looking for a contrast, a sudden change of direction.

A different and more controversial method to direct the 'internal camera' of a spectator is by pure intention. The dancers concentrate all their attention, all their energy on one person or one certain point on stage, and the idea is that the audience will feel the dancers' focus and follow it. If you try this method, some spectators will be able to observe the effect and some will not – probably depending on how sensitive they are. There is no doubt, however, that adding this mental focus to a visible movement impulse will make every movement more powerful.

Inducing a shift of attention through arrangement

Imagine a group of dancers in perfect unison. For the next image, you want two dancers in the back to become the new centre of attention. You can achieve such a shift of attention by changing the arrangement, for example splitting the group to leave only two dancers at the centre. You could also have the dancers in the front move in a different direction than the pair in the back. These are just two possibilities, you will find more on the topic of 'opposition' and 'compositional aspects' in more detail in the next chapter.

In an empty three-dimensional space, a choreography will have different focus points in the depth and height, between the floor and just above the dancer's maximal reach.

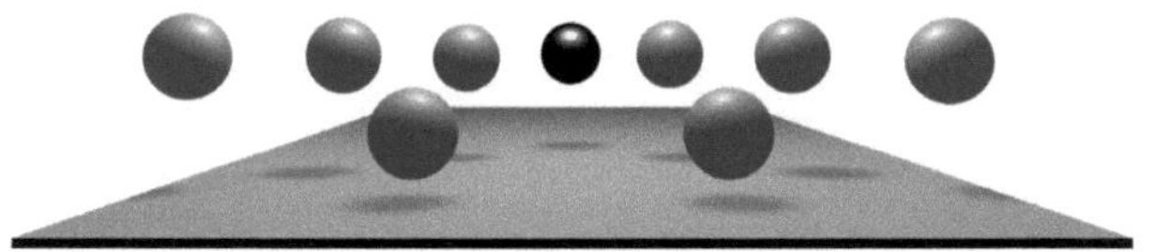

Switching the focus of attention from the front row to the back by dissolving the group at the front.

If you observe these focus points over a certain amount of time, they form a kind of 'focus line' in space. This line or curve will be more or less obvious at different focus points, depending on how much focus each point is getting. The spectators will follow this line with their attention, like a zooming camera, whether the dancers be entering or exiting, dancing a solo or in a group. The more aware you as a choreographer are of the dynamic of this focus line, the more possibilities you have to create contrasts, to draw an image on the empty canvas of your space.

Focus points in space

Anchors in space or stage design

You can use so-called 'anchors' to give your space a logical structure and make the spatial design more transparent for a spectator. If my stage looks like a scrapyard filled with random things, adding four columns will make them my anchors and the scrapyard landscape my 'carpet', because the columns all visibly belong to the same category. They give my space meaning. Were I to simply add four more random objects, my scrapyard would just grow larger and more untidy.

To bring order into chaos, such as in this scrapyard example, you can work with allocation. If the audience recognise an element on stage, they can allocate it. Looking at your stage like a landscape, you might think it more interesting to put in four very different columns instead of four exactly similar ones. While this may work well in a still-life, where you have time to take a minute to find all the columns, and another to realise that the four columns might represent a different level inside the image, there simply isn't enough time in dance for this kind of contemplation. We need our anchors to be more obvious.

The easiest way of setting up anchors is to make a recognisable design. It could be an arrangement of dancers that is repeated throughout the performance; another possibility is mirroring the position of a body or body part in different directions and places on stage, for example a horizontal arm position that is picked up by every dancer on different levels throughout the whole stage.

You can of course define your anchor points by movement alone, or you may decide you don't need any anchor points at all. It is perfectly fine not to use them if you don't need them. Look at them as a tool that is very useful when you feel the need for clarity and structure in your choreography, but do not have a concrete plan yet. The image of the columns in the wild scrapyard landscape serves as our metaphor for this phase in choreographing, but it can be used for many other situations as well.

Relations and relationships

Two people on a stage always stand in relation to each other. They cannot not communicate. If one of them changes, the whole stage changes. To describe the glittering facets of relationships between people, words often are not enough. Because it is the very nature of dance to express what words cannot, many people feel that it is the most appropriate language to represent the ever-changing connection between people.

When a new person arrives in a room, he or she changes the relationships in this room. The more people arrive, the more complex the network of relationships becomes. A change in one person always also affects the whole system. A decision inside a system never stands alone.

This idea inspired me to create my piece 'Sacculus Utriculus' for which we designed a floating, unstable floor sensitive to every single move of the dancers.

Working with a floor that reacted both to the directions of movement and to the changing positions of the dancers on stage changed the way I now look at spatial relations in my arrangements. The idea of the movable floor has become a tool for me to analyse how the relationships between the dancers go with their placement on stage.

Two dancers can stand close to each other without entering any relationship at all, or stand far apart and still relate to each other. The range between these two extremes offers divers possibilities for contrasting elements both in the arrangement and in the subtext of a choreography. Contrast can be expressed in many different ways: two dancers could dance close to each other without connecting at all, each in a completely different emotion; a duet could be torn apart by placing a group with a different choreography between the partners, and so on.

When we work on the variation of relationships in a choreography, we always work with the dancer's subtext. Key to the expression of the subtext is the dancer's ability to establish a connection with others through movement.

The construction of a freely movable, unstable stage floor for
'Sacculus Utriculus' by Kristine Tornquist

A and B choose movements they can only do when they are working together. Next, split up the pair and let them try the same movements at a distance. How do the movements change?

Develop duets of extreme closeness. Then unlock the duet by giving one dancer a path to follow while incorporating the movements found in the close situation.

A and B create two independent solo pieces which move continually inside their own kinaesthetic bubble. Connect the two pieces by stopping the movements and changing them subtly to establish a link between A, B and outside.

Integrate a third dancer into this duet.

Use the compositional elements from 1-5 to create the strongest contrasts you can from the material you already worked with.

Include a subtext.

Spatial relations	Qualitative relations
distance	tension
direction	subtext
level	action – reaction
number: group vs. solo, two vs. three	tempo
etc.	movement quality

The relations established in a dance sequence can be spatial or qualitative. Relationships form depending on how groups and soloists implement spatial and qualitative elements.

In 'Studies and exercises stages' you'll find exercises designed to to train your eye and feeling for relationships both in poses and during movement. The exercises focus on different aspects of relationships and relations. You will find that trying them out is a lot easier than trying to put them into words – but maybe you can do them in your imagination while you read. After all, Einstein pondered on his theory of relativity a long time before it was applied...

When you create a scene with more than one dancer, the audience will automatically perceive a net of relations and relationships on stage, even if your scene is not about relationships at all. Because it is natural for the spectator's eye to establish relations between objects or bodies on stage, you need to analyse your scene in terms of relations.

Repeat one of your scenes from a past exercise to consider the spatial tension between the dancers and the relations created by this tension.

Spatial tension created by the relation between space, direction and level

Imagine a stage with three dancers standing, sitting or lying on it. When the spectators shut their eyes, the dancers change positions, focusing on space, direction, and level. As soon as they have reached their new positions, the music starts and the audience open their eyes to take in the new image. The music fades out, the spectators shut their eyes again, the dancers change their positions, and so on.

Can you detect spatial tension and its rules in the different constellations?

Which images impress you most? Choose five to seven images.

Put these images into an order. Consider how one image refers to the next.

Next, we will focus on how space and movement quality can be used to express relationships in dance. Practical exercises will help us to implement our findings in our choreography work.

Closeness and distance as a choreographic statement

Imagine a theatrical scene in which a twenty-year-old dancer and a fifty-year-old actor are required to dance a short tango accompanied by a text recital. If you start by giving them dance steps to execute between the lines of the recital, the result will probably be a rather dull scene. The movements will look forced, the actor will never look like a dancer, and if the dancer is not familiar with tango, she will always lapse into the dance style she feels most at home with. The choreograph can react to this either by working on the weaknesses of the cast, or by starting out with the essence of his idea, trying to first find a 'tango feeling' in the emotional memory of the cast, and then developing the steps from there (see page 141, 'The direct approach').

Have you ever seen a perfectly styled, sleek tango performance that left you unimpressed and slightly bored, and then a dance scene that was technically inferior, but emotionally touching? If you want to create a dramatic, but reproducable scene, you'll need both. Don't start with the dance technique, though. Start with the essence of the tango. What is tango? You'll have to observe tango dancers, and try to feel their response to the music and each other, to find an answer to this question. Observing and feeling are two of the most important skills a choreograph needs to develop. Never mind the steps – focus on the experience. Seek the experience of the tango, and that is were you will find the steps.

When I worked on that tango scene with the actor and the dancer, the following questions were part of the text that accompanied their tango

- How close can you let your partner come before you oppose him?

- How much power do you grant each other?

- How much submission can you bear?

- How much closeness can you take?

In addition, it became clear from the text that the two protagonists were emotionally tied to each other by an unbreakable bond.

We started with an improvisational scene to collect material for a first choreographic study. The recited text was improvised, the musician tried out different tango pieces. The protagonists' movement were restricted by the following rules:

Stand on an imaginary line opposite each other, keeping eye contact all the time. None may step off the line.

Consequently, the movements were restricted to:

- moving towards the other

- moving with the other

- moving away from the other

- stop

This study opened up more questions:

- What is the intention behind 'standing still' and 'walking' (forwards and backwards)? How are the intention and the tempo of a movement connected?

- At which point can one partner enter the other's kinesphere?

- Does the scene allow touch? How much?

- What is the optimal balance between action, text, and music?

- How can we balance these elements to build suspense?

- How can we keep it up or release it?

Some of these questions could not be fully answered. They touch on the inconceivable, indescribable. Still, the questions need to be asked to create an awareness for them in the dance. This may not directly lead to answers, but to moments and experiences that can be discussed, and with each moment and each discussion, we move closer to what was out of reach at the beginning.

In every choreography, there are moments when we can work on the motif of 'closeness and distance'. Knowing how to to use the space between dancers on stage is a fundamental element of the art of choreography.

Movement to the motif of 'closeness – distance'

Create a dance combination that contains changes of spatial relations, different directions, and paths of varying length.

Two dancers stand close to each other. They start dancing the combination at different points in time.

The dancers may react to each other by stopping, changing or expanding movements to avoid collision or to provoke touching.

The choreographer than defines the dynamic of closeness and distance by changing

–	movement	–	action and reaction
–	direction	–	expansion
–	tempo	–	touch
–	focus	–	evasion

Extend the study by adding two more dancers.

As mentioned before, the first defining factor for relationships in a dance scene is space, i.e. where the dancers are positioned on the stage and in relation to each other. The other factor is trickier to grasp. It has to do with the dancers ability to give their movement a direction, to project and address their movement. You will quickly spot the dancers who naturally project. Some dancers just have this quality - they have a clear idea of their space, filling it by projecting their presence and movements. You can almost see them trailing glowing after-images of themselves, like a comet's tail, and energy seems to flow from their limbs into the space around them.

Just as we need language in theatre, we need to address movement when we work with relationships in dance. A piece may work without it, but it is an important medium through which we express emotion. The medium 'language' makes it unmistakeably clear who I am speaking to. My speech doesn't even have to be meant for one particular person. Even without a designed receiver, the medium language carries energy, a kind of internal movement, into space, to be shared by the audience. If dancers perform over a longer period of time without addressing their movements to somebody, the spectators will feel confused, as if they were listening to a speaker who doesn't connect with them as well as talking a lot without saying much.

It is difficult to train addressing. It is more than just projection. It is projection combined with a sense of meaning that is very personal to each dancer, filling his or her movements with purpose. But even if dancers have the ability to authentically fill their movements with meaning, they may be tempted to just pretend to feel it instead of really going through the process of addressing. The audience will feel it, though. When you are choreographing, don't try to verbalise each movement. It won't work. But it is your job – and this is far more than just working on relationships on stage - to make sure the dancers move with purpose, not at random. The easier you find it to inspire the dancers to move meaningfully, the more likely your piece will blossom during rehearsals. As relationships rely on action, reaction and the refusal to react, the development of body language is crucial for a successful dance piece.

Adressing

During a workshop, the dancers' movement language became vague and un-differentiated. I split the group into dancers and spectators, and asked the dancers to dance for one particular person from the spectator group. One of the dancers had suffered an injury a few months ago that had prevented her from dancing for seven months, and she moved with extreme care, anxious not to strain her recovering body. At the same time, she was longing to express herself after having been cooped up and not allowed to dance. When I asked her to dance for somebody, she still didn't throw herself into the dance. She basically moved very slowly from one position to another, but with an intensity that drew all the spectators' and even the other dancers' eyes. The power of her dance showed clearly where the source of true addressing lies. It comes from deep inside the dancer. What touches the audience is not primarily the movement, but the dancer's feeling behind the movement. This principle is important for both the relationship between dancer and audience and the relationship between dancers on stage. The audience will be fascinated if the dancers move with feeling and purpose, and dance partners in a duet will only truly feel each other's presence if they express themselves meaningfully.

Rely on what you see when you watch the dancers, looking for intention. Check each moment that strikes you as vague. Discuss vague moments with the dancers. Let them repeat the movements in slow-motion to find their intention, the feeling behind the movement.

I deliberately started this chapter with ensemble work because it is often neglected in favour of duet or partner work. Sometimes, 'relationships' is simply ticked off as 'man lifts woman, thank you, goodbye'. But on stage, relationships are developed all the time – between the individual dancers as well as between the dancers and the audience.

In 'Studies and exercises' you find techniques for developing duets that are commonly used in contact improvisation.
These exercises address all kinds of relationships between dancers and can be easily modified to suit any motif you might be working with.

Compositional cohesion between scenes

Apart from the relationships between the stage characters and the audience, there is also the relationship between the individual scenes of a piece. The arrangement of the scenes, the composition, creates compositional relations. The way the scenes relate to each other determines how the piece develops. It doesn't matter whether we are following a narrative plot or some more abstract arc of suspens; the scenes may well refer to each other on a more intuitive than logical level, but they will always react to each other in terms of intensity, rhythm and expression. This interplay between the scenes defines the dramaturgy, the flow of the piece that will either capture the audience or not. If your dramaturgy is faulty, the spectator will have difficulty following the performance, and will finally lose interest.

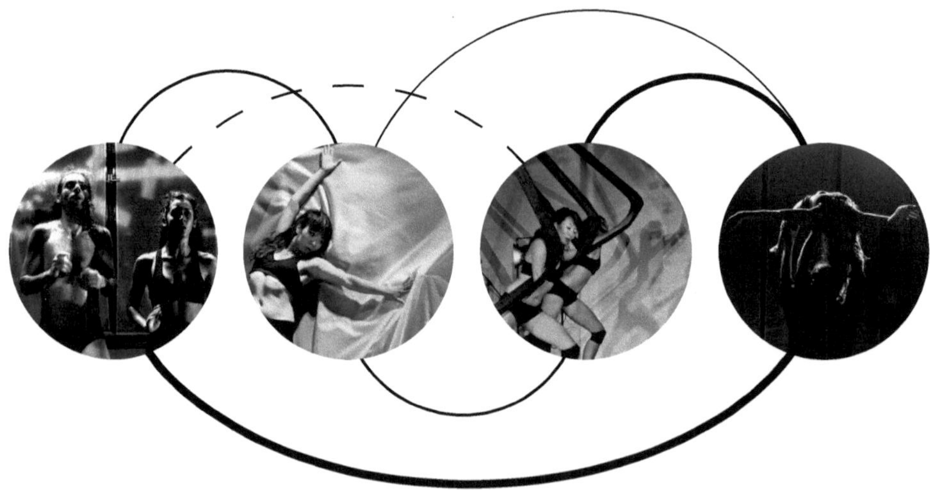

Just as relationships form between dancers, space, shadows, and music in a scene, the scenes relate to each other in terms of rhythm, density and expression throughout the piece, forming the arc of suspense.

Spatial arrangement

The previous section dealt with the relationships between the individual dancers on stage. If they didn't move from their positions, we could say the dancers are set in an arrangement – but of course they are moving, so what we see is a composition in space. A composition is something colourful, almost fluid, that moves in a spatial arrangement.

The arrangement consists of

There are harmonious arrangements, inconsistent arrangements, interesting, or boring arrangements. Arranging is the art of putting things in order. Wherever you are at this moment, look up from this book and take in your surroundings. Form a frame with your hands, as if you were taking a picture, and focus on different details through this frame. Decide which detail shots look harmonious to you, and which do not. If you've focused either on organic matter or on carefully arranged objects through your 'lens', you are quite unlikely to have found unharmonious images. A shelf filled with somebody's favourite things will in all probability look more harmonious than a shelf where everybody just dumps their stuff. Such a shelf may make an onlooker uncomfortable – we may wish to tidy up, or turn away, or scold whoever is responsible for the mess, and so on. This demonstrates how the way of arranging objects can affect a spectator. Naturally, spectators are different, and will react differently to the same arrangement, but there seems to be a collective limit to the scope of what is still perceived as 'harmonious'. Beyond this limit, the majority of the spectators will rate the arrangement as 'unharmonious', either because it creates too much or too little tension.

Arrangements that are too symmetrical often don't create enough tension to be interesting for longer than a few minutes. In musical or ballet, the wish to enjoy the pleasure of symmetry sometimes leads to over-harmonious arrangements which can grow tedious only too quickly. On the other hand, edgy, fragmentary arrangements will also lose their effect if they don't include at least some harmony. Fragmentation only works in contrast to wholeness, and the the eyes of the audience need an anchor to return to. Without an element of order to measure against, fragmentation just looks like any ordinary mess. This principle is true on many different levels. You could even apply it to look at Germany at the beginning of the 21st century: Most people live in relative comfort and safety. The shocking images the daily news show from all over the world boost our feeling of harmony – we realise how lucky we are in comparison. The effect of a fragmented, broken image is intensified by the contrast with a harmonious, whole image, which is why films such as 'The thin red line' start with images of happy children in beautiful green fields before everything is destroyed by the ensuing bombardment. On a much smaller scale, you can apply the same principle to a working environment, for example an office. If your office is chaotic by default, you probably won't notice a difference between slightly untidy and really messy. But if you are used to working in a very organised, tiny office, a few documents spread out over three desks will drive you mad. You have to love tidiness before a mess can affect you emotionally, just as you have to have known freedom to feel restricted by its loss.

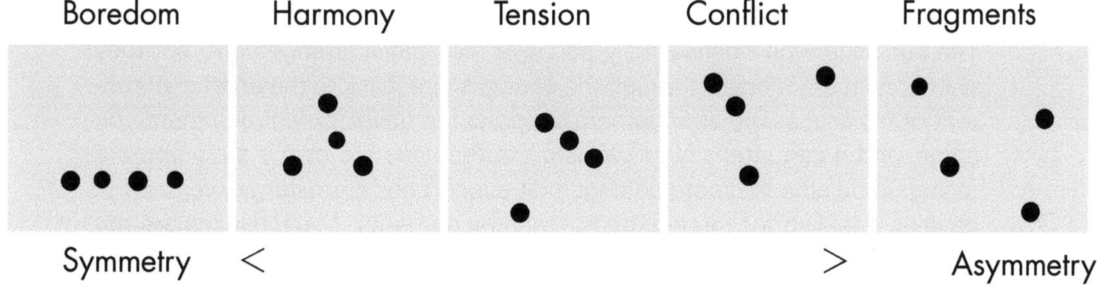

Different arrangements of four objects and their effect on the audience.

For our arrangement, this means that we can only destroy what we have built beforehand. If you want to disrupt an order, you first have to create it, and harmony will be felt more strongly if it is broken by moments of disharmony. This contrast of build-up and destruction has a temporal component we shall ignore at this point, and shall come back to in chapter 2, ('Dramaturgy')

Space within the arrangement

Visualise the following spatial layouts:

opening scene:
a harmonious arrangement

first scene:
the harmony is disrupted repeatedly

second scene:
the layout has shattered into fragments that do not fit together any more

finale:
the fragments try to reconnect again, but they keep falling apart, unable to unite

The arrangement reflects the expression and the atmosphere of the scene. The audience won't consciously perceive the spatial arrangement, but they will connect emotionally through the setting's direct link to the emotional content of the scene. The arrangement supports the development of a theme on stage, and it can intensify or weaken the dramatic arc of the story you are telling. To be able to create settings that support our dramaturgy, we need to develop a feeling for three-dimensional arrangements. Many dances are not truly arranged, they just fill space with random accents, exits and entrances, and coincidental formations that emerged during rehearsals, but they are far from using space like a language to express something.
In the following section, we will work on our sense of three-dimensional space and our understanding of different interpretations of space. The studies contain ideas you will only be able to experience and develop by watching and working with spatial arrangements.

Invisible space

Space in itself is invisible. It becomes conceivable only if it is framed or limited. The layout of these limits defines how much tension a space holds. It is the arrangement, the frame - not the space! - that creates tension. The space stays empty.

Try the following study:

Negative Space

Three dancers stand closely together at the centre of the stage.

The dancers only move when their names are called. The direction of the movement is defined by a number between 1 and 12, with 12 being the direction of the audience.

At their turn, the dancers slowly move in the given direction.

Observe how the tension changes between the leaving dancer and the other two dancers at the centre. The tension may rise at first, and then decrease at a certain distance. Sometimes it is enough to change the direction of a dancer's gaze to increase the tension again.

Experiment with a larger number of dancers to practise your eye and your feeling for arrangements.

Spatial relationships within the arrangement

Define different points of reference on the dancer's bodies.

The dancers' task is to link these points of reference in space. They can either focus on just two points or on all at once. This will result in individual positions connected by both isolated and whole-body movements.

Create three solo pieces. Let three dancers dance the first solo, two the second and one the third solo.

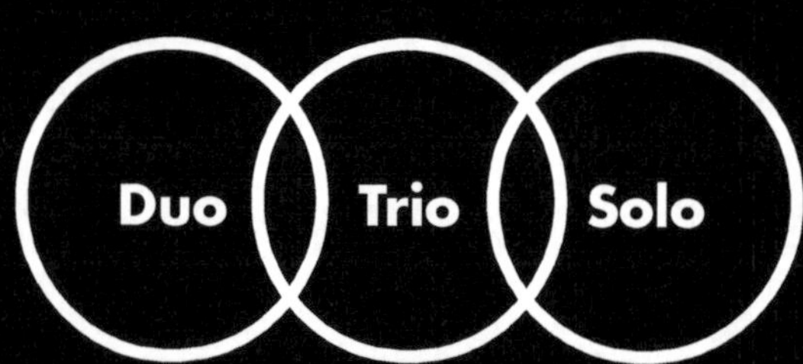

Now create different spatial relationships. Experiment with the arrangement of space and the arrangement of movement. Observe how the changes affect spatial tension.

Variation B

Creating different areas of conflict by changing the arrangement

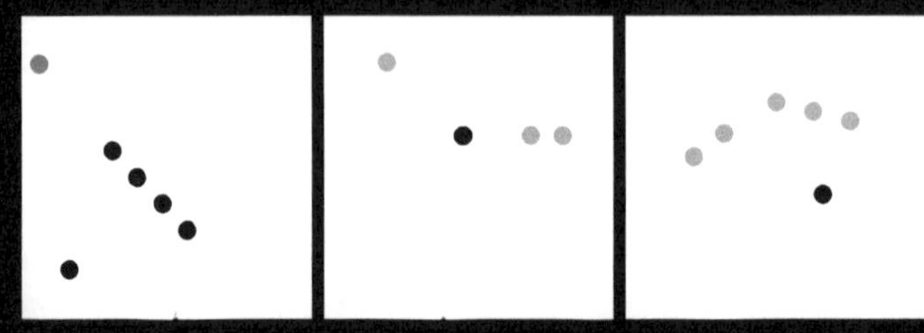

212

Establishing relationships

One way to create tension is to establish a relationship between two different parties.

This tension can be a form of expression and a central concept in a dance composition. For the audience to feel the tension, they first need to experience the relationship between the two parties. Choose an arrangement that visually supports your concept to make it more accessible for the spectators. If they cannot feel the relationships between the two parties, the space between the dancers will lose its function and all tension. It will be empty space, a black hole that sucks energy from your scene.

The spectator will have to ignore the empty space by fading out part of the stage. Naturally, the space is still there, the floor is still reflected, but it has become space in between without the function of an in-between space. The audience will have to actively suppress seeing what is uninteresting, which

is an effort they won't be able to keep up for more than a few moments. That means the audience will be able to focus on the parts of the stage where there is action for some time, but then the whole room including the 'dead' space will be back into focus, capturing the audience's concentration, thus taking it away from your scene. If you can work with movable stage light, creating islands of attention is easy. Or you may decide to fill the stage with action at all times and force the audience to choose for themselves where to look next, where to put their focus. In that case, the tension springs from the necessity of choice, the knowledge that while you are watching one detail, you might miss another. This kind of setting can work really well, but it is a risky business - the line between enjoyable tension and frustration is thin.
So you can choose between several options: you can work with the tension of the arrangement by allowing (meaningful!) distance between parties of dancers; or create islands of focus with moveable lights; or put simultaneous, parallel action on stage and challenge the audience to decide where to put their focus.

In a performance at Staatsschauspiel Dresden, a lighting technician pointed out to me how the 16 moveable lights he worked with gave each performer their own personal lighted space. When several performers met, their lights merged and formed a new, bigger, more brightly lit area. This kept the stage changing constantly, and the the whole performance was exciting and fascinating to watch. 16 moveable lights are a luxury, of course, and not something easily available in small budget theatres. But you don't necessarily need exclusive lighting technology. It is enough to appreciate, even treasure empty space, and learn to intuitively understand the language of arrangement.

Islands and paths of focus within an arrangement

Create an infinite movement loop of eight movements.

Set several points of focus on the empty stage. Change the movement loop to deliberately guide the spectator's gaze from one point of focus to the next.

Arrange islands of focus and 'zoom moments' in which the spectator's eye takes in details you want to highlight.

Levels

In 'Relations and relationships' we imagined two dancers standing on an imaginary line. This setting was two-dimensional. In the last section, we added another dimension to our space, namely depth. Let's add levels to our three-dimensional space. We can roughly divide them into three:

Floor levelMedium level   High level

Division of stage space in three levels along the vertical: floor level, medium level, high level.

Floor level

In some Contemporary Dance styles, the floor is considered a partner in dance. The movement vocabulary is extended to shifting the body's weight on the shoulders, hands, or head. Floor level is a whole dimension that can be added or taken away from your arrangement, depending on your own affinity towards floor work and on the possibilities of the stage you are arranging for. If the geometry of your stage renders the dancers invisible to most of the audience as soon as they drop to floor level, you might want to refrain from choreographing long floor work sections.

Medium level

While medium level offers almost infinite options of movements, gestures, and directions, it is also the level closest to our everyday lives. Even if you arrange your whole stage with fantastical contrasts, there will be moments when the audience's eyes will need to be challenged by more than just movements on medium level. Your task is to find these moments in your movement sequences and check if they could be improved by taking them to floor level. Develop your feeling for how much 'floor' you need to make your dance richer and more three-dimensional.

Try the following experiments: cut sequences from a choreography and fill the gaps with floor level transformations of the original sequences. Or do the opposite and insert floor sequences in between the original combinations. This technique is called 'sandwiching', because the 'sandwich' - the choreography - grows thicker and thicker with each added sequence.

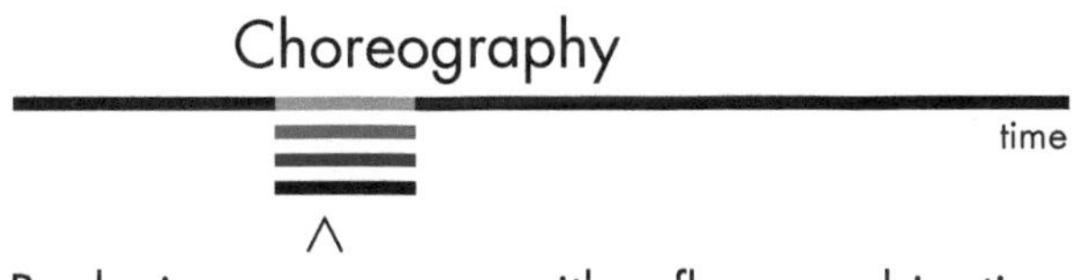

Replacing a sequence with a floor combination

Inserting a floor combination

Let's assume we have two groups of dancers on stage, A and B, who are dancing different combinations. Although the movements of the groups create an interesting dynamic, it starts to flatten after some time. To keep up the tension, you decide to transform part of the dance combination into a floor sequence. If both groups do their floor combinations at the same time, however, you will lose the element of contrast this situation offers you. Contrasts are the most powerful tool to create spatial tension in your arrangement, so go ahead and try to have only one of the groups switch to floor level. Can you feel the spatial tension rise?

The third level - high level

Every movement can be translated into a jump, and with every jump you enter the third level for a moment. If you want your dancers to spend more than just a moment on third level, you'll have to work with lifts. Lifts above shoulder level have to be approached with some respect – a two-meter fall may lead to serious injuries, after all. But you don't necessarily need strong men to transform your combinations into high level movements. There is always the option of using several dancers to lift one single dancer.
The following study shows how to explore the third level safely.

The living climbing frame

Define a small space in which a group of dancers lie, sit and stand to build a living climbing frame. Another dancer enters and uses the frame to support himself, distributing his weight on his hands and feet.

The frame dancers do not stay still, but try to actively support the climbing dancer. They take responsibility for the climber and share his weight among each other, thus reducing the risk of falling to a minimum. With practise, the frame will enter a movement dialogue with the climber, and will be able to change its shape more quickly. This is a good exercise to promote trust among the dancers and to test and develop the lifting potential of the group.

Now the frame turns into a wave that ceaselessly rolls forward. The dancers at the source of the wave start at floor level, progressing via medium level into high level and back to floor level. The climber scales the wave by stepping on the rolling, walking bodies until he reaches the end of the wave, where he lies down to integrate into it while another dancer starts climbing.

Develop isolated lifts from your living frame explorations and use them in a choreography.

Transforming medium level movements
into floor level movements, and the
compositional relationship between the
two levels

Create a movement combination at medium level.

Start on the floor. Adapt your combination to your
new position by trying to shift your weight to different parts of your body.

Use the floor like a dance partner. Explore the possibilities of transformation in all parameters of movement until the floor combination becomes independent from the medium level combination.

One dancer dances the medium level combination
and another the floor combination. Experiment with
the timing: Let the dancers alternately stop and start
their combinations, as if the stops and starts were
ping pong balls passing to and fro between them.

Composition and its elements

As you may have guessed by now, the line between arrangement and composition in dance is often blurred, and sometimes it disappears altogether. In dance, the arrangement can change the composition. Counterpoints are added, opposing elements run against the melody...
Individual parts, such as segments of a choreography, movement phrases or ideas, can be arranged, but they will change when other parts are altered, which in turn changes the whole composition.

Imagine space as a three-dimensional octave field in which all nuances of sound can be shown – shrill sounds, gentle notes swelling to orchestral thunder or plaintively dying away...the possibilities of motional composition compare to those in musical composition, and some of the tools a composer uses also work very well for choreographers.

Before we delve deeper into the choreographic aspects of composition, try the following study. I invite you to do the same study a second time, after you have finished this chapter, and see how it changes.

Compositions of space

In groups of four: One person takes the part of choreographer, the other three are 'givers'. Mark a space. The three givers enter the space and strike different poses in different positions.

The poses are dramatically different from each other: small gestures versus big, whole-body versus isolated, different levels, varying expressions and qualities. The givers keep entering, offering a pose, exiting, and entering again, choosing different positions and poses each time.

The choreographer chooses a few poses and puts them in an order. He may insert new elements as transitions, transform poses that have been offered, or move them in space.

The choreographer decides who enters when and with which movements.

When I work with a large number of dance students of varying skill level, I let two students work as a choreography team with only two 'givers'. Once they finish a creation, they switch roles. The finished pieces are then presented to the class and discussed. In these discussions it is almost unavoidable that there will be questions about divers compositional elements. Try to focus on one compositional element at a time – for example space, relationships, structure – to avoid wasting your time talking about everything at once and achieving nothing.

50 Study

Unisono

When a group of dancers performs the same movement in unison, the movement is given more power, more significance, more weight. It will feel more important to the audience, its symbolic value increased by the number of dancers performing it. Imagine sixty men, seated in a half-circle, all dropping their chests on their knees on the same musical accent. Such a simple movement, not very dramatic in a solo performance, is rendered exceedingly powerful just by this arrangement in the ensemble. If you let the sixty men perform complicated movements, the effect will be lost; just as it will be lost if the dancers do nothing but simple movements in unison throughout the whole piece.

The following rule applies:

The more dancers move in unison, the more important and symbolic the movement will seem.

The more dancers you add, the simpler the movement needs to be for maximum effect.

To tap the full potential of an unisono moment, it has to come as a surprise. The choreography has to build up to it without foreshadowing the idea. A surprise is always more effective than predictability or satisfied expectations. There will be certain moments when the audience expect the ensemble to dance big, synchronous movements, either because the music asks for big

movements, or because an unisono pattern has been introduced and repeatedly used with a certain line in the music. In such a case, it can be refreshing
to not meet the spectator's expectation. Here's an example: You choose a
song with a refrain for your choreography, and the refrain is always danced
in unison. After a few repetitions, your audience will expect the unisono moment when they hear the refrain – their expectations have been raised and
met. Another example could be a floor work choreography which keeps the
dancers standing up, pausing and throwing themselves back on the floor.
After a few repetitions, the spectator may well think 'Not again!' whenever a
dancer falls back on the floor. There is such a thing as too much recognisable
structure in a dance piece, after all.

Apart from the element of surprise, a unisono moment can also be used to
calm down a complex, multi-faceted choreography, making it seem more logic and more composed. You can play with raising and meeting subconscious
expectations, just as a Hollywood film raises and meets the expectation of a
happy end. Observe how much asynchronous movement you need to maxi-
mise the effect a sudden unisono moment, try out for how long you can build
up tension by putting off the calming reassurance of the unisono.

All in all, I feel it is best to use completely synchronous moments sparingly to
avoid the effect wearing off.

In a video clip or a film, you can break synchronicity by cutting or using a free
camera. The dancers move in unison, and the cuts or a fast moving camera
provide the necessary variety. If you work with simple camera effects and
less frequent cuts, your film will stay closer to your movement material and
the dancers, but it will require a viewer with a refined feeling for space, dynamics and arrangement.

Synchronicity in relation to dynamics

Create several movement combinations in place, travelling and on the floor, using

- small, rapid movements
- big, slow movements
- big, accentuated movements
- small, flowing movements
- big, flowing, connected movements

From this material, develop a study on 'synchronicity and asynchronicity'.

Opposition

The emergence of an opposing force always creates suspense – the kind of tension we enjoy in every good fairy tale, that keeps us glued to the screen in every action-packed thriller. It is exactly the kind of tension we look for when composing a new dance piece. The artful choreographer deploys opposition whenever he wants to replace boredom with excitement. Once you know how to create suspense in your composition, you will also be able to modify it to suit your needs.

Two opposing points or parties are connected by an axis. Shifting the axis allows us to shift to different points of view, which in turn define a reference point and its counterpart.

In the example on page 226, it is easy to imagine an axis connecting the two parties because we are looking at a static image. In dance, the axis will literally jump through space as the reference points switch and re-form.

Of course, the axis is not a real, tangible thing – it is an imaginary tool that helps us understand relations on stage. It allows us to order spatial designs into temporal sections. One section lasts for as long as a certain axis works, independent from music or motif. If you can define your axis inside a design and define for how long it lasts, you will be able to deliberately work with the two opposing ends of the axis, such as reducing or increasing spatial tension by reducing or increasing the contrasts between reference point and counterpart.

Do not let yourself be tempted to see this imaginary axis only where it is obvious. You can apply it anywhere you want! You may even find new, unusual perceptions of dance. Nobody forces you to stick with one defined axis for a whole scene, either. Use the different axes unexpectedly. Let them rotate. Experiment with several axes fading in and out of action. This will help to expand your imagination of spatial design.

The two ends of the axis can stand in harmonious or disharmonious opposition. Let me be clear about this: 'harmonious' or 'disharmonious' does not mean 'good' or 'bad' in this case. 'Harmonious' describes an opposition of two mirror images, exact opposites of each other. 'Unharmonious' means that while the ends of the axis do oppose each other, they are not exact opposites of each other.

Harmonious opposition   Unharmonious opposition

high	low
long	short
straight	bent
wide	narrow

high	low
long	
straight	no other differences

Examples for different oppositions along an axis

Naturally, there are no strict rules on how to set these oppositions, and no definitively 'right' or 'wrong' way of doing it. But by using the idea of axes to connect oppositions, we sensitise our eyes to new patterns, we learn a new way to look at designs, and this will help us develop our own personal standards and change the way we choreograph.

For more practise, you will find visual examples of axes added into dance positions on the following pages.

Symmetrical,
without opposition
Asymmetrical,
unharmonious opposition
horizontal axis
vertical axis
vertical axis
Asymmetrical,
harmonious opposition
Asymmetrical,
harmonious opposition

Spatial oppositions

Wide, outward   ... to ...   ... narrow, inward.

Opposition through number and relationship

Single, unrelated ...   ... to ...   ... two in relation.

Generating movement through axes

Working with oppositions offers more than just suspense. As every single gesture, every move of our body in space can be opposed somehow, any movement produces almost infinite movement material. At Laban Center, a choreographer once created a full-length dance piece from one single gesture – cradling an infant – and all movements she used were either oppositions or transformations of this one gesture.

You can set an axis inside a movement, a shape or a design. Actually, you can use it in all parameters of dance to define a contrast in general. You could, for example, use an axis to show differences in movement quality, density or use of space.

Example 1:
Setting two choreographies against each other: airy, dynamic, fluid movements at one end of the axis, heavy and static movements at the other end. The axis is not fixed in space, but rotates on stage, so that the the two groups of dancers switch movement qualities whenever the axis turns.

Example 2:
Opposing slow, regal movements with quick, lively movements.

Motif, counter-motif and counterpoint

We call the opposition of a motif – for example a shape or a quality – the counter-motif. They are the two ends of the axis. In addition, we have a third level, the counterpoint. The counterpoint is a free, independent agent that contrasts both motif and counter-motif, a little like a tiny flash of movement that renders the motif/counter-motif level more three-dimensional. Motif and counter-motif remain, and the counterpoint is added like a drop of colour, or a shooting star. It could be something new, an addition – maybe a new colour – or it could be like a memory, suddenly remembered, bringing up an aspect of the theme that has been forgotten or only briefly touched upon.

Let me give you an example for a thematic counterpoint in Mats Eks 'Sleeping Beauty' (1997): A woman giving birth. Nurses. The consultant , who will later turn out as the 'wicked witch'. This character is introduced thoroughly, obviously foreshadowing his double role. He takes up so much space that the birthscene fades into the background. Now, as a counterpoint, a trolley is wheeled across the stage, on it an embryo, still in the bag of waters (a dancer under a piece of cloth). This is what we call a thematic counterpoint, because it is used to lead the audience back from the sub-plot to the main plot.

We can also work with a 'non-thematic counterpoint'. Let's say our motif is 'poses on the floor', then an obvious counter-motif would be 'dynamic movements through space'. As a counterpoint, a dancer on stilts or hanging from a rope appears out of nowhere.

Opposing attributes

Wherever you are right now, observe what is going on around you and verbalise different attributes to describe your environment. Experiment with adding axes to your attributes to develop possible oppositions.

Developing a piece from a gesture

Choose an arm gesture, for example lifting the right forearm as if to shake hands.

The dancers create oppositional arm gestures to the original gesture, for example pulling back and lifting the left upper arm etc.

Check if and where the torso or the legs can support or oppose the original movement.

Find oppositions to the oppositions.

Link the movement material into sequences.

Experiment with moving your sequences through space. Some sequences will move naturally, others will stay in place.

Transform the gestures and sequences in the body and in space.

Now try to work out counterpoints to your material.

Embed your sequences in a structure, arrange and link them, making connections, setting up relationships and adding necessary images.

Symmetry – Asymmetry

The distinction between the two seems simple: if a shape can be mirrored along its central axis, it is symmetrical. But there is more to symmetry and asymmetry than just mathematical mirroring. Sometimes, shapes can seem symmetrical even though mathematically, they are not.
Symmetry is usually associated with feelings such as safety, stability, power, standstill, or boredom.

Symmetrical shapes can be mirrored along a central axis.

Symmetrical associations

- stationary

- safe

- powerful

- clear

Shapes that cannot be mirrored along their central axis are asymmetrical. The differences in the shape on either side of the central axis create spatial tension.

Asymmetrical associations

- tension

- insecurity

- hanging in the balance

- dynamical

- balancing

- mad

- quick

- fluid

If your dancers improvise with symmetrical positions only for a few minutes, chances are high that everybody present will get bored with the dance. Unbroken symmetry is not dynamic, it doesn't initiate movement. Suspense or tension comes with the uncertainty of asymmetry. It challenges, asks for movement, creates connections in space. Symmetry, on the other hand, calms down the excitement of asymmetry, gives us a break from chaos, and creates a quiet place from which new beginnings are possible.

Sometimes, a shape makes a symmetrical overall impression on stage even if strictly, mathematically speaking it is asymmetrical. Don't dismiss a shape as 'symmetrical' just because you can't mirror it along its axis. Trust the overall impression you get when you watch the shape on stage. Is the effect of the shape you show as asymmetrical as you want it to be, or is it just mathematically asymmetrical?

Depending on your choreographing style, you may or may not want to use the symbolism inherent in symmetry and asymmetry. If, for example, you want to express power, you can use strong symmetry in your scenes and images to evoke a feeling of power. But even if you don't like to include this kind symbolism in your choreographies, it is helpful to study the dynamics and effects of symmetry and asymmetry.

From symmetry to asymmetry

Give your students a simple movement sequence that is mainly symmetrical. Their task is to change it so it becomes asymmetrical.

Present the transformed combinations to each other. The audience rates the pieces on a scale from 1 for 'very symmetrical impression' to 10 for 'very asymmetrical impression'. Notice how symmetrical asymmetrical movements can seem depending on their context inside the combination.

Intensity

Some dance scenes overwhelm me while others feel lengthy and dull. Everybody knows that feeling – sometimes there is too much going on on stage for the piece to be enjoyable, and sometimes we miss the spark in a performance.

As a choreographer, I am constantly balancing between starving the audience to make them keen to see movement and offering action to keep them engaged. Boredom is what choreographers and directors fear most. Does this sound familiar? If yes, what do you about it? Most choreographers are aware of their fear and actively work against their natural over-activity. They force themselves to bear stillness, they tell themselves to trust in the quiet moments. The result, however, often seems rather forced and tense instead of calm and trusting.

It is challenging to withstand the pressure of the expectations coming at you from all directions – your own, your audience's, your peers', etc. - to sit at the throbbing heart of a theatre and stay relaxed enough to give room to necessary stillness. This challenge is part of your job as a choreographer.

Insecurity and anxiousness don't necessarily lead to over-action, however. They can also paralyse us and stifle our courage to follow the impulse to move. You want to fill the space with power and movement, but nothing happens. I mention this because we often don't realise we are not being 'calm' on purpose, but are actually paralysed by fear, and only self-reflection can help us find a way out of it.

You need the courage to keep asking yourself: 'Is this what I really want?'. The more you focus on this question, the deeper you will delve into working on your piece without being distracted. Constantly ask yourself: 'Is this really how I want it to be?', and you will never have to justify yourself later on – not before yourself or anybody else.
The compositional elements I have introduced here are ways of approaching dance that help to understand the individual parts of a piece. The more you are able to differentiate what you see, the more differentiated your own creations will be. Another approach is the concept of 'density'.

Dance, as we have seen, is a complex connection of numerous different elements. Some of them can be broken down into their single parts. As a concept, density comprises different elements such as power, energy, or other non-verbal factors. So when we deal with density, we have to bear in mind that we deal with a bundle of elements that, together, make up this concept. The challenge is not to let yourself isolate one of these elements to judge the density of a scene. 'It is too fast' may also mean 'the tempo is fine, but there are to many movements'.

In the introduction to the chapter on structure I used the image of a glider flying over a landscape. The spectator is a passenger on the glider, the piece is the landscape. It makes a difference whether we glide over a desert plateau or go thundering through thick undergrowth – this is density, the amount of action we see on our flight. Action on stage is closely connected to the number of dancers moving on it: more dancers usually create more density, and reducing numbers also reduces density, expanding your scene. But you can make a scene denser or less dense independent of numbers.

We can never fully predict when our audience will reach the limit of their attention. It also depends on the audience's experience, or training, in taking in complex movement compositions. The more important it is for us to reflect on how much action or absence of action we need to create the right amount of density in our pieces.

I already mentioned the risk of overwhelming the audience with too dense a composition. The same is of course true for the opposite. If you let your scene deflate, you will need a lot of energy to get back into flow. You don't have to rein in a piece the minute it is taking off just to avoid filling your stage with too much movement. Your first impulse might be to have two thirds of your dancers leave the stage to calm the scene down, but it may be an interesting idea to keep all dancers on stage and still calm down.

The question is, how, or rather: which elements can I use to make a scene denser, and which to reduce density?

'Density' is the combination of tempo, power, energy, and movement – or their absence – at a certain moment on stage.

It is one of the vital components for an effective dramatic arc.

<table>
<tr><td align="center">Expanding the scene</td><td align="center">Tightening the scene</td></tr>
<tr><td align="center">slow
small
in place
little
stationary</td><td align="center">fast
big
through space
a lot
dynamic</td></tr>
</table>

The denser a design, the less visible are its individual components. If you introduce a new element into an already dense structure, it will hardly be noticed at all. The structure will become a little tighter because it already is so close to its maximum density. If I want a new element to be noticeable, I have to introduce it at a moment when my design is less dense.

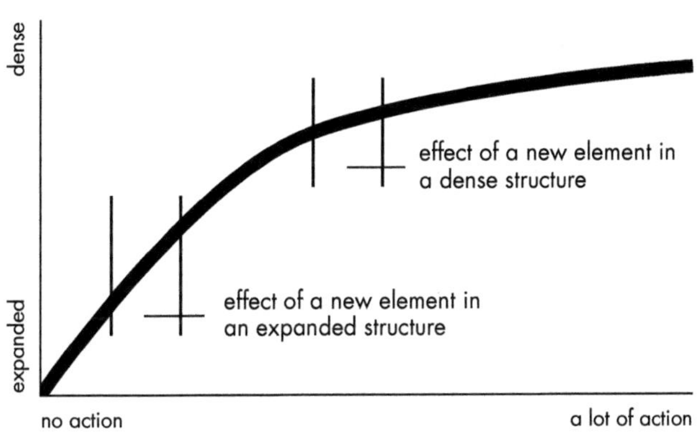

Correlation between density and action

In a denser structure, the overall expression of the scene will conceal the expression and movement of each individual dancer. In expanded structures, there is more room for individual characters and movements.

Tighten and expand

Create a movement sequence using the following chart.

Expanding	Tightening
– slow	– fast
– small	– big
– in place	– through space
– a little	– a lot
– stationary	– dynamic

Develop a structure for five dancers, that goes from expanded to dense and vice versa.

Work with different groups of dancers. Try to expand and tighten your scene regardless of the number of dancers on stage

Study the impact of abrupt versus slow transitions on the density of your movement sequences.

Observe how long an expanded or dense scene can last without losing momentum.

You can use this concept of density anywhere:

- music

- images

- a design in a shop window

- ...

Wherever somebody composed something, they will have used dense and expanded structures. Walk through your city and notice how the world grows wider in certain places and denser in others; how a single pneumatic hammer can fill up a square and block out every other sound. Train your senses to feel these different things. Sometimes, we oversee the process of tightening or expanding where it is most obvious, not seeing the wood for the trees.

Position – flow – transition

Everything flows. Everything that flows keeps changing forever. Dance is flow made visible, which is why it is so hard to grasp, transitioning all the time, transforming again and again. Images form and dissolve, overlapping, taking turns. If we freeze the movements, we find poses, statues. Are they part of the dance? The path to and through a position is the dance. Poses are static, the opposite of movement, which is the essence of dance. Dance is infinite transition.

A transition is provisional, something undefinable that lies between things. Many choreographers work with poses or positions – the actual destination of a movement - rather than the movements of transitions because it is that space between the positions that is so hard to grasp. Other choreographers find thinking in positions too limiting and prefer to focus on movement and its quality. Both approaches work fine, but very often choreographers stick with one of the two and never even think of working with the other. For well-balanced choreographies, we need both, poses and flow. So before you start developing a position-centred or flow-centred approach, you need to find out which one you prefer by habit.

Before your inner eye, imagine a dance scene. What do you see? Mainly positions, or never-ending movement? Are you longing for the clarity and strength of a pose, or the ease and flow of movement, or do you feel you are giving both equal attention?

Setting up positions in a movement flow

Create an organic travelling movement sequence using floor level. Try to avoid poses.

Create five to seven poses independent of your sequence.

Integrate the poses into your sequence, finding different transitions from the movements into the positions.

New paths into familiar positions

The aim of this study is to experience familiar positions as fresh, new sensations in which the path to and from the pose is just as important as the pose itself. The choreographer guides the dancers from the outside by setting them tasks. Together, they develop new pathways that lead to and from a position.

1. In pairs: one dancer, one choreographer. The dancers choose one of their favourite poses. The choreographers analyse how the dancers move to and from the position and change it. The pose stays the same, but the pathway becomes different: the dancers have to try to find into the pose from a new direction, or to start a movement from a different body part, etc.

2. The dancer choreographer duet develops into ensemble choreographer: the dancers start with an arrangement in space and transform it twice into other arrangements. The choreographer's task is similar to exercise 1, only with more pathways to work with. That means that another important element is added to the task, namely composition. Changing the movement of a dancer will change the whole composition. I encourage you not to just accept the first draft. Always search for more than one solution when you are exploring spatial design, positioning and movement paths.

Rhythm

Monotony kills. If a choreography's arc of suspense is failing, it is usually because of faulty phrasing. Before we work with rhythm and phrases, we need to understand how phrasing works. Phrases drive our piece and surprise the audience, whereas monotony slows down our composition and makes it predictable.

If you present different movements to a steady rhythm, they will start looking the same after a while. Even if you work without music, you will find that many dances and repertoires follow the same underlying rhythm, although if they were created without music. The rhythm of dance is the rhythm of action, independent of music. Every action, every change of position creates a beat, just like a pulse.

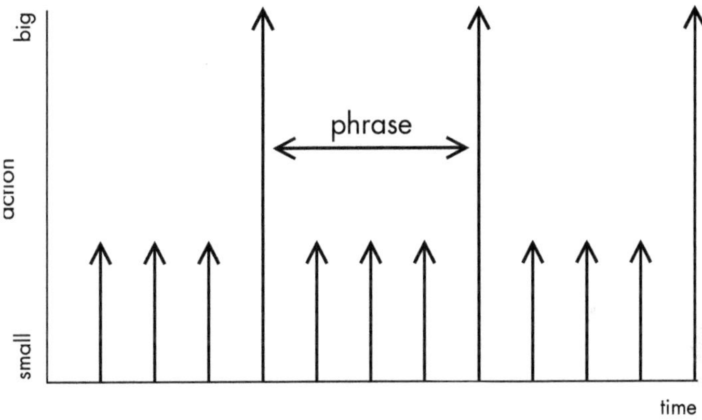

Temporal development of a dance piece with unchanging phrases and actions of consistent intensity

This pulse is the underlying rhythm we work with. We can create phrases by extending or shortening the intervals in which an action changes.

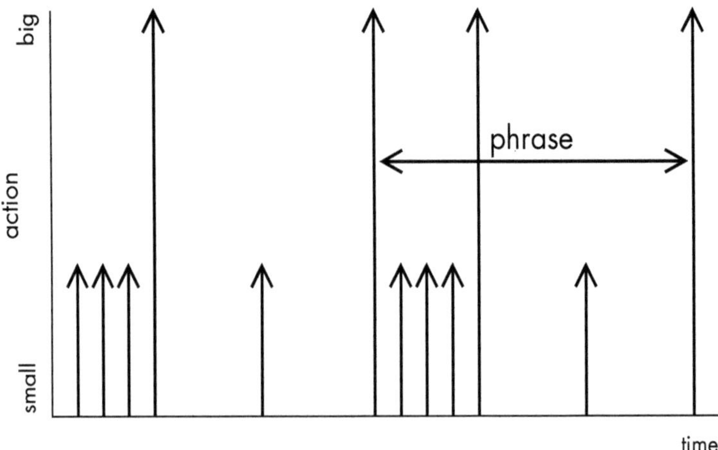

The phrase is a rhythmical pattern

But even this more complex, less predictable phrase will lose its sparkle after the fourth repetition. We often see choreographies that repeat the same rhythmical pattern in emotionally different scenes of a piece. Similar rhythmical phrases in different scenes may be a reason why the scenes you choreographed don't look and feel as different from each other as you would like them to.

Example: Imagine a first scene, 'the awakening'. The dancers move upwards from floor level to medium level and from there into space, taking up positions to dance the second scene in place. The third scene is 'destruction', the dancers move from their positions through space to floor level. The content and emotion of the first and the third scene are fundamentally different, but the rhythmical patterns are almost identical, which makes the scenes seem similar to each other. Although the dancers use different sets of movement, the emotional change between the two scenes doesn't translate as well as the choreographer intended.

It isn't obvious at first glance that the similarity of the scenes lies in their rhythm, it's just that they feel similar when we watch them.
To find out whether the fault lies in the phrasing, we need to limit the period under observation.

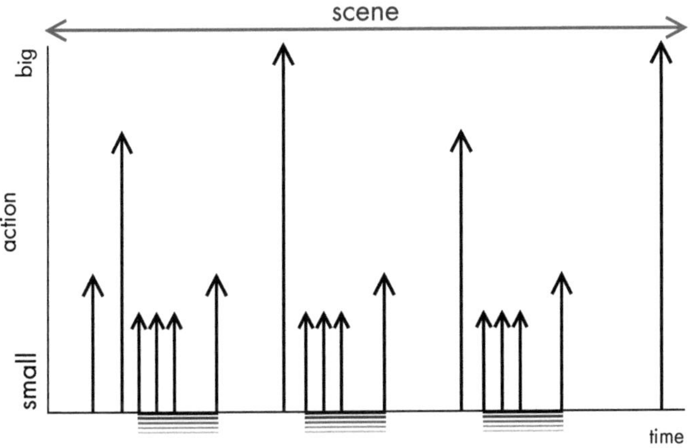

Temporal development of a dance piece with different phrases
and actions of varying intensity

The graph makes the pattern of the scene visible. It also reveals chunks of repeating patterns. If this rhythmical concept were repeated in two scenes that were meant to be different from each other, the scenes would seem similar even if they were set to different music and used a different movement repertoire.
There are several ways of detecting rhythmical patterns in your scene. You can use pen and paper, drawing a longer line for every big action you see and a shorter line for every smaller action. Or you can use your voice to express the movement qualities you observe. Count the beats one to eight, matching your tone with the movements you see: loud, low, high, deep, long, short, etc.

The actions represented in the graph as short or long arrows refer to all compositional variants. An action can be a change and/or a movement.
How we perceive rhythm and phrasing is not necessarily determined by the exact temporal structure of the movements, but rather by our subjective experience of actions, changes and movements in a certain time frame.

Let me give you an example: a dancer repeats a series of small movements and adds one big movement.

247

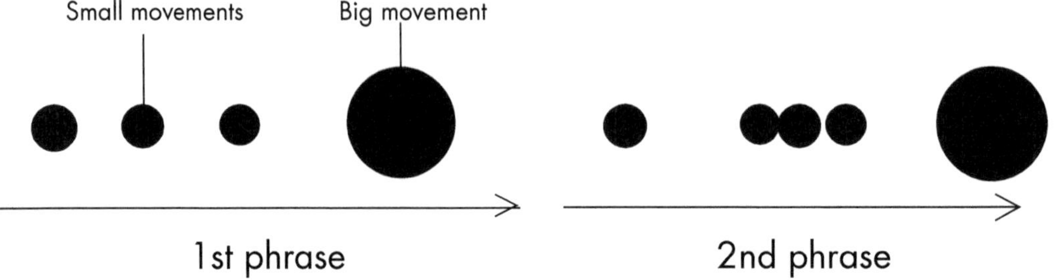

The mathematical and subjective perception of the phrase

The time intervals between the movement are different in both phrases, but the rhythm we perceive is created by the action 'change from small movement to big movement'. The change in movement size takes up more of our attention than the temporal structure of the movements.

This means that every action – a jump, dropping to the floor, change of movement quality or size – can be a rhythmical element in relation to other actions. So each change of action has the potential to create phrases and patterns that can be either predictable or surprising.

Example:

A choreography repeats a series of movements at floor level, some travelling movements and one jump. The phrasing of the individual sequences may be interesting, but the rhythm of the actions stays the same: floor – space – jump – floor – space – jump. At a certain point, the audience will have understood this rhythm – not necessarily on a conscious level, but they will feel familiar with the rhythm.

Depending on your spectators' sensitivity, spatial or qualitative changes in the choreography will be perceived as smaller or bigger. Every spectator sees their own rhythmical version of the same piece. But if you deliberately create phrases, the changes will be more visible and they will shape your piece with their structure.

The impact of a change also depends on how the choreographer balances the different phrasing parameters:

- movement accents
- change of quality
- change in space
- symmetry
- spacing of bodies
- relationship between dance, music, and projection
- synchronicity
- relationships on stage
- compositional opposition and solution

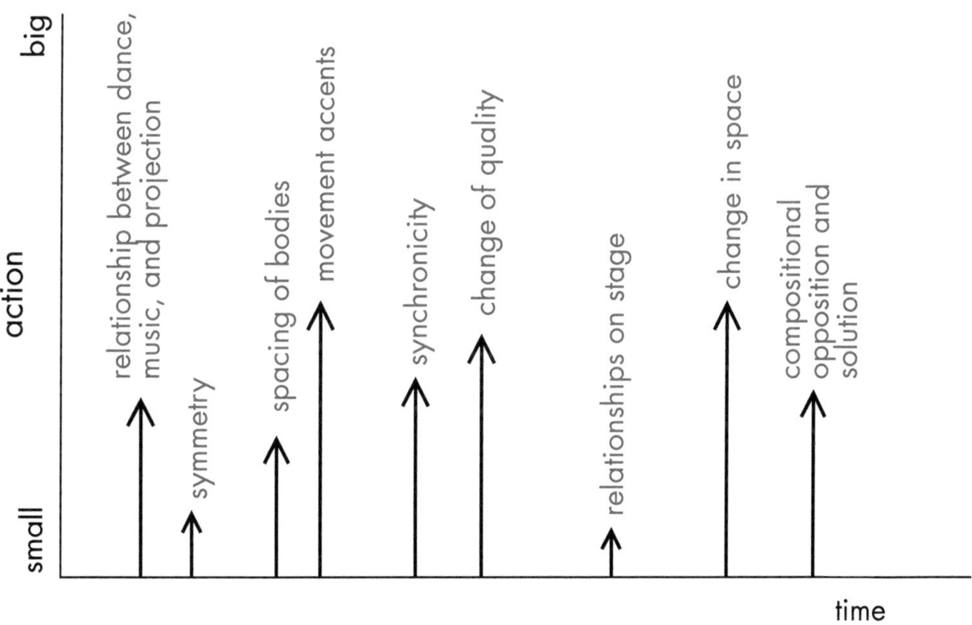

Examples for parameters that are part of a choreography's rhythm

If the spectators start feeling superior towards a choreography, it is usually because they think they have seen it all and that there are no surprises left. This feeling has to do with the design of the rhythmical phrases and the balance of phrasing parameters that together make up the rhythm of your choreography. Therefore be aware which actions in your choreography serve as rhythmical parameters. You have to learn to sense which actions are rhythmically relevant. Observe closely, with mathematical precision, and at the same time be sensitive and open to the speed and the rhythms of the world around you.

For some time I used a stop watch to measure the time frames of everyday actions of my friends. I found, for example, that in the action of 'leaving home', the time span between 'stopping to think whether I've forgotten something' and 'actually leaving' varied greatly. It changed depending on where people were going. I'm not sure this experiment changed my perception of time, but it was certainly funny (though admittedly quite annoying for my friends). If you want to try it, you'll need a stop watch that saves multiple reference points. Even if you just do it for fun, it will sharpen your perception of speed and rhythms. Whereas you normally concentrate on the content of a situation, for example a scary moment, you will now perceive different changes of speed. You will start connecting feelings with rhythmical patterns.

Another way of practising to analyse rhythms is to watch a film and pay attention to the pace in which the scenes are cut. When are the cuts faster, when slower? Is there a rhythm to the camera's movements? How do the cuts connect with the soundtrack? If you choose a film that touches you personally, it will be more difficult to keep an analytical distance, but it will be even more interesting to find out to which rhythms your emotions react.

The association of rhythm with emotion makes phrasing an important means of expression in dance. Just like space, it serves as a tool for the dancer and choreographer to express feelings. Rhythm is a way of articulating the emotional, non-verbal language of dance.

Phrasing with different parameters

Choose music with varying rhythmical density. Find different possibilities of relationships between music and dance.

Phrasing: create a sequence using a four-four rhythm. Then convert your sequence into a three-four rhythm, a five-four rhythm, and a seven-eight rhythm. If you have a group of students, let them all start with the same sequence, but give them different rhythms to convert the sequence to. Compare your results.

In pairs: A draws a rhythmical structure on a piece of paper, B dances the structure, either applying it to an already choreographed sequence or creating a new sequence.

Expand the study by adding rhythmical parameters other than speed and accent.
You can use the graph on p. 271 for reference.

Compositional variation

All compositional parameters can be used in contrast to each other. They make precision and in-depth work easier.

By focusing on compositional parameters you create tools with which you can develop variations.

The most important compositional parameters are:

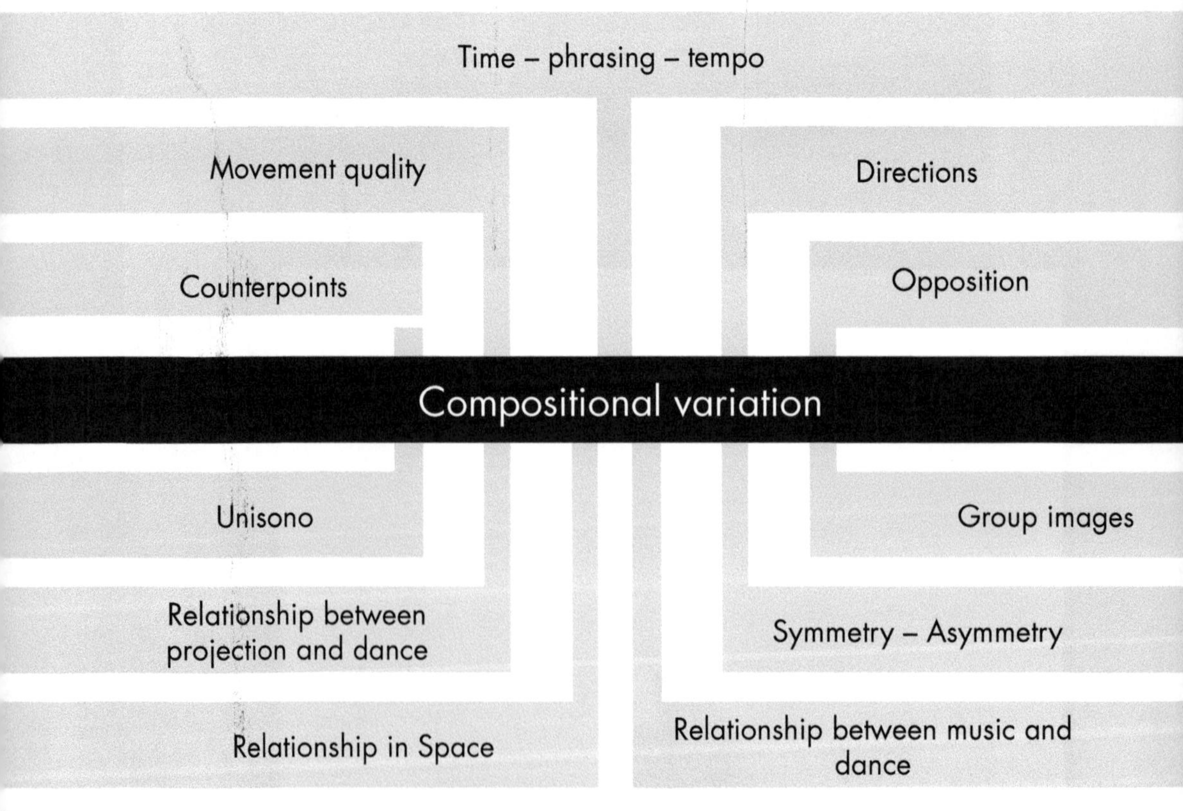

Compositional variation

6 Solo

The solo in contemporary dance

Choreography and development

Character work

A solo is a personal involvement with your own dance, your values, but also your own limitations of which you will become aware once you start solo work. First, you might find yourself technically challenged, because how you move in your imagination may look very different in real life, and you will be forced to bring the two images together somehow.

Another limitation is of a dramaturgical nature: either I want my solo to be exciting and full of surprises, or I want to create a moment of intimate intensity without any 'special effects'.

Is that what it is about? Publicly sharing an intimate moment?

Or do I want to offer good entertainment?

Maybe I want to touch or inspire my audience with my skills, or make them laugh, or maybe I just want to share my experience of the music with them for some time.

There are different approaches to a solo, different lenses through which we can look at our dance. We need to be clear about the starting point of our work.

Where do I start?

How do I create movements?
How can I develop contrasts and opposition?

Starting from the outside: I could first choose the music or a thematic source such as a poem or a story. Or I might choose 'contrasts' as my focus, when designing movement sequences. All these are approaches that start from the outside.

Starting from the inside: Do I want to add a personal component to my dance? Is there anything I want to tell about myself? Do I want to share an opinion about a certain topic?

Or do I want to start from the inside, without putting myself at the centre of attention? In that case, I could create a character for which I develop movements, shapes, ways of moving through space, qualities, subtexts and intentions.

The character may be connected to myself and my experience (in a way, of course, it always is), but it remains just a character, a role that I can step out of at any time. It is a little like writing a novel in which my own experience is mixed with many things that have nothing to do with me. The character will create its own reality and grow more independent, offering me more and more details to discover, allowing me to express my identification with the character in my solo.

Whatever approach I choose, the following questions will require some thought:

- How do I create a necessity for movement? I need to know why I choose a certain movement at a certain moment.

- When do I have to take step back to check on the dramaturgy of my piece? This outside perspective helps me decide what I can or should do for how long to keep the piece interesting.

How do I want to proceed? Either I dig deeper or I choose a break, that is, a contrast. If I switch into outside perspective too early, or permanently worry whether my dance is boring or interesting, I'm likely to miss the process that gives depth to my performance, thus making the solo superficial. If, on the other hand, I lose myself in the depth of my character, the solo's dramaturgical structure may suffer. If you have seen solo dances before, you will certainly remember performances that did not work because they were stuck in one of the two extremes.

The clearer you are about your approach, the easier it will be to get into a work flow.
If you want too much at once, you will only create blockades, but if you learn to distinguish your approach from your material, you will always discover something new and fascinating to work on.

As people are all individuals with their own priorities and opinions, it is impossible to generalise or judge, so don't worry what people might think about what you do. Instead, try to develop a work approach that allows you to keep shifting your focus onto different aspects of your process. That way, you will keep up your flow.

Whichever approach you choose: I highly recommend using a score. It will make it easier for you to shift your focus between parameters.

In the score, you fix individual parts or even movement sequences and chart them in an overview. In each row you can note keywords for the parameters to which you want to give special attention in that particular sequence.
This will help you to not lose the thread in your piece, and also to decide where you want contrasts and how to structure the dramaturgy of your solo.

Example of a solo score:

Stageing Space	Subtext	Quality	Level	Tempo/ accent	Form	Symmetry/ Asymmetry	focus audience	Tension/ Release
1. scene	Waking up	soft	Floor	slow	flat	asymmetry	introverted	release
2. scene								
3. scene								

Often, it is only through analysis that you realise that certain parameters remain unchanged for too long. The potential for a break or a visual change only becomes obvious through analytical examination.

The score is also a useful tool for scaffolding a structure you can use in rehearsals. It helps you keep an overview and better understand sequences that have already been choreographed.

Structuring space

If you have prepared a score for your solo and are ready to work on its spatial structure, this would be the ideal moment to sit in the auditorium of the theatre where you will be performing and envision yourself dancing the piece on stage. This will make your rehearsals on stage much more precise and intense than only preparing on paper.

If you cannot access the theatre before the performance, I recommend making a scale model of the stage, for example from a shoebox. Add a small object that represents the dancer in proportion to the stage. Now you can simulate the audience's perspective. You will change your positioning according to their point of view – looking down on the stage from above in an auditorium, or up from below if you are on a raised stage.

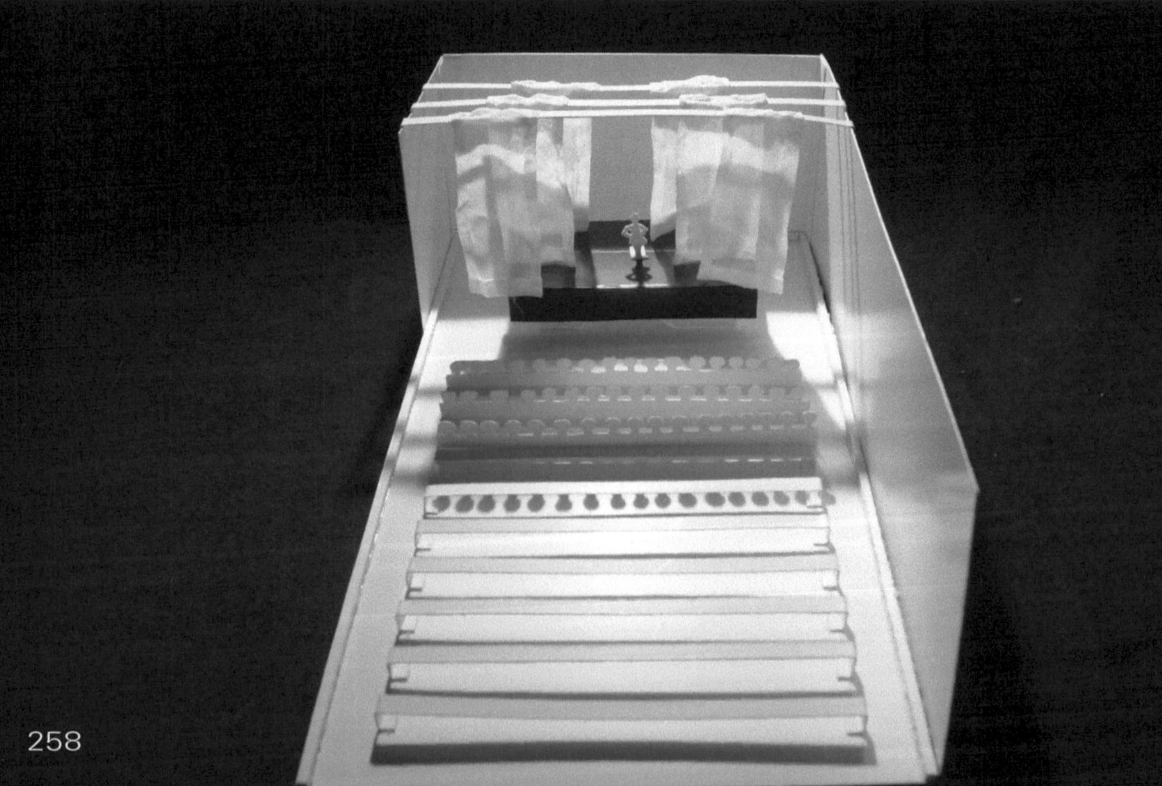

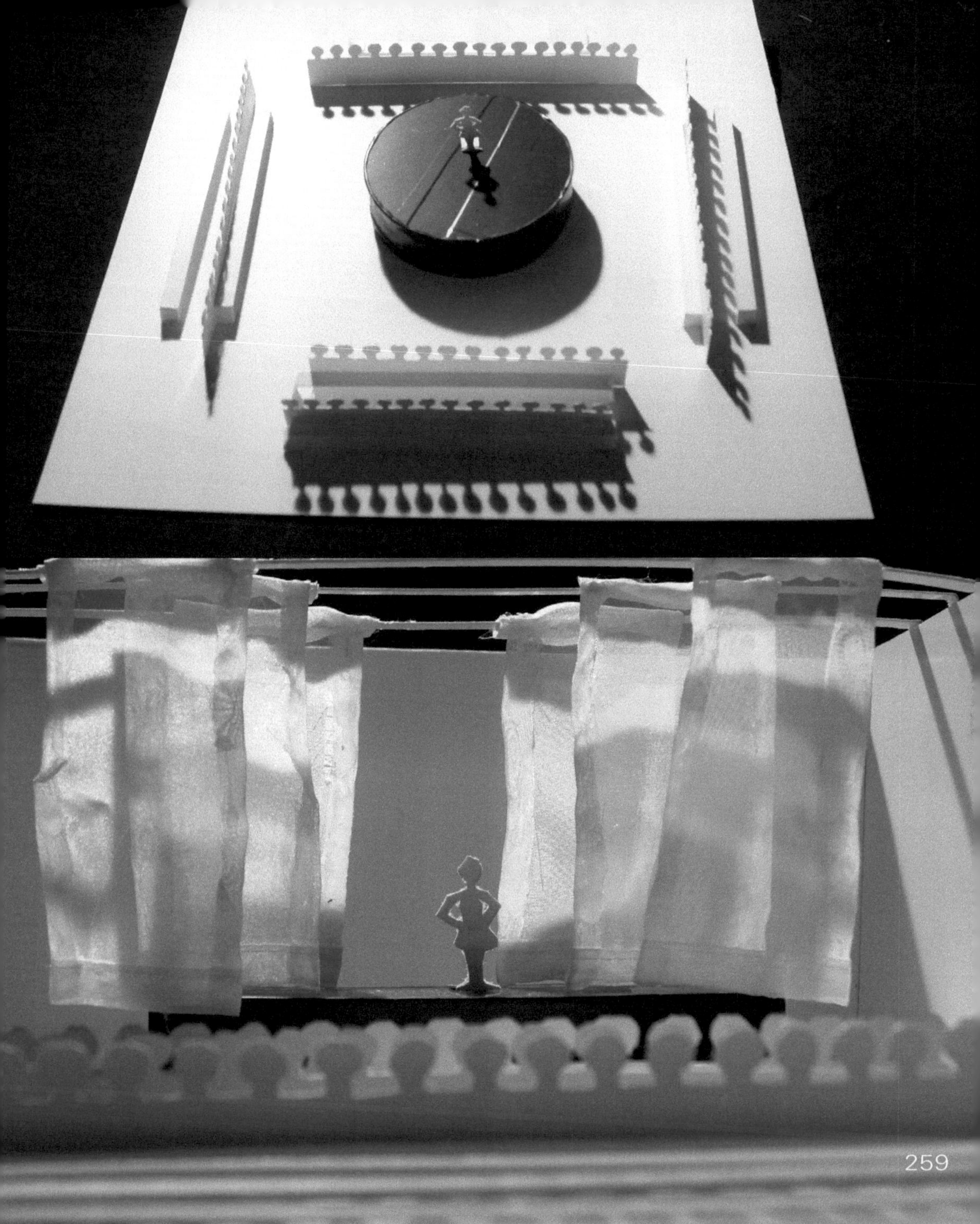

A basic choice of approaches

I Creating movements and their variations through technical and visual approaches such as gesture, manipulation, opposition, movement quality and composition.

II Linking emotion and body. Distinguishing different body parts.

III Developing a character.

IV The personal solo: weaving important personal milestones, emotional moments, and life-changing experiences into a dance.

V Translating source material such as music, text or images into dance.

VI Working with objects.

Let's examine these approaches more closely.

Technical approaches: Gesture, manipulation, opposition, movement quality, and composition

At first glance, the technical approach seems the easiest and most obvious:

You collect movements and skills you find interesting, you manipulate them, contrast them with each other, experiment with movement quality; you translate the movement fragments into your concept of space, and you add musical and movement contrasts, creating a scaffold for your composition that you can build on.

Great! Whether your solo touches your audience, however, depends on your awareness of your theme and its potential, on the subtext of your solo that lends intention to your movement fragments.

This process does not have to be logical at all. Actors often look for a certain logic that corresponds with the psychological process of their character. As a dancer, you are free from this logic. You may confront the audience with a conglomerate of emotions and yearnings. Leonard Cohen once said the secret of his success was that his songs confronted the audience with their own inner chaos and held up a mirror to their own imperfection.

Many artists work like this. It doesn't agree with everybody, but it always gets a lot of resonance. I remember chatting to a theatre intendant, and we came to talk about Freddie Mercury's songs. He told me how he used to sing along to Bohemian Rhapsody with great enthusiasm in his youth, and that it was only in his thirties that he realised, much to his surprise, that the lyrics didn't make sense at all. The logic of lyrics and poems, it seems, is associative rather than an intellectual, reflecting the difficulties of approaching and expressing emotion.

For your solo work, this means you cannot go wrong once you have your scaffold and are working on subtext, emotion, association and content! From here, you are free to explore the associations of emotions and content with an open mind. Sometimes, you will remember things you have observed in others, and sometimes you will remember experiences you have had yourself. Use these thoughts to fill your solo with inner images. One single thought may inspire a movement, or even a whole movement phrase.

Some dancers experience their own bodies and their movements so intensely that it is fascinating to watch them dance and share their awareness with the audience. It takes confidence and courage to dance like that, and it is risky to rely on this quality alone when preparing a solo.

Consider different approaches, and choose what suits you best. However you choose to approach your solo: leave all arbitrariness behind, and make every movement necessary.

Take a look at the next few pages Examples for 'generating movements' and 'developing contrasts' without any thematic requirements:

Examples for spatial approaches

Drawing figure eights or circles in the air: with your head, shoulders, chest, hips, legs. Varying size and dynamics. Adding contrasts with other body parts, directions, and floor patterns. Explore your personal space with different parts of your body.

Experimenting with the idea of pushing

Imagine pushing parts of your body - elbow, heel, palm, hip
head - against different surfaces.

Imagine being trapped in a bubble. Move around in that bubble.

Pushing against the imaginary bubble with different body parts, varying the intensity and dynamic of your movements.

Find ways down to floor level using the following images:

- Melting chocolate Easter bunny
- Dynamite in a skyscraper

Coming down on the floor from standing or jumping: Try
different dynamics and qualities, e.g. collapsing, floating, in
stages, tearing, melting ...

From open space into the floor with the idea of reaching out
for something, then releasing, and reaching out again.

Moving through space:

- Armour poses: wear an imaginary armour or shield.

- Develop poses from this image. Then translate the poses into movements.

In a strait-jacket: Gathering strength and pushing out agains the jacket to tear it apart in different places.

Bringing dynamic release movements into a flow sequence, using different directions and levels.

Gathering energy in the contraction and releasing it into space.

Open and close in contrast.

Contrast choreography:

- Choose a movement.

- Develop a movement that opposes the first, either by its quality or its direction in space.

- Find a next movement that contrasts the second.

- Use this contrasting principle to create movement through space.

Magnifying glass:

- A looks at B's upper body through an imaginary magnifying glass. B only moves the part of her upper body
  that is magnified.
- Develop movements with this idea and link them into
  a sequence.

Imagine a square on the floor, divided in several smaller squares:

- Try to touch the squares with different body parts.
- Use the movements from this exercise to create dance sequences.
- Add accents and tempo changes.

Examples for qualitative approaches

Theme: Insects

- Moving through space, try to emulate the movement quality of an insect:

- quick, fragile, light-weight, your bones filled with air....

- Include the parameters of time and accent.

- Develop movement variations by translating individual elements from one level to another: floor, table, and higher levels.

- Create a short movement combination. Notice how your body fills the dance space in the combination.

- Now turn your attention to the negative space in the combination you have just created – the space your body does NOT fill when you dance your combination, the space in between.

- Experiment with stilts and sticks.

Theme: Octopus

- Experiment with the range of motion of your pelvis: lying down, sitting, standing up. Try to find circles, twists or tilts, making the movements as muscular as you can.

- Let your pelvis movements flow into strong, sinuous arms and legs, visualising the movements of an octopus.

- Keep working on sending the muscular impulses from your pelvis into the rest of your body.

- Find movement combinations that contrast a large range of motion with moments of centering and gathering energy.

You can expand the octopus theme and use it to connect one body part with your core. Take your elbow, for instance, and apply the octopus movement quality to its movements to and from your core, and also to the contraction of your arm muscles. In a next step, integrate this octopus quality with the spatial concept of spiralling and and the body concept of turn-in and turn-out.

II   The connection between emotion and body

Divided in body parts

As a starting point, let's assume that the human body has certain energetic fields, similar to the concept of the chakras in yoga (if you have never heard of the chakras, you might like to search Youtube for 'chakra activation meditation' to get an idea). In dance, my division of the body parts is slightly different, and I don't necessarily associate certain emotions with a specific body part. My goal is to provoke a profound experience by focusing all my attention on a single part of my body. This approach is based upon the observation that the energy or prevailing mood of a person often concentrates in a certain body part. This usually unconscious body focus may manifest itself in a heightened muscle tone or stronger presence in that particular body part.

If you observe extreme personalities, you will notice that body regions and character are inextricably connected. Somebody with a bull's neck or prominent jaw muscles seems to have shifted the centre of their body into that region. People with their centre in their elbow and shoulder region will have a different energy than somebody with their centre in their chest. Maybe you can spontaneously recall someone you know whose energy focuses in their chest? This kind of body focus doesn't necessarily have to mean more tension in the region in question, it may simply be given more attention than others. Inner organs, for example, may express themselves through a soft, gentle energy.

Sometimes you will encounter a negative focus, i.e. a body region that stands out because of a pronounced lack of energy. There are quite a few figures of speech describing this: 'to hang your head', 'to become weak at the knees', 'to feel queasy (in your stomach)', 'to have a frog in your throat', 'to have no backbone', and many more.

If you want to give a certain body part more attention, one way of doing it is to breathe into that particular part. Becoming fully aware of an area of your body is a good starting point for creating movement from this area or finding a different movement quality. If, for instance, you choose a story, a historical personality or a literary character as your source material, you can approach it by connecting it with a certain body part.

Examples

I once created a solo sequence about the Austrian empress Sisi. In her life, corsets played an important part. So my first step into that character was to completely tighten up my core and observe how this affected my emotions and my experience. From there, I could explore possible shapes and movement qualities.

In a project on Bernarda Alba, my focus lay on hand movements, because I felt that the hands best expressed a sense of separation and guidance.

Another possibility to work with energetic fields is to start with an emotion. Allow the emotion to express itself, and try to feel where it manifests most in your body. You can then use this part of your body to initiate the movements you want to create.

This approach is very open, there aren't many rules to it – what feels exactly right for me may not work for you. Consequently, I would like you to think of the following ideas as creative inputs rather than detailed instructions.
If I want to focus on one specific body part, I mentally divide my body into different areas:

- centre: pelvis

- solar plexus

- ribcage

- back

- shoulders

- elbows

- legs and feet

We can access our bodies' energetic fields in various ways:

From the inside out: creating a shape or movement quality by visualising and breathing into a certain area.

From the outside in: imagine pressing your body against the 'walls' of your own kinesphere. Observe your emotional response.

Via contraction and release.
By exploring different stereotypes, for example 'bull-necked', turtle-shell, elbow-type...
Through spatial concepts such as opening, closing, spiralling of body parts such as back, ribcage, haunches, or sexual centre.
By connecting a body part with the body system, for example opposing a muscular movement quality with the quality created by imagining the movement of bones.

Once you have found access to your energetic fields, you can add theme, space, time, focus, and levels.

III Developing a character

Character work

1. Approach

During the first phase, you don't work. You contemplate and let things evolve.

You develop a character or figure by creating an emotional connection with it, even though you don't know yet what it will be.

The search for a suitable character can start anywhere:

- on the tram

- taking a walk in nature

- in the city

- while meditating

- in a noisy club

You might find access to the inner atmosphere of the character by trying to feel your way towards it. The goal is a feeling that is not connected with an environment, an image, or anything physical at all.

Or the other way around:
Start with the image. See the character before your mind's eye – hair, eyes, posture, how it move. See how it carries its head, see the back of its neck, its hands, how it touch things and itselvef.
Or you see an environment and its atmosphere, the play of light and shadow, colours, and other characters that may mean heaven or hell to your character.

2. Vita

Now is the time to write things down, because writing can change everything.

In keywords, write down the following aspects (you could also write this in the style of a curriculum vitae):

- the character's age, appearance, social environment,

- its best friend, secret lover, closest relation etc.,

- its habitat and its relationship with it.

Example:
My character is a woman who lives in a deserted tunnel of the underground. She neither hears the trains nor does she see the masses of commuters boarding and leaving the trains, but she recognises a policeman's step by the sound of his shoes on the pavement. When she leaves her tunnel, her movements seem slow and considerate, but inside, she is on her guard and as tense as a cat ready to pounce.

Their secret:

What is your character's secret?
Does it have secret desires or an experience it do not wish to reveal?

Their dream:

What are its dreams, hopes, longings?

Turning points and consequences:

What were the turning points in your character's life, and what are their consequences?

Formative influences:

What has your character seen and heard that made it what it is today?

Emotion:

What is the character's appearance and the impression it makes on others?

How does it really feel inside?

3. Interview

After having worked on your own until now, it is time to take up a dialogue with a partner.

 A talks about her character. B listens and asks questions.

Many things that were undefined before become much clearer during or after the interview.
Our speech and story change when we have somebody who listens.

4. Improvisations and Approaches

I have collected different approaches with which you can develop your character. If one of them works particularly well for you, it may not be necessary for you to study others. Still, every approach that you try will unearth different movement material, and may help you to explore more deeply that character in the making. In the end, the different approaches are but ways to understanding and maybe even loving your character (or at least parts of it).
If that is not possible, then you should at least be fascinated with or curious about the figure, and you should feel a desire to find it. Otherwise, there won't be any reason for dancing a solo, nothing to express, no story to tell.
At this point in the process, it doesn't matter how detailed the images are that you see before your mind's eye. Let go of all expectations.

5. Dream and Strength

From visualisation to improvisation to movement.

Dream

We create an improvisation called 'the dream', starting with developing the character's dreams and longing, and translating it into dance.

Using an emotional-meditative approach, we try to identify the character's big dream. Parallel to that, we will also discover the character's inner strength, its 'centre of power'.

This takes us into free improvisation.

To become receptive for the essence and the impulses of the character, we require an emotional emptiness that comes with total relaxation. You will first have to free your mind and body from everything to do with your own life before you can really listen to the character and make space for it.

As a first step, I try to guide the students into a state of deep relaxation so that they can let go of any expectations for their next step. We try to emotionally connect with the characters, feel close to them, but without expecting to see them or their environment yet before our mind's eye.
'The character's big dream' is a particularly useful introduction if I don't want to expose myself to the yearning and needs of the character. Instead, I trust in the power of vision and inner strength.

Starting character work with the big dream and the inner strength of the character usually has a positive effect on the participants and their project. It feels as if you were laying a strong foundation for future development.

If you can let yourself sink into deep relaxation during meditation, you may gain access to the inner world of the character. You can imagine diving through layers upon layers: first, an outer layer, then the layer of words and thoughts, and then they layer of the soul, which you only find after having passed through the layer of words, leaving it behind. Only then will the soul of the character reveal itself to you. It is quite easy to show a character's surface and its thoughts on stage, compared to the complexity of emotional identification beyond the world of verbalisation and thought.

When you are on the stage, by your movements the audience will feel and acknowledge the layers you have pushed through. They will be able to follow you to the same level. They sense how much you identify with your character. There are many meditation techniques which will guide you into deep relaxation. If you work on your own, you can use Youtube to find relaxing music tracks or meditation channels. However, if you can work with a partner to guide you into relaxation and then take you closer to your character, I would definitely recommend this option.

Once you have reached deep relaxation, try if you can see your figure.

Perceive the colours, smells, and other characters that surround them, guess their mood. Follow the character as they rise and walk away. Where does it go? How does it move? What does it see?

If you work with a partner, your partner can represent the outside world of the character or a counterpart and you react to it as the character.

Now the character settles down. Where do does it make its bed? What are
its thought and its emotions? Where in its body does it feel tension, where
relaxation?
Now that both you and the character are lying down, look for physical identification. Let the character its their position. Let it dream, find a solution for a
problem or enter another world.
See if you can split your consciousness: lightly keep in touch with the character and at the same time, be present as a dancer. Let your body be the
reflection of your character's dream. Trust your body to find a way to tell the
story. Let go of all expectations.
Everything is allowed.

Strength

As a theme, 'strength' combines very well with the dream theme we have
just dealt with. When working with groups, I try to wake the participants' inner strengths through games and exercises that work as triggers and activate
all muscles in the body.
One option to trigger strength is competition.
Here's a partner exercise:
Sit on the floor, back to back, with your feet and hands on the floor. Engage
your whole body to try and push your partner away from you.
Another trigger for strength is anger.
Play aggressive, fast, powerful music. Develop movements by imagining you
were smashing walls or kicking in styrofoam sheets. What is the meaning of
the walls? From what is your character breaking free? What is it they want to
destroy?

Painting fury

On a big sheet of paper, paint a picture of fury. Put in everything that hinders
your character, all it hates, the injustices it has suffered, everything that would
make it angry.
Hang the picture on a wall in the studio. Stand with your back to the painting,
inhale deeply and exhale with a loud 'Ha!' to activate your diaphragm. Slowly
walk backwards towards the picture. Gather energy from the floor and plant
your feet. Exhale on 'ha!' again and imagine your painting. Then turn around to
look at it, letting your body move intuitively in response to it.
Create a powerful combination with pushes, pulls, and kicks. Add subtext and
images that reflect your character.

6. Shapes

In this section, you will find four poses that characterise your figure.

Choose four different emotions, moods, or key words that you connect with your figure. Write each of these on a piece of paper.

Pin the sheets to four different places in the studio.

Start in the middle of the studio. Feel the distance between you, the dancer, and the words on the sheets.

Experiment with walking towards one of the sheets, trying to approach the emotion written on it both physically and emotionally. Look for emotional connection without losing yourself in it.

Practise letting go as well. When you move away from the sheet, you also distance yourself from the emotion written on it.

Now step towards a sheet again. This time aim at full identification with the emotion Keep the emotion alive in yourself. Don't let go. Train yourself to stay with it.

From this emotion, start moving into different poses or shapes. You can work in the middle of the room, against the walls, or using a chair. Hold each shape for some time. These poses reflect aspects of the character's emotions.

7. Interview

You can implement interviews at regular intervals – in fact, you should! Only afterwards will you realise how important they were for your process.

A declaration of love

B asks A:

> 'What do you find exciting about the character?'
> 'Why do you it?'

Try to unearth everything that makes the character loveable in your eyes. Understanding the character means understanding why it acts how it acts. Because it has no other choice. Its behaviour stems from its personal history and its emotions.

Defence

A is the inspector and asks uncomfortable questions. B is the advocate in defense for the character, for example:

'How can it be that nobody noticed this?'

The inspector questions the plausibility of the character, the advocate defends its story.

The character develops

It can be surprising to see the spectrum of emotions and actions of a character come to light during the process of working on a piece. It develops a life of its own, and its reactions may prove quite irrational at times. I myself have been surprised by my characters many times. They make decisions without consulting me, and reveal aspects of themselves that even I who created them did not know about. Insofar, a character is not just a construct of my imagination, but a being with its own impulses. I imagine it like an energetic field that I can step into, a field fed by the character's environment, era, personal history, social norms, expectations, longings, disappointments, bitterness and hurts as well as moments of happiness, serenity, opportunities, and chances. When I read Tolstoi or Lorca, for example, I can feel the character's environments. The great writers of any era all condense the energies of a certain age in a certain place around their characters, creating a mirror of their time in their works that is, albeit realised through language, a non-verbal process in itself. Character work will always have a non-verbal aspect, whether your medium is dance or language. A character is more than words can describe. Therefore, it is important to make space in our work for the ineffable, to allow for ways to stay on an intuitive level. If you are looking for the intuitive, look deep into somebody's eyes. The eyes are the mirrors of the soul, and dance the extension of its movements.

In relation to and by influencing objects

Identification and empathy after Lee Strasberg

Caution: this exercise may trigger more emotions than expected or desired. Remember: you decide how far to go.

Arrange several pairs of chairs, standing opposite each other. All participants move through the room, thinking of their characters. Finally, A and B each take up positions standing behind a chair, facing one another.

A says: 'I, the dancer A, now take the role of the character XY (insert character's name). Then A sits down on his chair.

B does the same.

A and B sit opposite and look into each other's eyes. While they do so, they try to become their character, gaining access to a deeper level of their soul. This may lead to changes:

- movements that transform into posture

- a change of the body's centre of gravity

- a change of the way somebody sits

Sometimes a word or even a few sentences might find their way out.

To finish, A says: 'I, dancer A, now leave this character. '
A then leaves his chair, resumes walking through the room and focuses on separating from his character.

When A is ready, he finds a new chair and a new partner B.

Sometimes, two characters may engage in a dialogue with each other, at other times they may stay silent. Amongst other things, it is very interesting to see how the character behaves on their own and if or how they change when they meet different opposites. It shows in their posture, the tension in their bodies, their gestures and, if they choose to speak, also their words.

Impulse points in your hands

Your hands and their leading points are a great tool to start moving, to connect your own movement with the character and to vary the size and levels of your movements.

Develop different impulse points from which to move your hands.

Examples:

- leading with the edge of your hand like a karate fighter, cutting, severing, war-like, powerful, direct, fast.

- leading with the back of your hand, with a lyrical feeling. Light, free, indirect.

- leading with your palm, changing from direct to indirect, pushing away the air.

- leading with your finger tips that divide space. Clarity, form, focus.

- leading with your thumb, cutting as well, but with a different quality.

Check which impulse points go with your character, and how the movements affect your shoulders and elbows.

Further develop the movement quality from these hand impulse points by transferring it onto other body parts.

Gestures

Gestures differ from impulse-led hands in that they underline a verbal expression, whereas the impulse led hand rather reflects moods and emotions.

Compile a list of different figures with whom your character interacts, for example the landlady, policeman, their worst enemy, the love of their life.

Sketch a short, emotional dialogue between your character and one of the other figures. If you can, work with a partner.

Act out your dialogue, taking the role of your character, and look for gestures to match with your statements. Then leave away the dialogue, and focus on your gestures alone.

Manipulate the gestures until they move your whole body.
Add the original gestures and their manipulations to your collection of movement material.

Costume or object

You can keep the object with you every day and access your character through it.

Choose a piece of clothing that you find typical for your character, for example

    a scarf, a hat, a glove, a sock, a belt …

In addition, choose an object, such as

    a cup, a pebble, a lighter …

Best are objects you can easily hold in your hand or put in your pocket. Look at your object as often as possible and give it a story, such as

    'My character always drinks from that cup in this or that place …'

Then put your piece of clothing or object down and leave it. Approach it again, recalling its story.

You put on the costume, take the object in your hand, and find your way into the character.

Top Bella M
50x

Top Bella M
50x

Walking and moving

Develop different ways of moving through the studio.

For example:

- swaying your hips
- as if you were drawn upwards, with elevated shoulders
- flaring your ribcage
- walking fast
- walking leaning backwards
- shuffling on the outsides of your feet

Experiment with different ways of walking and how they match with your character's situation and environment.

Now add the parameters of space and time to your walking: changes of direction, speed, expansion and accentuation.

Movement quality

Play with different themes and suitable movement qualities. It is advisable to choose music that will support the quality your are looking for.

Example: fragility
Create a movement sequence imagining you are standing on a frozen lake. Carefully place one foot before the other and hear the ice crack under your feet, its breaking continuing into your bones.

What is the fragile side of your character?
Which movements show this fragility?
You will find more examples for translating themes into movement qualities and improvisational approaches in the chapter on movement synonyms.

The better you know your character, the clearer you will be about which themes will help you to develop a movement quality.

For inspiration, I compiled a list of themes.
It is very likely that you will find a few that have something to do with your
character.

– lust	– vulnerability
– focus	– symbiosis
– fear	– love
– hunter and hunted	– dependence
– victim	– freedom
– permeability	

Body parts

Work with different body parts while you moving across the floor.
Examples:

- draw up your shoulders

- walk with a heightened focus in your upper body, like a football
  player

- use your elbows

- let yourself be pushed forward by your back

- imagine your ribs as a fan that opens and closes and initiates all
  your movements

- alternate between being led by your head and your sit bones

- imagine wings on your shoulder blades

- imagine a protective shield on your back, like the shell of a turtle

- imagine having one particularly vulnerable spot somewhere on
  your body

- walk with your legs squeezed together

- walk with your legs wide apart

Does your character favour a certain body region?
What do the different body regions mean for your character?
Attribute movements and movement qualities to the different areas of the
character's body.
Alternate your main focus within a body part, for example by proudly puffing
up your chest or shyly hiding it.

Developing solos

From all the parameters we have discussed so far, pick one to focus on. Choose positions in space and decide on movement qualities. Work with the dreams, the power, and the vulnerability of the character and develop a solo that matches them: expansive, gestural, with varying dynamics and on different spatial levels. Draw up a score and use it to check your variation options.

Systemic constellation

To get even closer to a character, you can assemble its family in a systemic constellation.

Work with a group. Tell them all you know about the character, and describe its family.
Then assign roles – mother, father, sister, brother, etc. – to members of your group, In character, they will take up positions in space according to their relationships with each other. Observe who stands where, how close they stand to each other and where they are facing. At last, you yourself take up a position and let a moderator take over. The moderator starts by asking each character how they feel in this constellation and how they experience the distance between them and the other characters.

In a next step, the characters can

- change the direction in which they are facing

- change their posture, for example by squatting down or extending their arms, etc.

- get in physical contact with other characters

In this more improvisational phase of the exercise, the moderator may offer verbal inputs or play some atmospheric music to inspire the characters into a free movement improvisation.It is important to then consciously finish the improvisation by inviting the participants to find a final pose and hold it. After that, the moderator instructs them to let their character go and return to their own selves. Shaking out and relaxing the body, breathing, body percussion, and free improvisation to a different piece of music help to find the way back.

IV. Autobiographical solo: important stepping stones and emotional, life-changing experiences collected in a dance

In this kind of solo, you are looking to translate your personal experiences into a dance. Your research may take you deep into your own soul, and it will be a challenge to express your findings through dance. You can keep yourself from getting lost by painting or sketching an abstract selfportrait to which you can transfer everything you have found inside your mind.
Once you have finished this process, you can translate the portrait into movement quality, space, time, and effort, and develop your solo from there.

Before you start painting your selfportrait, you need to connect with yourself, your memories and the turning points in your life. This is a difficult task, especially if you are working alone. It is much easier with some support, for example through guided meditation in a setting in which you feel safe. Maybe you can find a coach, or a group who are experienced in meditation and mind travel, who can take you to deep relaxation and guide you through different stages of your life. Once you do start painting, let the colours and materials inspire you, and let go of all expectations. If you'd rather develop your solo on your own without implementing guided meditation, then find a place where you are undisturbed for a while, put on some music that makes you feel good, take a big sheet of blank paper, some beautiful painting colours, and let your thoughts and feelings flow. Do not expect anything, just be open and curious to whatever comes up. Once your painting is finished, take it to the studio. Working without music is more difficult, but can be even more interesting. No music means less guidance, but also less distraction from your process. If you feel you cannot work without music, then focus on one aspect of your painting and find a piece of music that helps you access this aspect without being too dominant.

Contemplate your painting. Sink into it and connect with the emotions, memories, and stories it contains. Then, try to translate them into movement.

Bernhard Mohr:
"Slam", 2013,
acrylic on canvas, 95 x 105 cm.
Owned by the artist.

V Translating music into dance

At first glance, it seems that the easiest way to choreograph a solo is to choose a song, divide it into parts, and then assign a theme to each part. The themes are developed with movement synonyms, and the resulting dance combinations are set into an interesting relationship with the music. There is nothing at all wrong with this method, after all, it has a clear structure and is great fun as well. The only problem is that you are less likely to develop a dance with depth and a personal note than if you use character work or any other approach that requires you to investigate your own personality and biography.

In my experience, most of the other approaches described in this chapter produce stronger solo choreographies than the approach in which you start with the music. It is a tendency, of course, not a rule, but it seems it is a risky business to start your process by choosing the music. In the end, it only matters what you want to gain from your work.

In the following paragraphs, I have compiled a list of movement synonyms which might help you to develop approaches towards different themes.

Movement synonyms

Suppression

In pairs: A is lying on the floor and tries to reach upwards with different bodyparts.

B pushes A back towards to the floor.

Develop this approach on different levels, in different directions, in place and travelling.

Combine your ideas into a sequence.

Devotion

Experimenting with the concept of 'fall and recover'.
Let a body part - your head, shoulder, arm, pelvis, etc. - fall in different directions. Try extending that body part's trajectory into movements through space. Connect the movements into a sequence.

Dance with a partner. Take away the partner. Look what's left.

Working from your inner self:

Connect with your inner self. Give it space to expand. Rather than generating new movements, become aware of the tiny movements that are already present in you. Follow these movements. Surrender to the impulses you find, let them ripple through your body, from joint to joint, muscle to muscle. Maintaining the connection with yourself, try to let the impulse expand into space.

Using the inner image of 'softening':

Standing still, scan your body from head to toe and feel the tension in your muscles. Map it out as if it were a landscape. Without collapsing, try to soften certain regions of your body. Lengthen and soften your muscles. To this, add the idea of surrendering to gravity: falling to the floor, rolling, letting the energy continue through the movements.

In pairs: trust your partner to support you.

Structure

Pick body parts:

- edge of your hand

- fingertips

- elbows

- coccyx

- crown of your head

Draw straight lines, like sunbeams, from these body parts into space, and let your body follow them.
Choose linear paths through the room.
From this, develop a sequence A.

Add an opposing sequence B that fills the empty spaces of sequence A.

Look for parallel lines in your extremities. Find two-dimensional shapes with different directions of your forearms, calves, upper arms, thighs, back and head and connect these elements with a staccato quality.

Awakening

Using imagery:

Enlarge the small movements you find in your joints.
Start from using minimal muscular effort and work up to maximal effort.

Become aware of the movements of your inner organs.
Transfer them into a movement combination.

Picture your blood coursing through your veins. Imagine how that flow expands into movement.

Working in pairs:

A is standing still.
B touches A in different places.
The places B touch wake up and fall silent again.

Aggression

Inhale deeply, sending breath and energy into your belly.
Exhale with a deep 'O' sound, let it swell into an explosive 'A'-sound. Combine the swelling sound with movement.

Send impulses from different places in your body into space. Find connections between body parts and finish with explosive movements.

Experiment with jumps that express an explosion.
Experiment with jumps that express the shattering of an object.

Imagine yourself surrounded by styrofoam sheets. Break these sheets with different parts of your body, for example your foot, heel, knee, elbow, fist, the edge of your hand, or your head.

Love

Tenderly embrace the air with your arms, experiment with different levels and directions.

Imagine somebody you want to be close to standing next to you.
Rest your upper body against him or her.
Try different directions.

> – Visualise something opening inside you.
>
> – Move opening sensation around in your body.
>
> – Experiment with your pelvis and your legs.

Finding vulnerability

Look for reliable places in your body. From these places, develop positions that are vulnerable, sensitive, and permeable.

Being supported

Imagine you are carrying a partner. Express this feeling with powerful positions.

Protection

Imagine your body is protected wherever you move.
How does this idea affect your movements?

Create positions that express trust, feeling protected, supported, embraced.

Freedom

Freedom as an active state.

Look for spiralling movements.
Explore how your arms follow your hands and your arms your torso.
Move out into space. Start with your upper body and let your legs and feet follow.

Introduce a feeling of opening to your movements, letting the opening expand beyond your kinesphere. Become aware of the whole dance space and use it.

Start with small, opening movements. Let them grow bigger, add explosive movement qualities and different directions.

Implement imagery and your emotional memory:
In your mind, re-live a moment in which you felt free and open.

Which parts of your body resonate with this memory?

Try to expand this feeling into movement through space.

Grief and despair

Standing.
Let various parts of your body grow heavy.

- head

- torso

- core

Develop pathways towards the floor from these body parts.

Breathe deeply into your belly. Exhale through your mouth, intoning a dark, heavy 'A' sound.

Explore movements that share the same dark, heavy quality.

Body percussion:

Choose places on your body.
Touch them with your hands.
Aim at fast, powerful motions and abrupt rhythms.
Develop a sequence that expresses despair.

Unwrapping

Imagine being wrapped in a big cover. Find two different movement patterns
to strip it off:

> Slowly and with a lot of effort, with the cover continuously growing back.
> Feel how the endless re-growing takes its toll on your strength, how
> frustration turns into aggression. Let these feelings shape the quality of
> your movements.

> In a fast, ripping motion. Again, the cover grows back as soon as you tear
> it off, enclosing you. The harder you fight, the more covers grow around
> you, so you double your efforts, ripping them off faster, more violently,
> exhausting yourself.

Hope

Standing still. Focus on your breath. Visualise an ideal inner state, a feeling,
something you are longing for.

Stay with this feeling.
Try to locate it in space.

Is it next to you, below, or to your diagonal?
Move in that direction and finish with a shape that corresponds with your
ideal inner state.
Abandon the shape and return to where you started.

The feeling remains.
Compare how you feel in your start position to how you felt in your second
position. Repeat the process. Make room for changes.

Look for new positions and shapes. Keep the feeling, but enlarge the shapes.
Let them flow into movements by focusing on the pathways into the shapes
rather than the shapes themselves. Pay attention to movement quality and
dynamics. Be mindful and gentle, do not lose yourself in motion. Stay with
the feeling.

You can use this approach with all feelings and emotions. But be careful –
when we feel under pressure to create something, the movements tend to
take the lead and leave the feeling behind.

Cocoon

Take up a sitting or lying position that takes up as little space as possible.

You are the butterfly in the chrysalis, trying to hatch. The time is right, and you long to be free, but you are also scared. You rush forward, retreat, and gingerly feel your way out again. With each time you retreat, your initial position changes.
Develop a sequence from your hatching movements.

Subservient, dependent

In pairs: A moves B slowly, but unorganically, going against the grain. The movements don't flow into each other naturally at all. Only try a few movements at a time.

A can switch B's body parts on or off. The switch is quick and mechanic.
Then, B repeats the movement elements on his own.
A helps B to find an expression of dependence.

Focused

Define a point on the wall and imagine being pulled towards it. Approach it slowly, as if the air had become a thick, glutinous mass through which you have to wade. Moving against this resistance, focus on different places on your body. Then focus on points in space. Connect the places on your body with the points in space in unpredictable rhythmic phrases.

Falling

In pairs: A transfers his weight from one body part to the space out of his body's axis, on the verge of falling. B catches A. From this off-balance position, A tries to find a way back to the starting position.
Create several movements and link them in a way that eliminates all centred, balanced positions.

Fear

Explore contracting movements. They can be quick and jumpy or cautious and wary, as if you were trying to remain unseen.

Engage your emotional memory, letting yourself remember scary situations while you move. Shiver and shake, either with your whole body or with parts of your body. Develop movements from this.

Worshipping the earth

On the floor, explore different stroking and touching gestures and ways of opening your body towards the floor. Add contrasting rhythms, directions, shapes, and qualities.

Create movements that relate to the sky. Work with the emotion you associate with the sky, but mirror the gestures you found exploring the floor by 180°.

Link the two parts, worshipping the earth and the sky movement material. Focus on the connection.

Danger

Walking on a straight line, move as cautiously and tensely as you can. Evoke the feeling of being stalked by something dangerous. Swiftly turn around, not by 180°, just a little, so you never fully see the danger that is lurking behind you. Resist the urge to fully turn around.
Try to feel the impulse to turn around from your nerves, not your muscles. Then develop the movements of alarm further, make them bigger, transfer them to different areas of your body.

Running. Starting from running, create fast avoiding movements. Connect them to a sequence and find suitable directions in space.
The floor is hot, your feet are getting burned. With this visualisation, develop

- jumping

- rolling

- running

with the subtext of danger.

Fragility

Develop a sequence in which you move as if the floor were made of brittle ice. Gingerly put one foot in front of the other, imagining the sound of hairline cracks running through the ice beneath you, your bones resonating with the quality of the breaking ice.

Working with objects

Physical energy

Researching matter, i.e. physical substance, you will at some point encounter the theory that all matter is a concentration of energy. According to this theory, every material has a specific primary quality with its own energetic charge. In principle, you might feel the different charges of wood, concrete, ceramic, paper, clay or a precious stone, just as you might hear a musical note, see colours or changes in the brightness of light. However you interpret the material in your hands, you will perceive its uniqueness.

As a first exercise in working with objects, I suggest you start with the material's primary quality. Choose different organic and unorganic materials and explore the corresponding movement quality, ignoring shape and colours at this stage of the exercise.

You can put the objects in different places in your studio and move from one to the other, observing their effect on you. In a second step you try to establish a connection between the object and your breath. From there, you can move on to establishing movement qualities.

Shape

Use objects of different size and shape. Translate the shapes into three-dimensional space. You don't have to be too precise in your adaptation, feel free to play with the structures, using the shapes as inspirations rather than restrictions.
The narrative approach:

Now, you let the object speak. Use it to develop associations with a story that will in turn inspire you in free improvisation.

Poses and movements with and through the object

Implement the object work on different body parts, on various spatial levels, travelling and stationary. Remember the idea of addition and integration: How could you add or embed the object to a pose or a movement?

Work with connecting different parts of your body – in balance and travelling, turns and jumps – and pay attention to the relationship with the object. Does it break or continue a line? Experiment with the spatial relationships between the object and your poses and movements.

In the end …

… your solo will present a part of yourself: your ability and your courage to dive down into the depth of your soul to create a connection with dance. And yes, the audience will see your dance skills as well. What matters is linking technique with self-expression. The first will impress your audience, the latter touch them.

Try to free yourself from the urge to please the audience.
Tastes vary, and everybody lives their own truth.
Make it your goal to love your work and have fun.
Never, ever let yourself lose pleasure in what you do.

7 Pedagogical aspects

A dance company is just like a big, complex organism that depends on the cooperation of its individual parts. Each of these parts in turn consists of many facets with different kinds of energy.

The most important groups are:

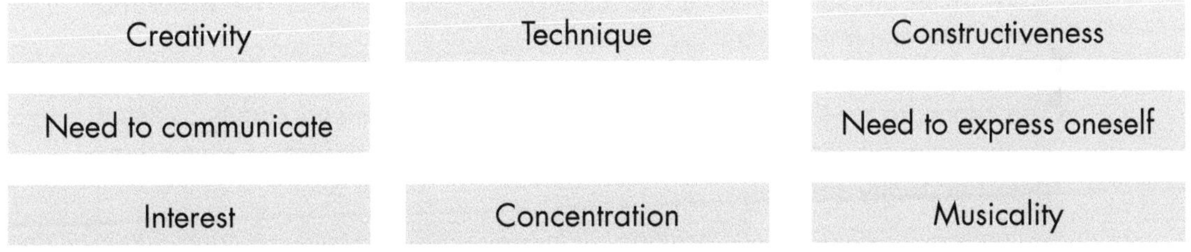

The energy levels will never be the same in two dancers, and nobody can be at a 100% all the time. Everybody has different strengths and weaknesses at different times in their lives, seasons, or times of day, and the company as a whole goes through different phases as well.

The choreographer has to feel where the energetic focus of his company lies to be able to react pedagogically and ask the right questions at the right moment:

-     What does the group need?
-     What do the individualdancers need?
-     What challenges are we facing?
-     What kind of environment do I have to create?
-     Where does the group stand?
-     Where is it going?

From these questions you can develop pedagogical concepts for every moment, day, and production.

The concepts are both a challenging task for you and an opportunity to develop for the group, and they will develop well if you take the job of giving them this opportunity seriously.

Often, the ambitions of the choreographer clash with the abilities of the dancers. They can't meet the requirements of the choreography. The only pedagogical approach the choreographer knows is to order the organism to function, or to demand an element such as creativity, technique or musicality. But just being demanding doesn't necessarily help the group to reach the goal. In fact, it may even prevent them from doing so.

By telling the company what they can't do, by focusing on their weaknesses, we stoke their fears of failure. We celebrate the problem, but don't create a situation that invites a change to the better.

Training for a new choreography is hard work for the dancers, and you usually see straight away how they have trained and if the elements you need for your choreography have been included in the routine.

The training process is always changing, and if you feel it lacks something, you will have to find a way to include what you need. Try to introduce new material playfully, easily, to draw the dancers' interest and motivation. Be enthusiastic

about what you do, and never lose the whole picture: your piece and its progress, but also the company and each individual dancer.

If a scene or an image in your piece seems stuck, you can try to make it more
dynamic by either working on the movement or by using the subtext of the
scene.

The same instruction given individually to different dancers will be perceived
differently by each dancer. If the company are all on the same level, one instruction given to everybody will suffice.

8

Acting, language and dance

If we add language to dance, we create something new from two elements. The individual elements are not required to work separately, but to merge. Working on a piece that combines language and dance, you need to be mindful of both components being parts of a whole. It is easy to lose focus during rehearsals, and forget either to perfect each individual element or to keep the elements connected to each other, which usually leads to one of these two extremes:

> Each part, dance and language, are rehearsed separately, as if they were two independent pieces. On stage, we end up with two strong parts which do not make for a strong sum, rather the opposite – they seem to reduce instead of complement each other because they are not connected and balanced. The acting gets in the way of the dance and vice versa.

> The parts are rehearsed with the constant, acute awareness that 'there is also the other part that needs space'. This can hinder a part's development, which leads to a piece that presents two weak parts with little content. Example: audio play meets choreography without meaning.

The biggest risk you run when combining language and dance is that the dance can easily be reduced to illustrating the text. But this takes away the

8

effect of both text and dance. The text is stripped of its associative potential and becomes limited instead of enriched, and the dance becomes an uninspired rehash of the text, losing its depth and non-verbal power. If, on the other hand, we take the dance too far away from the text to avoid the illustrating effect, it will look isolated, leaving the audience to wonder 'Why are they dancing?' or 'What does that text mean?'.

If the posts of director and choreographer are filled by two people, their cooperation is vital for the success of the piece. Cooperation means that both are able and willing to understand and support the other's part without limiting each other or themselves.

Each has to be dominant enough to take their space, but emphatic enough to grant the other enough room for development. If the two parties cannot work together harmoniously, it is best to opt for scenes that are not joined together, but work in parallel.

Before you develop a scene, be it parallel or joint, ask yourself: 'Is there a general theme both parts share in this scene that we can use as a guide line?'

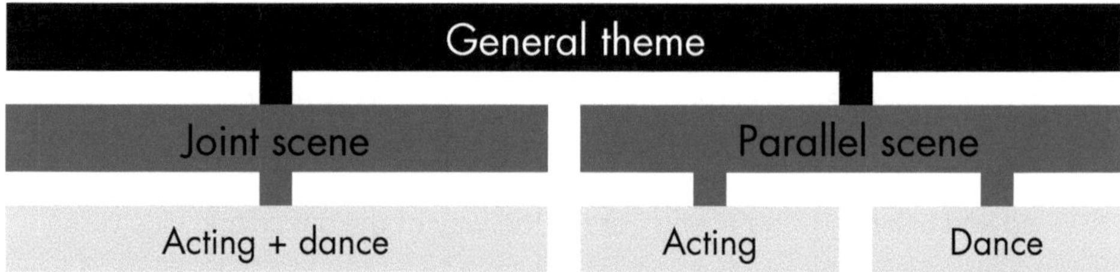

Example for parallel scenes developed from a fictional title

Author: George Tabori. Play: "Peep Show".
Will meets his nanny to get answers to all the questions puberty brings with it. The title of the scene is 'Secret wishes and their straight-jackets'. While Will is speaking to his nanny, two dancers perform an erotic duet. Will and his nanny could just as well be talking about something else, they seem reserved, do not move much, and express a certain shyness. The danced love duet is part of their thoughts. The scenes work in parallel, no part illustrates the other, but they complement each other in a common context.

Example for parallel scenes with acting and dance

Little John is suffering because his parents fight all the time. He longs for a pet to brighten up his lonely hours. Finally, his parents give him a goldfish in a fishbowl. Looking at the fish trapped in its bowl, John recognises himself and his own hopeless situation. He begins to imagine the fish's world view: how the world curves in on itself behind the glass, how the sounds outside filter through glass and water, the muffled shouting of his parents. Before his eyes flashes the mental image of his unborn self in his mother's womb, listening to the fighting and screaming, himself a tiny, desperate, trapped fish. The fishbowl slips from his hands and smashes on the floor. The fish dies.

We started working with this setting for a film scene, and our motto was 'John's life is determined by his parent's constant quarrels'. So we needed to show consistent fighting on one level and John's fishbowl revelation on another. We solved the problem by giving the parts of mother and father to two dancers. They danced a never-ending loop of aggressive movements against each other. Because the movements kept repeating, the dancers could stay on scene the whole time without taking up too much of the audience's attention, and there was room for a parallel scene with John and the fishbowl. In addition, we used different camera angles to show the dancers reflected in the fishbowl, as shadows on the wall, etc.

Example for a joint scene

In *Romeo and Juliet*, the long-standing feud between the rivalling families of Capulet and Montague peaks in a violent brawl at high noon. Tybalt of the Capulets duels Romeo's friend Mercutio, who is stabbed when Romeo tries to separate the two. Romeo avenges Mercutio's death by slaying Tybalt.

The scene was set statically. The transition from the narrative into dance was simply walking. The actors walk past each other, glaring, seizing each other up. From the individuals two groups form, dancing their opposition against the other group. From the two groups, smaller groups step out to dance a fight, interrupted now and then by verbal aggression. The choreography tightens when more and more fighters step back, leaving the three protagonists at the centre of attention. Mercutio takes the brawl to the next level by ripping up a board from the stage and attacking Tybalt with it, who in his turn wrenches a curtain rail from the door frame to defend himself. The fight is still stylised, but it is growing more and more realistic as the dance elements are replaced with actual weapons. Again, the actors threaten and mock each other, then they fling their makeshift weapons away to attack each other with their bare hands, pulling each other's hair and kicking each other across the stage. This third level marks the transition back from dancing into the narrative.

The challenge of linking acting and dance scenes is finding a way from the narrative into the abstract level of dance and back. In the battle between Montagues and Capulets, we used the division of the fight into three levels of brutality to make this transition.

You could make a faster transition by changing lights, music and movement all at once. In such a fast switch, the audience don't have time to think and decide whether they want to go with the change – they either get it or not. With a more even, slower transition, you seduce the audience into following you to the new level.

Dance as an interlude in a play

In theatrical plays, dance is mostly included as an interlude, rather than in parallel scenes. As a concept, interludes are much easier to apply than parallel scenes, and they work well when dance and acting come together naturally. Including dance gives a scene more body, making it sensual and also opening up the audience to take in the scenes that follow the dance. Also, it gives the spectator a break by targeting the kinaesthetic instead of the text-processing parts of the brain.

A director hires a choreographer to create suitable interludes for her play. She'll already have a concrete vision or at least an idea of the dance and its place in the play, having worked on it for a long enough time to have a mental image of the aesthetics associated with it. In her head, the play has already taken a shape which the choreographer cannot know.

It would be possible for the director and the choreographer to go through this shaping process together. In my experience, however, the choreographer is usually called in when most of the creative process is already done. It is good to first read the play to know what it is about, but you need much more information than just the text. Most importantly, you need to know which feelings and mental images the director associates with the play so you can tune into the atmosphere she wants you to create. You don't have to like the director's interpretation – your job is to understand the play from her point of view and create a choreography that supports her vision.

Once I understand the director's interpretation, I dig deep to find my own version of the same interpretation. Is there something I find particularly interesting about the material? Then I can start bringing together the text and the director's vision, looking at it through the lens of movement. Frequently, this is the moment when the choreographer and the director clash for the first time, with the choreographer calling the whole interpretation into question and the director defending her vision. As a result, the production loses focus and momentum. We don't have to avoid conflict at any price, we don't need to agree all the time, but for an interdisciplinary setting to succeed, it is crucial to sincerely care about each others visions. I can only develop my own opinion if I am ready to engage openly and intensely. Doubting another person's idea does not create a new vision, but your enthusiasm and interest in a challenging idea will. Dig deep, and you will find something new and surprising.

Mini plays

Choose a scene from a play (I recommend Karlheinz Braun's book "MiniDramen"). This scene is the starting point for an improvisation for dancers and actors. Find a motto or title for the scene that will serve as a focus for the participants.

Try the following variations:

Actors and dancers are on scene simultaneously, but without acknowledging each other.

Actors and dancers are on scene together, interacting with each other.

Actors and dancers do not share the stage, improvising separately.

9 Dance and film

Dance in film was kick-started the moment a free camera moved between waltzing couples for the first time. It developed continuously, up to a point where it is not even necessary to really dance anymore, even if it is a film about dance. Connecting film and dance offers us an unique opportunity of being able to control the perspective of the viewer. It is almost like adding a fourth dimension to our stage: the adjustable perspective of a camera and the possibilities of montage. There is no stage where you can direct the audience's gaze like in a film. They have no choice but to accept the perspective and the speed of the camera.

Film exponentiates the divers expressions of dance. Because there is so much potential in camera perspective, cuts and effects, it is sometimes enough to just work with basic dance elements.

This is the main reason why there are hardly any choreographers who work in video clip productions – there is no dance dramaturgy at the shoot itself, it is composed at the editor's desk. The stars and the songs have to look good in the clip, and movement and sex appeal are used support the effect. If the singer can't move, the dancers do it for him, and the camera will zoom around him, shooting seemingly dynamic scenes that will later be edited in between the dance sequences. That is usually enough to sell a song. Should the star dance, the movement material needs to be easy so it can be learnt quickly – big, clear gestures determine the genre of the piece, often and quite unashamedly copied from other clips and modified to suit the song. Video clips with sophisticated dance material are fairly exceptional, but there is a chance of these exceptions becoming more and more frequent as the gestures become over-used and stale, and the music scene is always trying to set new trends.

An entirely different approach we find in so-called 'video dance'. Here, dance is not just a filler helping to sell some pop star's records. Dance and film meet in a dialogue, creating a joint performance. Examples of video dance pieces can be seen at international dance festivals and found on the internet.

The compositional factors of dance are similar to those used in editing and camera work. In addition, there are rules for the photographic composition of images that deal with countering the two-dimensionality of the medium. I strongly recommend all choreographers to experiment with dance and video, as it is an excellent tool for understanding the visual aspect of our art. As a plus, you can edit your scenes and add countless filters and special effects to create a certain look or atmosphere in your film. You need to be careful though: the viewers will accept almost any special effect as long as it is consistent with your theme and your idea, but if you only use effects to improve the material you recorded, it will feel as if your material wasn't very good to start with. A special effect is, after all, just a click on the computer, and may soon feel like a cheap trick. Many dance film makers shoot 16 or 32mm videos, but you do need a professional camera man to do that, and not every company can afford it. Others consider editing a part of the artistic process, and count on it from the beginning when creating a concept for their piece.

A significant advantage of combining dance and film is the intimacy we can create by using close-ups and detail shots. While we can't translate the energy and feeling of a live performance into a film, we can compensate for it and make the viewers feel they are in the moment with the dancers by means of film-making.

Another advantage of film-making is that you are free in your choice of location. When you are considering different ideas for a dance film, your eye for suitable dance locations will help you. A staircase or a row of houses become shapes and rhythms. A foreground and a landscape become part of the choreography. When you put yourself in a dance video mind-set, you will look differently at cities or landscapes, even if you don't actually plan to realise a video project and are just toying with the idea. Suddenly, the buildings and shapes of the city will speak to you in choreographic language and open up a visionary space that will expand your sensitivity, not just for film, but for all kinds of choreography.

In a film, the cuts and montage determine the rhythm and the phrasing of the choreography. A professional cutter will edit mediocre material into a good film. It is very, very rare to find an untrained cutter who can do that. But there are many cutters who trained themselves, just learning by doing, and choreographers can use their own trained sense of rhythm and phrasing to analyse and understand cutting and editing.

Before you start editing a dance film, try to spot the cuts in other films. Spot them – all of them! - and observe their emotional and compositional effect. Basically, the cuts connect different perspectives. They may range from long shots to close-ups such as a droplet of sweat on a dancer's face. In addition, the camera can switch between different characters and an invisible observer, creating relationships between the characters.

You will quickly develop a feeling for the cuts and their effect, which will have an impact on your screenplay and your work on set.

Many film makers from the experimental film scene ignore the component of craftmanship in film-making, partly because they don't want to restrict themselves, partly because it is a frightening amount of work and study. It is easier – though not necessarily better – to just grab a camera, film and then edit.

If you only focus on theoretical knowledge alone, then it might indeed hinder your creative flow and feel restrictive, but if you sharpen your senses and put to use all your knowledge about relations, design, shape, dynamic and emotion, your sensitivity will change more than just the cinematic aspects of your project.

Film

1 Analyse different dance films.
Observe closely the following aspects:

- relation between location and choreography

- camera work

- aspects of image composition:

    - foreground – centre - background

    - depth of focus

    - camera perspective

    - camera movements

- dynamic of cuts, rhythm, phrasing

- relationships between the characters through cuts

- resolution of movement through cuts

- special effects

- light and colour

2 Draft a video adaptation of a stage choreography, adhering to the aspects discussed under **1**.

3 Draft a concept for a dance film based on a location. Adhere to he aspects discussed under **1**.

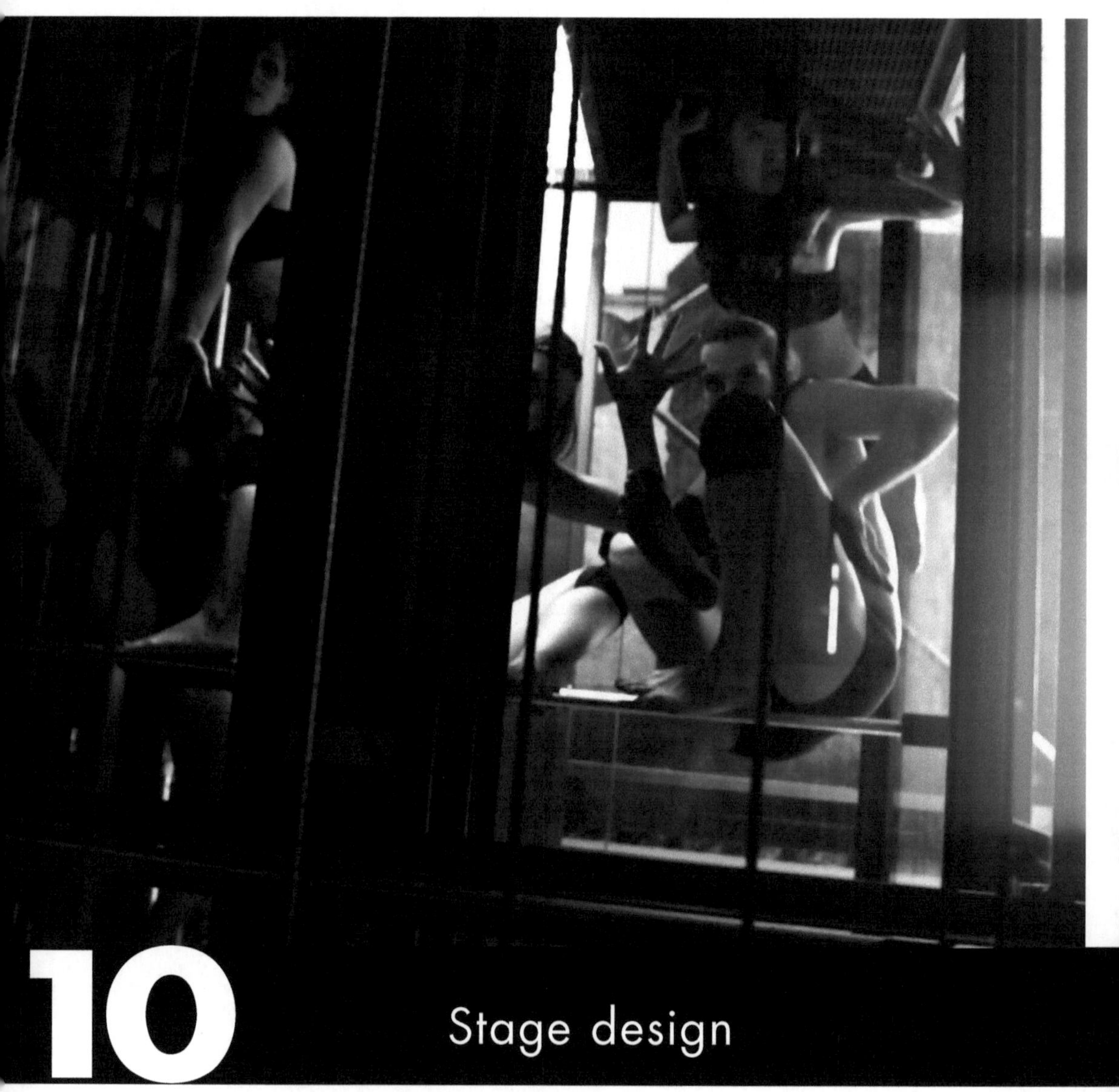

10

Stage design

The importance of stage design

Stage design is a profession, so it is obvious that you cannot substitute a trained stage designer with just anybody. But because many productions can't afford a professional stage designer, it's often the choreographers who have to step in, because they can use their knowledge of space, dynamics and composition for designing the stage. The advantage of this emergency solution is that the choreographer can adjust the stage design exactly to his vision. However, working together with another professional usually makes for richer, deeper results than working on your own because you'll always inspire each other, sharing ideas and giving each other new impulses. The stage designer will be involved in the dance piece, and his involvement will show in the shapes, colours and the overall design of the space. His work is a process, and he will provide you with a draft to work with that will develop into the final design with the progression of the piece.

In this chapter I will digress – let's explore the relationship between body and energy to get a glimpse of how visual design affects the spectator.
In a low-budget 'Freie Szene' production, you will ask how much stage design is actually necessary. Isn't there a way to make the most from what little you have? The advantage of not having much is that you won't clutter your space and take away it's clarity. If you love materials and objects, you don't need to express this love by quantity, you can just as well express it by how you make use your materials.

I have danced, for example, for a choreographer who used costumes made out of metal who could be used as clothing, means of transport, podium, and as a prison.

In dance performances, the stage design is hardly ever illustrative. Even in the classical narrative ballets it is very rare nowadays to see dancers perform 'in' a painted forest. Images – usually projected on the stage background - are mostly used to create a perspective, or to put the dancer in relation with space and colour.

If you do your own stage design, you shouldn't be asking 'What do I need?', but rather 'What can I leave out?' If, after having asked yourself with how much stage design you can dispense, you are still convinced the piece needs four podiums, two ladders and ten cubic metres of rose leaves, you should ask yourself two more questions:

- How does the design change the look of the piece in relation to the choreography's theme?

- How does the design affect the dance physically?

These questions make you enter into a dialogue with the stage designer - even if it is only yourself – which will help you with the details of your stage design.

Personally, I mix the first impression of the room I want to use as a stage with my thoughts on the theme of the dance. Then I check whether the dance and the room contrast or complement each other.

Example
A baroque piece doesn't have to be performed in a choral shell or the entrance hall of a palace. Under certain circumstances, its effect may be increased by a contrasting setting such as a junk yard or a storehouse.
I need to decide whether I want to contrast dance and setting, such as placing a baroque dance in a junk yard, or whether I want the setting to embrace and support the dance, like a baroque dance on a palace's staircase.

This is a simple example, but often it is hard to define the look and content of a choreography. A lot of it happens in the spaces between, and the clearer I am about what is happening on stage, about the energy of the piece and what its language has to be, the easier it will be to decide whether it needs a contrast or support from the setting.

Shape, idea and contrast

The overall shape and the look of the space are determined by variables not unlike those we have already used when discussing the thematic development of a choreography.

Which shapes do you connect with the theme / the choreography?
Are they:

– sharp	– dotted
– soft	– two-dimensional
– flowing	– three-dimensional
– brittle	– separate
– round	– connected
– square	– static
– symmetrical	– dynamic
– asymmetrical	

Which levels do you associate with the theme / the choreography?
Are they:

– horizontals	– floor level
– verticals	– eye level
– diagonals	

The stage design can transport the dance to different levels, giving you more options for contrast. Especially the use of the vertical level that goes beyond the physical reach of the dancers gives the choreography a whole new dimension.

Implementing ropes, climbing frames, platforms, staircases, or ladders will radically change the range of the dancer's possibilities – after all, dangling from a rope or dancing on a stepladder demand a wholly different set of movements.

Which materials do you associate with the theme / the choreography?

- wood
- cloth
- metal
- rubber
- paper
- glass
- styrofoam
- water
- natural materials such as leaves or flowers

There are two aspects we need to bear in mind when choosing materials: the purely physical aspect on one hand (e.g. you can't dance on a stage made of paper), and an expressive aspect on the other (wood speaks a different language, has a different effect than metal). Too often, materials are chosen only for their physical qualities because it is easier or cheaper, ignoring the energy they bring to the stage. Wood, metal, or glass can have a mitigating or intensifying effect, depending on their combination.

Composition

How do the segments link? Are the transitions:

- defined
- connected
- linear
- curving
- hard
- soft
- brittle
- melting
- fading

Like dancers, the segments relate to each other on stage in different compositional arrangements.

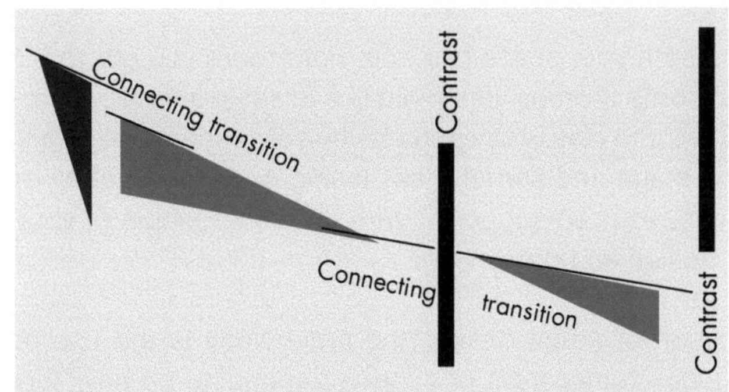

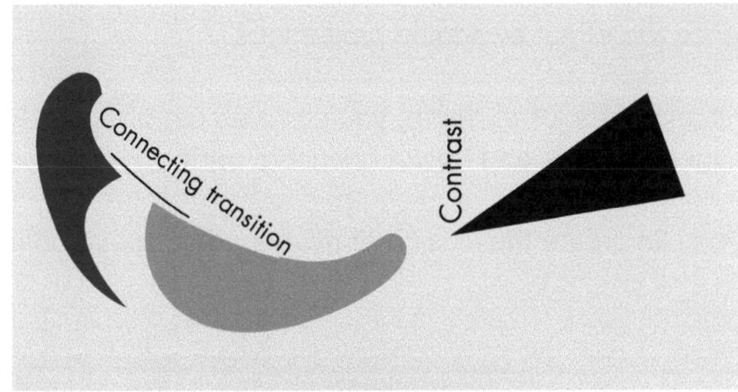

Are you looking for depth or width?

The more depth your space has, the more room you get to build a spatial dynamic. But some themes you might like to set in a wider, more defined space. Or do you want to play with contrasts by sometimes opening the space at the back of the stage and sometimes closing it? Is depth at all relevant for your piece? If it is, you can support it with the composition of your choreography, the stage design and projections.

A combination of stage design and projections is the use of gaze curtains which can look transparent or opaque depending on how they are lit, giving you the possibility to switch between the effects of depth and width. You can even enhance the effect by adding projections.

If you are aiming at a lot of depth, you can also set up several gaze curtains, project images on them and let your dancers perform in between them.

Like this you can create the illusion of never-ending space behind your stage.

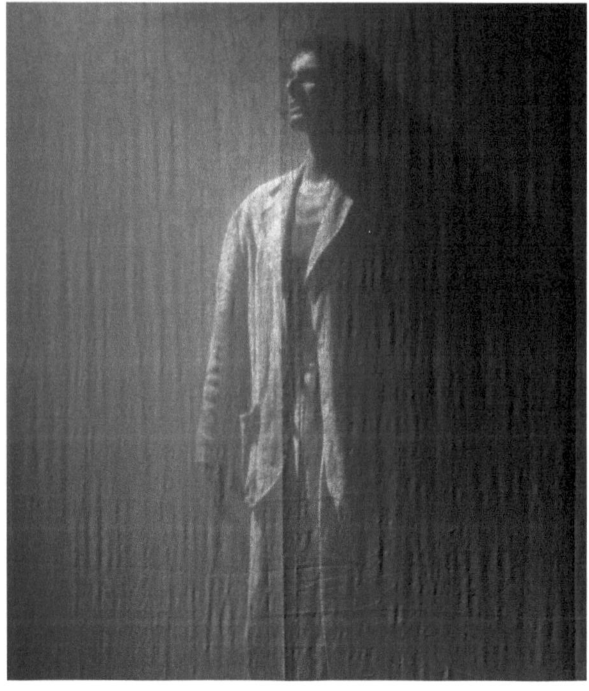

Example of a gaze curtain lit to look opaque

Example of a gaze curtain lit to look transparent

Which objects related to your theme can be integrated into the dance, and how do they change the repertoire?

Let's say your theme is the biography of a person who has had to spend a lot of their time in bed due to an illness. Obviously, an appropriate prop would be a bed. The stage could:

- depict a huge bed,

- be a landscape made from metal bedsteads,

- be a landscape made from mattresses,

- be a landscape made from the feathers out of the mattresses,

- be a landscape made from a huge number of pillows,

- hold a single bed with wheels,

- be strewn with torn pillows, feathers spilling out.

Depending on which stage design you choose, your piece will appear in a different light and with a different emotional background. You can compare the stage design to the weather: it makes a difference whether you spend your day under grey, dark winter clouds or looking up at a clear blue sky in spring. You are creating an emotional landscape. When deciding between rusty bedsteads and feathers, you are also deciding about springs skies or winter clouds, a kiss in an autumn storm or a death in spring.

The emotional content of your landscape will show itself with the development of your concept, and it will not only have an impact on the look of your piece, but also on its repertoire.

The setup of the stage will influence the movement language of your piece. A strong stage design will limit the endless possibilities of how you can move in your dance space, so if your design reaches into the dance space, it will become a central feature in your piece and your rehearsals. It will not only limit movement options, but also focus the choreographer's mind on using as much of the design as possible. If, for example, you have the moveable metal costumes I mentioned earlier, and your task is to create a hunting scene, your mind will fix onto the use of the costume, and only allow associations that work with moveable costumes. Expressing the hunt through gestures alone will not be an option because the costumes are a central focus in your work.

On the one hand it is pleasant to give yourself a direction by creating limits with a stage design, as it can be paralysing to have too many options; on the other hand, a dominant stage design will limit our changes of trying out unexpected ideas that we didn't even come up with because we limited ourselves with our focus on the relation between stage design and dance. I advise you to try and altogether forget about stage design to keep your repertoire broad and open.

What colours and contrasts come with your theme?

Colours can be alive or dead, differentiated or flat. Even black and white can be divers, interesting, or dull.

Dance isn't as directly associated with colour as it is with the dynamics of shapes or space. It takes effort and sensitivity to identify the colour scheme you need for your choreography, and maybe also the help of people who are experienced in working with colours.

Because they are emotionally charged, colours and contrast are very powerful. And they are everywhere, from the stage design and lights to costumes. There are millions of colours and millions of possible combinations with which you can create a world on stage that sets off your theme.

Stage design, lights and costumes determine the overall expression and emotion of a scene, and it is this overall expression we need to decide on first. Do I want a soft, flat world without any contrasts, such as a white floor, white walls, white lights and twenty dancers all in white? Or am I looking for stark contrasts, placing dancers all in black on a red floor, harshly back-lit? Or maybe contrasting colours, with dancers in yellow, green and red moving between gold leaves?

The contrasts and colours will spark emotions in a spectator because they trigger memories. Hardly ever do we remember a feeling as such, what we do remember is a situation or image that gave us the feeling, which is why we can access feelings via visual inputs. The visual experience we create on stage with lights and colours has to connect with our audience's personal experiences if we want our scene to be emotionally strong. Colours serve as a link to the spectator's emotions. Sky blue will always make us feel different than ash grey. Because this is so obvious, there is also the danger of lapsing into cliché. If you choose too obvious a colour scheme, your audience will lose interest instead of engaging with your piece. You can't relax into an image or atmosphere if you can spot the director's intentions from a mile away, trying worn-out visual metaphors to trick you into feeling love or pain. It is just like that type of cheap, would-be naturalistic oil paintings you find at street markets, where the painter shows a young couple on the beach and you know what you should be feeling is 'romance', but you don't. You are put off it because you know you are supposed to feel romance.

To avoid obvious, worn-out images, try not to focus too much on your intention. Don't look for an effect to present the concept of 'love', rather, go through your own experience to find your own associations of love. The shape you give your own experience will give your audience a visual impulse which, ideally, will conjure up images and memories, which in turn may spark emotions if they connect with the experiences of an individual spectator.
But your piece is meant for more than one spectator, and every single person in the audience has a different set of experiences. Any image you offer will address a cluster of experiences in each spectator, and everybody will react with different associations. What we choreographers and stage designers create on stage is a visual experience, an impulse that continues in the spectator's emotions.

There are many experimental productions that refrain from trying to trigger emotions with their images on stage – the whole point of the piece is the experiment, not the expression of a specific content.

Although I love this kind of project, to be fair I have to admit that in eight out of ten pieces the audience will be bored at some point. If you leave the overall impression of your piece to chance, the outcome will be unpredictable. Spontaneous experiments are helpful inasmuch as they allow things to happen we may never have imagined, making space for new ideas, but to create a strong visual experience we usually have to dig deeper. We need to be able to react to form, colour, and association so we can find out how to change images in order to open the door for different associations.

The difficulty lies in the task of transforming a vague feeling into shape and colour, and then detaching to observe the shape and colour. By stepping back, I avoid being tricked into seeing what I expect to see, and instead let my mind react to the image that is there.

Experience – association – feeling – understanding – connection

As it is the goal of most choreographers to evoke emotions in their audience, or even expand their consciousness, it is interesting to study how feelings are generated in our brains. Which experiences and impulses trigger emotions?

A simplified description

A store of colours, shapes, faces and movements are mixed with what you perceive at the moment to produce an emotion.

	Store of memories
Emotion	
	Perceptions at the moment

This emotion will impose itself on the next decision you make or how you perceive a situation. It is a concentrate of all the experiences you have had so far.

Depending on its make-up from

- shapes   – acoustic stimuli
- colors   – movements

the brain will translate it into a different emotion, which means that shapes, colours, movements and acoustic stimuli are inextricably linked in an emotional context. These contexts are not entirely universal, every person will interpret the contexts of a colour, movement or sound slightly differently – but only slightly. Depending on my personal experience, some elements will seem more important to me than others. Still, there is an intersection: Some colours, sounds, and shapes have either a soothing or an activating effect on most people.

As a choreographer, director, stage designer, costume designer, light designer or musician I need to be aware of the signals I am sending out. Scenes that completely capture the audience usually hit an emotional 'trigger point' both visually and musically.

Trying too hard to bring out each individual element separately often makes us miss the trigger point. As a director and choreographer, I have to work together with the stage designer to find that place where everything fits together. You might need to meet half-way to achieve it, but it will be more than worth it. Let yourself be encouraged to let go of your ego for a bit, to not only see your piece as a platform for different dance elements, by the thought of how a performance of dance, colour, shape and music can subtly, but really change people's consciousness.

Stage design

Spontaneously decide on a theme for a choreography and create a stage design with the help of the following questions:

- What kind of shapes do you associate with the theme?

- Which materials match your theme best?

- Are you looking for an impression of depth or rather width?

- Which props / objects can I integrate in the dance, and how do they change the movement repertoire?

- What colours and contrasts come with the theme?

- What are your requirements for an outdoor location?

11

Lighting

Dance and light are visual. Volatile. Elusive. Magical. Stage lighting poten-
tiates dance. A scene that seemed rather unspectacular at the studio may
move audiences to tears with proper lighting.

Objects reflect the light and become visible. We never see light - we see its
reflection on smoke, dust, objects, or people. Because we see reflections,
it is possible for a green tree to appear blue under a certain light, and blue
will have a different impact on our psyche than the original daylight green.
As a spectator, I won't think I'm seeing a tree that is normally green, yet at
the moment reflects blue light. I will accept that I see a blue tree. What we
think we are seeing shapes our reality. Mountains, at a distance, seem blue
even in broad daylight. Although we know that mountains are green, brown,
grey etc., we look at the scenery and call them 'the blue mountains', simply
because they look blue to our eyes.

Lighting parameters

Brightness

Dimmed, soft light blurs the details of a structure and accentuates the outlines of a shape. We see a different image and make different associations.

Example
Consider a shrub in the afternoon sun. You will be able to detect branches,
twigs, leaves, the veins on the leaves, even from a few meters away. You
will take in countless details that allow you to form a differentiated image of
that shrub. This image contains so many shapes that each individual shape
distracts your mind from the next, giving you not one image of a shrub, but
hundreds. In this situation, you won't feel the need to associate at all, because your eyes and your brain are far too busy processing the myriad of
impressions coming in.

However, if we set the shrub in pale moon light, you won't see individual leaves. The details disappear and the shrub will seem one big outline containing different shades of dark. Objects in the moon light may trick the eye and seem to be what they are not. An ill-lit shrub can look like a sleeping animal. Or – far more inconvenient – a sleeping bear may look like a shrub in semi-darkness. It is very likely that anybody who survives mistaking a bear for a shrub will afterwards think many a shrub a bear, just in case.

The rules of analogy invite associations. The visual reduction of a shrub to its outlines releases images in our minds because we are not distracted by detail. If I put a burning torch into a shrub at night, I will highlight its inner structures, offering the onlooker a new perspective without distracting him with the shrub's outline or background. Again, concentrating on one out of many possible perspectives makes for a strong visual impression.

Light gives us the means to show things one way or another. It determines our vision. What does this mean for our work on stage?

In plays, we are required to meet two expectations at once: the actors' facial expressions must be visible to the audience, while at the same time we want to create a striking, clear image that doesn't distract the audience with to many details. It is possible, but difficult. It is asking us to light the shrub from our previous example so that it could be mistaken for a bear, but at the same time shows each individual leaf. Can you spot the dilemma?

In dance, the shapes of the dancers' bodies are essential. Facial expression has its place, but the central means of expression is the body. For lighting, this means that the overall brightness of the stage can be much lower than in a play. Shapes and movements appear clearer when distracting details fade in dim light, and it is usually easier to direct the audience's attention towards the dancer's bodies.

In general, dance can be lit to show associative images, or, to use our example again, shrubs in moon light. The brighter the light, the more details will become visible:

bright	dim
variety	concentration
details	outlines
closeness	distance

Colours

Try to skip the basic colours red, blue and green for now. Think past them and look for a colour shift. Imagine a scene and mentally tint it with a different colour. Observe how the new shade changes the intention of the scene.

Example
Imagine creating a piece on the theme of 'exclusion'. One dancer is expelled from the group and becomes an individual in the following scene. The interesting question now is how we light the two parties. Are we visualising the process of expulsion from the group's point of view, or from the shunned individual's perspective?

If we assume that the initial atmosphere is one of cold-heartedness and brutality, the scene could be lit like this:
Hard shadows dominate the scene. The main source of light are the backlights creating harsh contrasts of black and white. All colours are cold: stark white, icy blue, acid green.

What happens, though, if you want to stress the protagonist's longing to be part of a community, and experience love and understanding? Maybe you feel this longing is best expressed through the soft colours of autumn light, that golden light that seems to spend itself entirely one last time before winter, and makes the earth glow with content? Will this lighting serve to highlight the feelings of the protagonist, or will it distract from the process of expulsion? Will it water down the basic emotion of the scene, sharpen or soften the contrast between the parties?

So this is where we stand so far:
The harsh black-and-white lighting option is too literal, it leaves too little space for interpretation. The autumn light option, however, weakens the drama of the process.

Exploring further the emotions in the scene, you may decide to highlight the pain of separation. Pain associates with blood, so the obvious colour is red. But there are thousands of shades of red, and you can't find the perfect shade that expresses what you are looking for. You return to the first two drafts of your scene, cold blue and autumn light. The scene and the lighting become more and more intertwined. You adjust the layout of your scene to the lighting concept. At this point, dramaturgy and lighting start interacting. Even if you wanted to distance yourself from all technical issues, you would still have to integrate your lighting design into your dramaturgy concept to create a well-rounded piece.

Perception

You need to train your perception of light to develop a feeling for it. Being able to distinguish daylight from artificial light is not enough! Observe different artificial lights in different places, such as office complexes or shopping malls (where the lighting proves relevant for sales figures).

Light doesn't just light the room, it also affects our minds and emotions. Have you ever stepped into a room and instantly felt at home? Observe the light in such rooms and how it makes you feel.

In the course of one single day, the light changes countless times. Our eyes adjust consistently, without us even noticing. But we do notice how the things we see every day change with the light. Consider the infinite colour range of the sky and its effect on our emotional state. Our perception of the world is determined by the light. How the sky turns black just before a thunderstorm, how the setting sun breaks through, fiery red between the inky clouds and the dark earth. Maybe it was this kind of light that inspired the first sidelights in theatre, its flat angle making everything seem more three-dimensional.

If you see a light situation that strikes you, and you want to use it in a project, you will have to analyse it in order to reproduce its effect on stage. Simply adoring it won't do, however touched you may be by it. You have to be willing to exchange the magic for skill. It can be tough, but it is part of the job.

When an image captures you – imagine, for example, a night-time street with one single street-light, and a solitary figure passing under it – your reflex should be to observe where the street-light is located, what it's radius is, and at which moment the light on the figure was most dramatic. Sobering, I know - but while disillusionment is part of the job, it doesn't have to keep you from being fascinated by the magic of a scene.

Stage lighting

200 years ago, the stage and the auditorium were lit equally bright. Then, somebody came up with the idea to dim the lights in the auditorium to direct more attention to the actors on stage. The light of an average lamp, however, was undirected. So new lanterns had to be invented with which the light could be directed where it was needed.

Floodlights

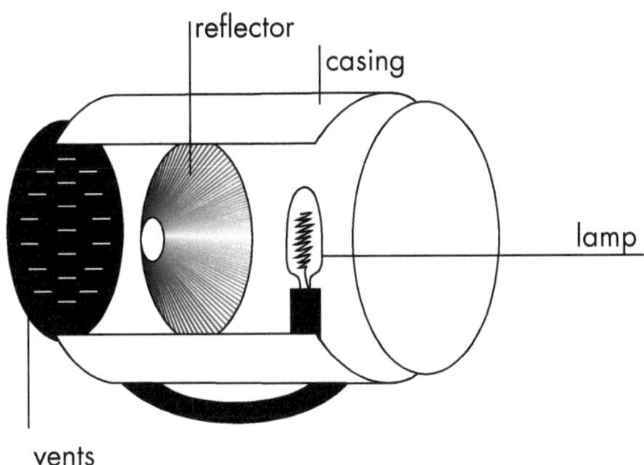

Basic structure of floodlights

Floodlights light big spaces. Their beams are broad and unfocused, so they can't be used to only light a certain area on stage. If they are used at all on stage, it is usually to light the background.

Common floodlight

Spotlights

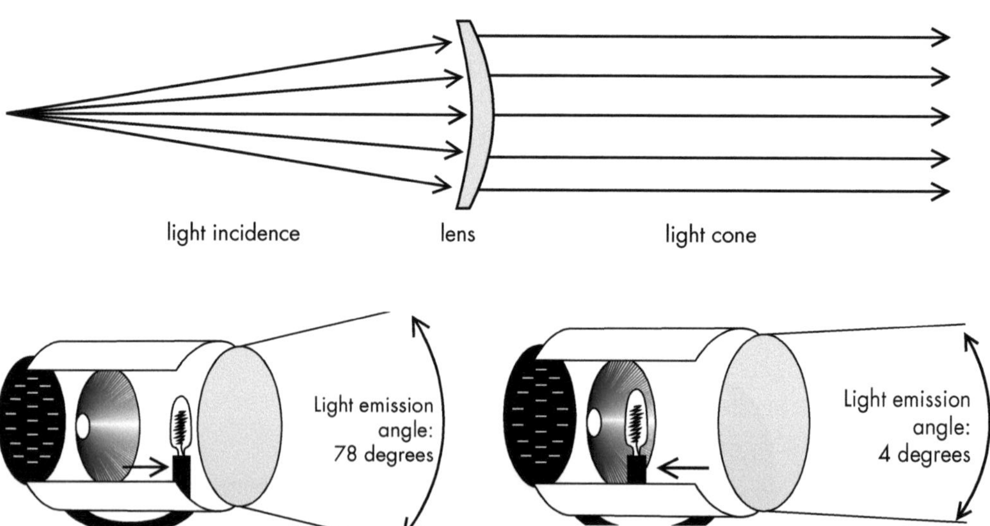

Changeability of the light drop angle in the lens headlight by moving the lamp

Lens headlamp

To focus light on a certain area, you need a lens. Depending on the lens type, its strength and its distance to the source of light, the light beam will be more focused or more diffuse.

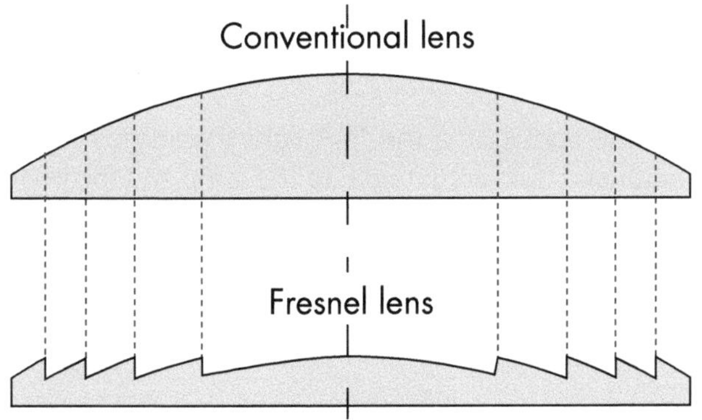

Cross section through a fresnel lens

Fresnels

The Fresnel lens has the same effect as a normal lens, with the advantage that the formerly thick and heavy lens has been reduced to a thickness of a few millimetres.

Spotlights are the most common type of lighting instrument on stages all over the world as they give off a beautiful stage light, are versatile in their use and at the same time affordable. They can be used with different light bulbs depending on the size of the stage, ranging from 100 to 1000 watt. Average stages are fitted with bulbs between 500 to 2000 watt.

PAR lights

A simpler version of the spotlight is the PAR light (Parabolic Aluminised Reflector). Lens, reflector and bulb are integral to the lamp and the beam spread is fixed. Because the beam spread is not adjustable, the PAR lights are somewhat limited, but then again there are different versions with different beam spreads available. They are very robust and affordable. Due to its appearance, the PAR light is often called PAR-can.

PAR-Can

Profile spots

The most beautiful light for dance is created with profile spots or 'profilers'.

Profile headlights

The profile spot doesn't just have one lens like the normal spotlight, but a system of lenses that is highly adjustable.

In addition, they can be used like a huge slide-projector to project shadow images on walls, curtains and the floor by inserting metal slides (so-called gobos or irises) that shape the beam of light. The only two disadvantages of the profile spot are its heavy weight and its expensiveness. But if you can afford one, then the world, or, in our case, the stage, is your oyster!

Dimmer

The spotlights are powered by dimmers. The dimmers determine how much energy goes into a lighting instrument, i.e. how bright it shines. The simplest kind of dimmer is the manual dimmer, a control board with twelve slides that manage twelve spotlights.

In one of our dance performances, the light technician used only 10 hand-dimmed spotlights although he could have had a full 100 at his command. This demonstrates, once again, how quality is not the same as quantity.

Lighting board

If you want to avoid the finger acrobatics involved in operating a manual dimmer, you will have to invest in a memory board. Memory boards are control panels that can digitally store light settings, so that you can activate a pre-programmed light setting including different spotlights with only one slide. This can of course also be a computer, connected to the dimmer by USB. But let's keep working with the control panel for the sake of simplicity.

More advanced control panels are computer-based and show the settings on a monitor. At the push of a button, a pre-set light setting can be activated, or it can even be timed beforehand. How light settings are stored varies from board to board, but it usually won't take more than a few minutes to understand if somebody explains it to you.

With a control panel that is not computer-based, you'll just take notes to re-member where you want the light to switch on or off suddenly, or fade in and out softly.

Control panel

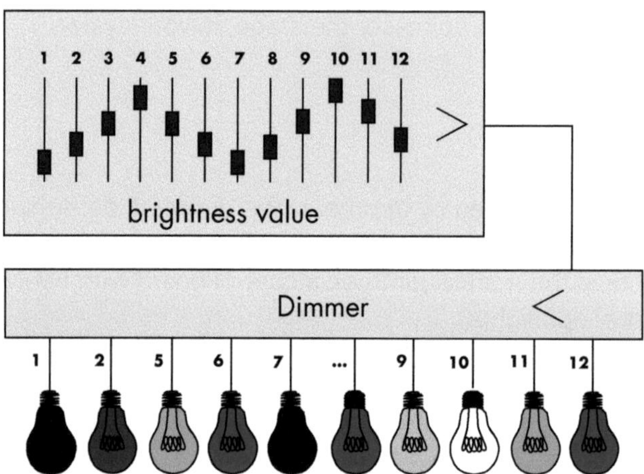

Channel allocation

Each spotlight is connected to the dimmer and the control board by a so-called 'channel' (an electronic connection). You can plug several spotlights into one dimmer channel so that all of them light up together when you operate the switch of that channel.

The dimmer's load limit determines how many spotlights it can manage: a dimmer channel of 2 kilowatt, for example, can take four spots of 500 watt or two of 1000 watt, etc.

Because the dimmer supplies the spotlights with electricity, it needs to be plugged to a high-voltage circuit system. The plug looks the same as the ones you use every day, just thicker.
The cables from the dimmer to the spotlights are normal electric cables sim-ilar to your common household cable. If you need to connect a great number of spotlights, you can avoid getting tangled in all the individual cables by using a multi-core cable, a thick cable that ends in individual plugs.

Control panel

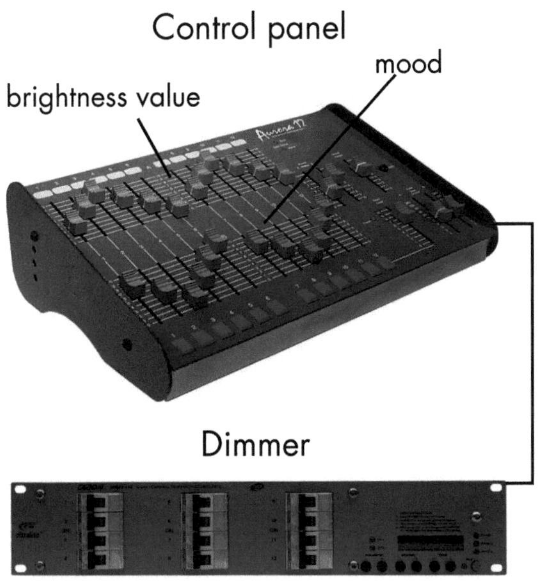

Control panel

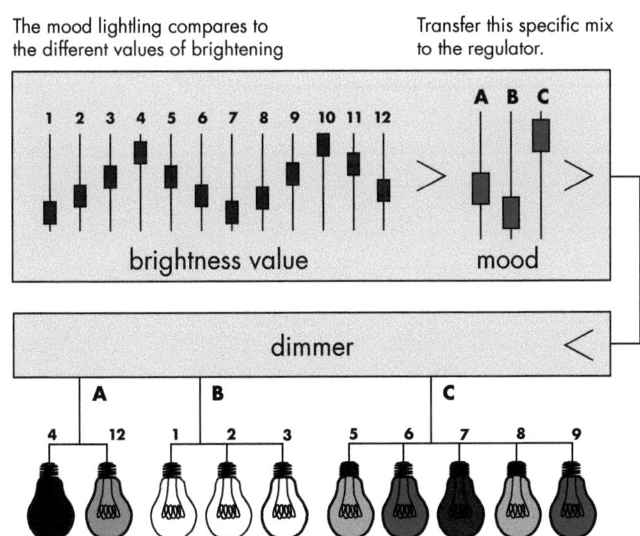

Light design

What equipment you need depends on what you want to see. Ask yourself: How many spotlights do I need, and what kind? Where do I need them? In addition, there are a few basic principles for lighting dance performances you should consider when planning your lighting.

Frontlight

1. Principle: dance does not need a lot of frontlight.

Frontlight (usually from above or from each side of the stage) makes faces visible. If it is too bright, the space appears flat and two-dimensional. Use as little frontlight as you can to preserve a sense of depth on stage.

Headlight position

Position of spotlights in perspective of brightening

Sidelights

2. Principle: not the face is the main lighting center but the whole body.

Sidelights are the most important lights for dance performances. They make the stage and the bodies on it seem more three-dimensional, giving the performance more plasticity. They also allow you to light the foreground, centre, and background separately, which visibly divides your space into different levels, supporting a sense of depth. In dance, space is is an essential means of expression, so the more visible and differentiated it becomes to your audience, the better.

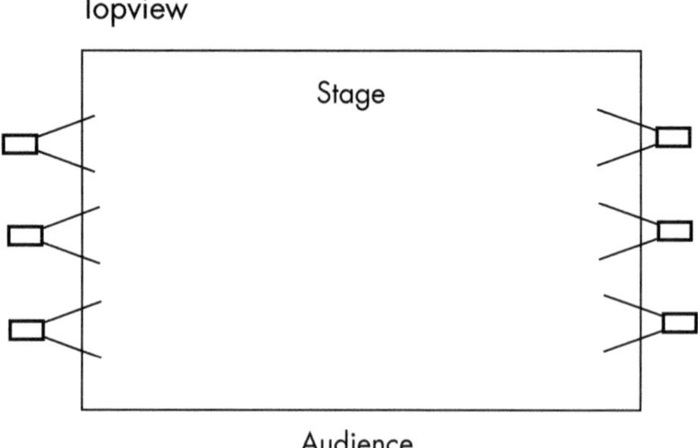

Position of spotlights in perspective

Ideally, the sidelights are not placed too high up, so they don't cast a shadow. The spotlight itself, the source of light, is not visible, and there are no visible cones of light on stage. The advantage of this arrangement is that dancers can appear 'out of nowhere' just by stepping from the shadow into the light.

Profile spots give the best sidelight, but you can also use common spotlights or, at a pinch, even PAR lights with a small beam spread. If the only thing available are floodlight PAR cans, you can mask them with aluminium foil to limit their beam spread: simply cover the opening of the can with the foil until you see the cone of light you want.

Sidelight: spotlight position

On both sides of a stage there are usually lengths of black fabric, so-called masking legs, that hide the wings and all equipment placed there from the audience's view. Standing on the stage, you can see the openings between the legs and use them to enter or exit. For sidelight, the spotlights are placed behind the legs. Overhead lights are hung up in the rigging; low or 'boom' sidelight is created by stacking spotlights on stands. Their light beams coming from each side of the stage may overlap at centre stage, or leave a dark path between them. You can create interesting effects by lighting alternating openings, so that a figure walking from upstage to downstage will be lit from one side, pass through the dark, and be lit from the other side the next moment. Whichever option you choose, using low sidelight is practically a must in a dance performances today.

Backlight

3. Principle: the dancers should stand out from the background, lending the space more depth!

On dance stages, there is usually a backdrop screen that can be lit in different colours indirectly from behind. You can also backlight a dancer standing in front of a black backdrop. The backlight will outline the dancer's body and make for a dramatic halo effect.

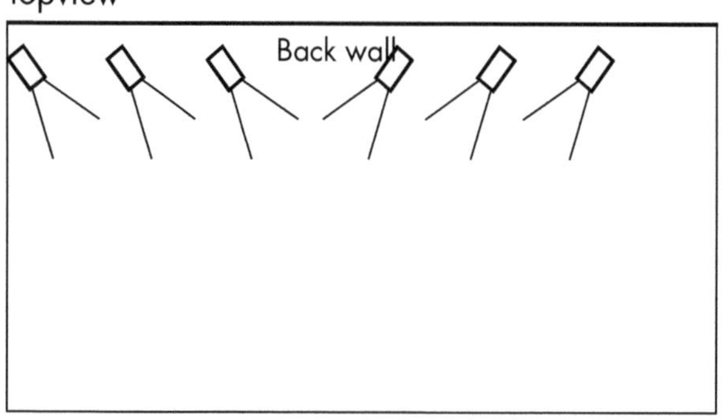

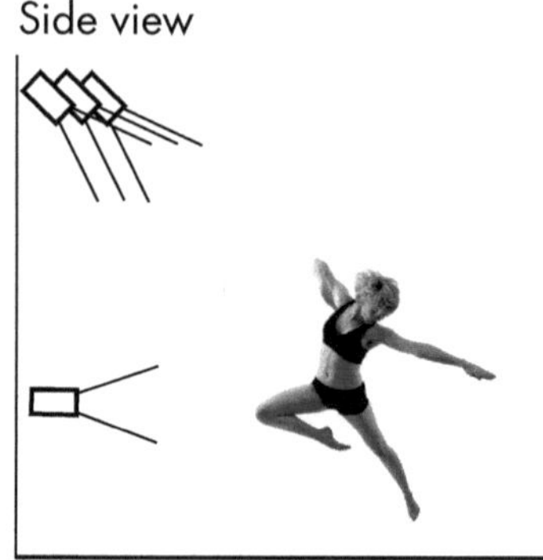

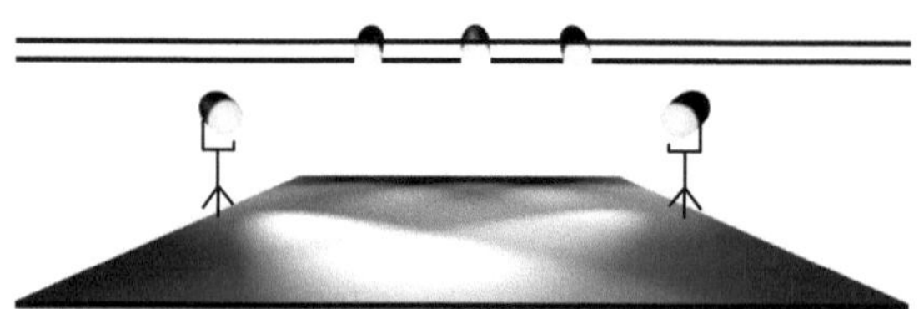

Position of backlights

Highlights

A further element of lighting that requires your consideration is focus. The audience's eyes are directed by the light. You can literally highlight a figure or object on stage, literally put them 'in the spotlight' by using a separate lighting instrument just for them.

Example

While the main plot is developing at the centre of the stage, a few dancers lie off to one side of the stage for several minutes. You want the audience's attention to shift onto the dancers lying in the dark without changing the scene. You could achieve this by slowly fading in light and colour on the faces of the lying figures while the scene continues.

For such moments, you will need to set up spotlights that have no other use than just this one particular scene. This means that a whole dimmer channel will be dedicated – all evening – to a scene that lasts a minute or less, and you won't be able to use that channel for anything else during your piece. Think twice whether you really need to set up a highlight, or whether you can use the spotlights that are already there for a similar effect. Setting up special highlights will have an effect on your budget because you will need more equipment if every second scene needs its own dimmer channel.

12

Studies and exercises

Choreographers will automatically coach their dancers. Whether the training stays on the surface or includes the development of inner qualities is a question of style.

Always remember that a set of exercises may work wonderfully with one group and end in total disaster with another. There is no direct transferability. I once worked successfully with a group of dancers, taking them through a series of exercises going from utter stillness to maximal movement. One of the dancers was a teacher for 'movement' at an acting academy, and she used my lesson in a class with her actors, where it proved a huge disappointment.

If you are working on a set of movements to understand its mechanics, you don't need to tune in much with the dancers. Developing emotion and inner attitude is a different cup of tea entirely – there, you can only start where your dancers are at that very moment.

Timing:
Implementing these exercises requires sensitive timing. Your own perception may be quicker than the group's, just because you already know what you are aiming at, and they hear the instructions for the first time. But if you go too slowly, you risk losing momentum and the dancers' attention and it will be difficult to re-establish the flow.

Repeating and developing:
Repeat your instructions, in the same words or re-formulating. Don't leave any space for thoughts outside the exercise. Feel free to further develop all exercises.

Always keep your eyes on the aim of the exercise, but allow for it to evolve and change.

The better the dancers become at feeling nuances in their movements, the better the choreographer can fine-tune the details of the choreography.

It is the fine-tuning that keeps the choreographies alive, and it's often the tiniest of details that decides whether a choreography works or not.

If as a choreographer you come to the point where you can see details that need changing, but your dancers cannot feel and change them in their movement, you need a method to develop the dancers' feeling.

I. The internal spaces of the body

These are exercises that focus on the inner space, but also serve as links to kinesphere and general space. They raise body awareness and sharpen perception.
Hearing
The coach gives the following instructions:

Stand still. Close your eyes and bring awareness to your body and your breathing. Stand still. Tune out any sound you hear. Listen to your breath. Hear your heart beat. Hear your breath and your heartbeat together. Breathe easily, normally, don't let concentration stay your breath. Let it flow freely. Can you hear the rhythm created by your heartbeat and your breath? Do you hear any other noises in your body?

Now expand your attention to the space you are occupying. What noises do you notice? Now try to hear both your heartbeat and the noises around you at the same time.

Expand your hearing and notice the noises from the city around you. Separate the noises of the city, this room, and your heartbeat from each other. Develop an awareness that allows you to be within yourself and with your environment at the same time.

1 Partner work – divided attention

A gives B a massage of about 20 minutes. B begins to react with small movements to A's impulses. The movements expand to create a duet.
B who receives the massage focuses on his own body at first. With the visible reactions to A's touch, he begins to expand his body awareness from inside to outside. The duet is led by touch, always changing between inside and outside focus.

2 Different circles of attention

Partner exercise

A with eyes closed.

B touches A, for example putting a hand on his right shoulder.

A answers to the touch by pushing into it.

B brings A's shoulder back to its original position while touching another body part with his other hand, maybe the left hip.

A attempts to feel the connection between his right shoulder and his left hip as his right shoulder is being moved back into its original position. Repeat with different points of contact.

Establish a sequence of points of contact, e.g. hand, hip, knee, back, stomach, back of the neck...

A repeats the sequence without B's touch and tries to

- transfer the movements as far into space as possible,

- keep the movements close to his body,

move just inside his own kinesphere.

You can repeat points of contact and change the sequence according to the opportunities that present themselves during the transformation of the movements in space.

3 Guided improvisation – composition – group exercise

The basis for this exercise is the collective change of a movement in a group. It is particularly useful when you want to steer your group into a certain direction while still staying open to experiment and change in the movements. It takes some skill for the dancers to keep moving fluidly and still focus on the ever-changing tasks the choreographer gives them from outside. The choreographer has to collaborate with the group by verbally supporting the dancers, giving the right inputs at the right moment so they can realise his idea without breaking their flow.

Below you find a basic form of guided composition. You can develop it further and fill it with content suitable to your goals.

During the exercise the group is constantly moving through space. As coach, you walk with them so you can gauge how much time you need for each exercise. Always give the group a little more time than it takes you to do the task – you already know what the exercise will be when you explain it, so you will be quicker in realising it. The dancers hear your instructions for the first time. Direct their attention towards

- their own bodies
- their perception
- the group
- a creation

1. Level – Being aware of your body

The coach gives the following instructions:

Walk through the room at your own pace. Keep your eyes low and unfocused. Direct your attention towards your body. Before your inner eye, watch your feet lift and connect with the floor again. Notice which parts of the soles of your feet touch the floor and which parts don't. How much tension can you feel in the soles of your feet? Now try to relax them into the floor when walking. Can you feel the area of support expanding? Where do you put the most weight? Now shift your weight on the outside of your feet. Try the same with the weight on the inside. And now back to centre, rolling the weight from your heel through the middle of your sole and your second toe.

How much support do your toes give you? Can you relax them more during the swing phase, and engage them more at the moment of propulsion? Feel how your foot pushes against the floor. Increase that pushing feeling to change your speed of walking.

Now direct your attention toward your ankles. How much do the ankle joints move? How does their tension change throughout your gait cycle? Try out different walking speeds to feel how your ankle movement adapts. Try walking with more or less muscular engagement. Feel the link between ankle and the sole of your foot in motion.

Now travel upwards with your attention. What sensations come from your knee? Can you feel your calf swing from your knee? How far do you extend your knee while walking? Can you feel the extension at the back of your knee? Send your patellae forward. Make as much space in the joint as possible. Now connect your knees with your ankles and your feet. Are the feet and ankles still working with the same intention as before? Give all three equal attention now. Drop your weight into the floor. Allow your joints to pass on your weight to the floor instead of holding it up.

Let your attention travel further up. Put your hands on your hips and feel the sway of your pelvis. Try to relax your pelvis, taking calm, gliding steps, as if your pelvis was floating. Let the weight of your pelvis drop into the floor through your heels. Visualise a connection: draw a plumb line from your sit bones through your heels. Breathe all the way down into your pelvis. Notice how your thighs swing from your hip joints.

Now focus on your breath. Let it flow freely. Fill the front of your body with air. Fill your back with air. Observe your spine, try to see its shape before your inner eye. Feel it resonate with the motion of your walking.
Drop your weight through all joints into the floor. Feel your feet push into the floor. At the same time imagine a soft upwards pull through your spine.
Visualise all your vertebrae separating and lengthening while your weight drops into the floor. Feel the two directions in your body: dropping into the floor, lengthening towards the sky.

Instead of tensing muscles, imagine lengthening from your sacrum to the crown of your head.

Balance your head on your spine, as if you were balancing a balloon on a finger. Allow for minute balancing movements. Remember your breath, flowing freely. Drop your ribs, relax your stomach without crumpling in on yourself to let the breath flow. Find an elastic overall muscle tone that feels healthy to you.

Let your arms swing freely from your shoulders. The sit bones drop, the spine rises, the head floats, the feet roll over the floor. Push off with your feet to increase your walking tempo. Visualise drawing a line between your heels and a spot between your shoulder blades. Let your feet push you through this line with each step.

2. Level – being aware of space

Walk. Focus on your field of vision. How big is it? Notice how what you see changes constantly even if you don't focus on anything. Perceive the whole room in front of you: people, colours, light. Widen your field of vision to 180°, as far left and as far right as you can. Now, as a contrast, focus on details in the room. Notice what colour your fellow dancers' eyes are.

Open your field of vision again. Mentally map the space you are crossing. Where in the room are you? Where is everybody else?
Can you feel the air moving when you walk? How its movement changes when you walk past another dancer? Hear the rhythm of their feet. Compare it to you own. Is there a common walking tempo in the group? Is it slower or faster than your own?

As a group, try to find a collective tempo and walking rhythm. Use your widened field of vision and your hearing to synchronise your walking without falling into a marching step, just walk rhythmically. Walking is by nature a two-beat-movement. Find a four-four beat inside your step by saying 'Hey!' on each 1, starting at the first step. I shall count you in by giving you the first 'Hey!', then you all take over after the first phrase. After 'Hey!' on 1, silently count 2, 3 and 4 in you mind. From now on, I will give all instructions between the 'Hey!'-s.
Make your 'Hey!' louder. And louder. Shout it. Take it down. Even quieter. Whisper.

Some of the dancers in the group keep up the four-four beat, others improvise along using sounds. Don't lose the beat! Switch roles several times, giving the four-four, improvising, and going back again.

3. Level – Qualities

Walking.
As one, the group suddenly stops, i.e. if one dancer stops, everybody else in the group stops as well. At the same time, the dancers have to fill the space evenly, leaving no gaps. The group keeps moving and stopping unpredictably.

Leave it to the dancers' imagination how they want to move on after stopping. One option are different speeds from slow motion to full speed, but you can also try out different spatial patterns or movement qualities such as free, restricted, fluid, staccato, big, small, etc.

Restrict the number of different qualities in the room, and the dancers will form groups. Start adding inputs from the theme you want to work on.

When switching between movement qualities is working, part of the group can oppose the quality like so: after a stop, one dancer may initiate a fluid movement. A part of the group follows into fluidity, but the other part move staccato-like, opposing the fluid quality of the first group. You can do the same exercise with associations.

4. Level – Themes

Let the group split up into two to three smaller groups. Ask them to move with the same quality in their group, but oppose the other group(s).

There is also the option of exiting and entering the dance. Exit by stepping to the side of the room, enter by taking centre. Try to incorporate movements and qualities you associate with the theme you are working on.

4 Inner spaces – mental journey

This Alexander technique exercise has found its way into dance and is used every day by many teachers all over the world. It takes between three to ten minutes.

The coach gives the following instructions:

Stand with your feet hip-width apart, knees bent, arms hanging by your sides. Close your eyes and bring your attention to your body.
Let your breath flow freely. Feel the air flowing into your torso. How much space does the air take in your body? Let this space expand by relaxing your abdomen. If you like, you can make your breath audible. Relax your face, your eyes, your tongue. Comfortable, open, friendly, awake. Your breath flows right down into your pelvis.

Send your attention into your feet. Where is your weight? Centre it right over your feet. Relax the soles of your feet from front to back, right to left. Put 60% of your weight into your heels. Your ankles are soft and relaxed, your knees slightly bent. Let your weight drop through your joints into the floor. For a moment, make gentle little movements in your ankles and knees to ascertain their elasticity.

Let your breath flow freely down into your pelvis. Drop your pelvis through your heels into the floor, distributing your weight evenly on both feet. Feel the pull of gravity. At the same time imagine a soft upwards pull through your spine. Your head floats atop your spine. Feel the two directions in your body: dropping into the floor with gravity, lengthening through the spine towards the sky. Let your ribs sink, relax your abdomen, lengthen your neck.

Finish the exercise by smoothly continuing into whatever exercises you do in your training. Experiment with different visualisations to develop body perception.

However you transform these exercises, always remember to give the dancers time to tune in with themselves.
It is your job to create an atmosphere that allows for personal growth and creativity.

5 Visualisation

A choreographic study you can implement with companies of different dance levels and styles.

A piece on animals or the beast inside yourself

- Avoid plain miming of animals

- Evoke a kind of animal magic

This exercise is about finding animal movements and lending human movements an animal-like quality. It is also valuable for training dancers how to assess their own movement quality. In this particular task, dancers need to mentally and emotionally engage to find authentic expression.

Procedure

Prepare the dancers with a relaxation exercise that finishes with lying supine, deeply relaxed but wide awake. Give the following instructions:

Picture a sleeping animal.
What is it lying on?
What do its surroundings look like?
Look at the animal's pelt. Is it soft and warm, or sleek and shiny, or shaggy? How does it feel?
How does it feel when it draws its limbs close to its body, rubbing fur against fur?
Imagine the animal's face, how it's snout protrudes and the eyes are set back. What are its teeth like?
How big is its mouth, in what relation to they stand to the eyes?
What emotions does this trigger in you?
What size is the animal's head?
How is it proportioned with the body? Examine its legs.
What are its paws like?
What kind of tension do they hold?

Now let the animal wake up. How does it move its head?
How do its eyes and ears react to its environment?
What does it see, smell, hear, and feel?
Is it confident, superior, or shy and wary?

How does that show in its movements?
How does it place its feet?
How do the legs move?
What is the animal's emotion, what kind of energy emanates from it?
Visualise the animal's face and eyes as it stands and looks, as it runs and slows down again.
How does it move when it moves quickly?
Does it make any sound?
Does it expression change when it speeds up and slows down?

Picture the animal's natural environment. Then change it and observe how that changes the animal's way of moving. What are the animal's strengths? Does it have any advantages over other animals? Feel it grow hungry and look for food. Let other animals appear and watch them meet your animal. How do they react to each other? Watch how your animal retreats and goes back to sleep.

In your mind, enter the animal's body. Transfer the image of the animal's limbs onto your own arms and legs. Let your nails grow into claws. Feel how your paws tense and relax again. Let your eyes recede and your nose and mouth expand into a snout. Look for the animal's tension in your face, find its strength and flexibility in your back. Stretch your back and wake up as the animal. Cross the room looking for nourishment until you grow tired, then go back to sleep.

6 Subtext 'Mama'

Standing in a circle. Utter the word 'Mama' with different subtexts. The group repeats. Then add bodily expression. Repeat with a new subtext, etc. At some point, leave out the verbalisation and just use movement.

II. Structure and dynamics

7 Exercise for structure and dramatic arc

In groups of three. A paints a picture of an island with a dramatic landscape rich in contrasts. B plans a journey through the landscape, creating a map, an outline with a dramatic arc that lays down the dynamics of the movements, the number of dancers in space and their association with the landscape. From this, A and B develop improvisations. C gives them feedback as to how visible their 'travelling itinerary' became in the improvisation. Find different travel routes for the same island.

III.   Stage spaces

8 Spatial tension deriving from the relation between space, direction, and level

Three dancers on stage, the rest of the groups are spectators. The dancers take a position standing, sitting or lying down. The spectators close their eyes, and the dancers change positions, focusing on space, direction, and level. When they are in position, the music starts and the spectators open their eyes. When the music fades, the spectators close their eyes again, the dancers change positions, etc. .

What different kinds of spatial tension do you notice in the different constellations? Which images stay with you? Choose five to seven images. Put them into an order, observing how each image refers to the next. Spatial tension between three-dimensional positions. Stationary. A enters the stage and takes up a position, B enters and places herself in relation to A. Let the image stand for a moment and observe its effect. Then A exits, leaving B. Again, look at the new image and its effect. Now let C enter, forming a new image with B, then B leaves, C stays, D enters, etc.

At first, the dancers will decide rationally what position to take, but after a while, their bodies will start to react intuitively.

Notice which positions and placements create dramatic tension.

9 Spatial tension – stationary

This is basically the same exercise as the previous one, but the dancers don't leave the stage once they have entered, i.e. they will create a group image, not unlike a tableau.
Notice changes in tension, how the relation between positions and groups (three to one, solo to group, etc.) change the dramatic effect on stage.
Are there discernible rules as to how you have to place to group to increase or reduce tension?

10 Spatial tension through movement quality and tempo

Two dancers on stage. Starting from the previous exercise. As soon as the duet has formed an image, A slowly moves into a new position. B reacts by also finding a new position. A reacts, B reacts, etc. . In the course of the exercise, the dancers may begin to use the pose as transit instead of stopping, flowing through one pose into the next.

There will be moments in which the tension is lost and the dancers look the same even though they are moving separately. Movements tend to merge with space, while positions stand in relation to space, so there is more potential for tension in positions than in movements. Still, you will find that some movement sequences are more interesting than others. Look out for dramatic moments in the improvisation and try to analyse what makes them dramatic.

11 Different relations between action and reaction

A dances a sequence and stops. B answers with another sequence.

Observe:

- the relationships between the dancers,

- the effect of different moments of overlapping exits and entrances,

- how much energy A needs to muster to make B react,

- how B's reaction changes A's intention.

IV.   Structure and dynamics

12   Exercise for structure and dramatic arc

In groups of three. A paints a picture of an island with a dramatic landscape rich in contrasts. B plans a journey through the landscape, creating a map, an outline with a dramatic arc that lays down the dynamics of the movements, the number of dancers in space and their association with the landscape. From this, A and B develop improvisations. C gives them feedback as to how visible their 'travelling itinerary' became in the improvisation. Find different travel routes for the same island.

V. Scene, language, and dance

13   Plot

In pairs. A and B take turns telling a tale. Nobody knows where the story leads, it develops while it's being told. The narrators dance while they tell their part of the story, improvising freely. Watching different pairs dance their tale will give you a feeling for how dance can illustrate or accompany language.

14   Storytelling

Groups of three. One person is the narrator, telling a short story. In the background, the other two dancers improvise to the story. When the story is over, the narrator starts again. The two dancers now have the opportunity to try out different ideas and / or integrate movements from their first improvisation.

15   Gestures

Choose a story, a film, or a book. Watch it unfold before your inner eye. Notice the moments that touch or impress you most. Let these moments inspire a gesture. Don't mime! Keep checking in with yourself, asking whether the experience of the movement rings true with the story you connect it with.

16 Image

In pairs. One paints a picture. The other develops a series of movements that match the picture. Create a solo from these movements.

17 Poem

In pairs. One dancer reads a poem to the other. What images linger? What feelings? Develop movements from these images and feelings and link them to create a solo. Read the poem again and dance the solo to it. Do any connections form from the combination of movement, text, and silence?

18 Personal story

Tell something about yourself, a short, personal anecdote or story.
What associations does the story raise?
Dreams, hopes, etc.?
Develop associations in movement and link them to create a solo. ,

19 Colours

Variant A: Use coloured foil to tint the lights in your room. The dancers move through space. What associations or feelings does the colour raise? How does it change the atmosphere? Collect movements and movement qualities you associate with that colour.

Variant B: The teacher / choreographer gives the dancers a set movement sequence. The dancers 'colour' it red. How does the quality of movement change?

VI. Music

20 Movement combination

Listen to an excerpt from a concert. Decide on a title that suits the piece. Without listening to the music, develop a movement combination that goes with the title you set. Then dance the movement combination to the music. Experiment with starting your combination at different points in the music.

VII. Relationships

21 Impulses

Level 1

Walk through the room in pairs. B gives A impulses to change his body position. A has to try and keep moving across the floor with the altered positioning. B gives more impulses on different parts of A's body, A tries to include the new information into her movement through the room.

Level 2

B still gives A impulses, but A instead of trying to move on while staying in the new position, A can now move through the position into movement. B needs to time his impulses carefully so as not to overwhelm A, but still give her enough material to dance with. A can make B's task easier by slowing down at the end of a movement to invite the new impulse.

Level 3

A now sometimes opposes B's impulse. Leading and following develops into more equal interaction.

Level 4

At some point, the impulse to change a movement won't need touch any more. The partners now constantly react to each others movement without touching. Add an 'observer' who watches the dance, taking note of interesting movement sequences that occur during improvisation. These can be used to create a composition.

22　Towel impulses

In pairs. A lies supine, blindfolded.
B gives A different impulses by touching him with a towel,
A reacts to the touch.
The towel can stroke, tap, fold, wrap, etc. .
The aim is to find movement and sensations beyond A's usual movement
habits.

23　Mirroring

In pairs, standing opposite each other. Synchronise with each other energetically before starting to move very slowly, fluidly and alternating between leading and following. An observer should not be able to detect who is leading.

24　Rolling Point

In pairs, sitting back to back. Concentrate the pressure of your body weight on one point on your backs, approximately the size of a ping pong ball. Reduce pressure to approx. 100 grams. Now try to let the imagined ball move along your backs without determining who leads the movement. Do not increase pressure or speed, and don't lose the 'ball'. In unison, try to stop and start again.
The 'ball' moves on over the rest of your body. The duet changes position from sitting to lying down to standing up and through space. You can expand the exercise almost endlessly by integrating weight shifts, lifts, etc. . Practise this exercise every day for a month, and you will improve every day.

25　Obstacles

Group exercise. Half of the group take up positions as 'obstacles' on the floor. The other half finds ways to dance around or over them. After some time, the 'obstacles' start moving and reacting to the passing dancers.

26 Taking weight

Level 1

In pairs. A slowly moves through different positions. B adds himself to each
position by putting his weight on A: leaning on A, hanging from A, sitting on A
as if in a deck chair, whatever comes naturally. A gently takes B's weight by
slightly giving in his position and then pushing back to indicate a switch.

Level 2

In pairs. After going through exercise 1 for some time, the dancers will have
tuned in to each other, creating a kind of pulse. Two bodies fluidly connect in a
position, where they slow down, never stopping, to dissolve the image again
and transforming into the next.

Level 3

In pairs. Without actively planning, A and B transit through different positions
without stopping. One of them is weight bearer, one is weight giver.

Level 4

In pairs. The weight giver takes all his weight off the ground every now and
then, floating with the help of the weight bearer. If possible, the weight giver
floats for a moment before gently touching down again.

27 Absorb - divert

In pairs. A dances, B keeps the contact. Then B starts to try and divert A's
movements into the floor. A is lead down by B and gets up again, is led down
and gets up again.

28 Support

In pairs. A dances, adding jumps to her repertoire. B follows, supporting A
in all jumps. B has to feel when A prepares to jump and lift her at the right
moment or offer her body as support. A jumps when she feels that B is ready.

29 Nodes

In pairs. A part of A's body touches a part of B's body, for example A's elbow touches B's knee. Both move without losing contact. What movements are possible? Develop movement combinations from different connections.

30 Connection

In pairs. A with eyes shut. B touches A with his hand. A pushes into B's hand and develops that push into a movement towards a position. While A is moving towards his position, B touches another part of A's body to provoke a change of direction. A's task is to send his movement energy through the body part touched by B, following the direction with absolute clarity; and, as soon as A feels B's hand on a different body part, to connect with that body part before sending it into the new direction. The exercise is about connecting outside input with inner impulse.

B's challenge is to time the shifting of his hand so that A can move fluidly on one hand and still has enough time to feel and follow the change of direction. Start small before developing movements through space.
As a further step, B can start moving as well, either supporting or opposing A's movement, turning the exercise into a duet.

31 Snapping

Exercise to develop the mapping of space.
A closes his eyes. B stands next to A and snaps her fingers. A tries to localise where the snap came from and catch the snapping fingers.

32 Push and release

In pairs, facing each other. Without touching, A pushes B away, using different parts of his body. A pushes with varying strength and intensity, and is free to use his breath to 'blow' B away, or to use his voice to indicate the strain of pushing. B reacts with the same intensity. Switch roles. Develop into a duet

33 Balls – Trio

In groups of three. Imagine throwing a ball of changing quality:

> steel ball
> air balloon
> ping pong ball
> football

The dancers catch the ball with different parts of their bodies, reacting appropriately to the different qualities. From this, develop a trio combination.

VIII. Movement quality

34 Light and heavy

From standing:
A part of your body becomes heavy and pulls you down towards to floor. Try not to bump against anything, find an even, smooth transition. Notice the path your body takes going down, what your points of contact are once you reach the floor. Find places on your body you can roll over without hurting, massaging muscle instead of hitting bone. Try a few times until you have found the most efficient way down.

From lying down:
A part of your body fills up with helium. It becomes very light, pulling your body behind like a balloon. What unusual paths can your body take on its way up? How can you use momentum to make your ascent feel like falling upwards instead of struggling up? Try different options and dynamics.

35 Rolling and gliding

Lie supine. Pull your elbow towards your knee, turning your body to one side. Let elbow and knee relax, roll back to centre. Now increase the impulse until the motion turns you into a kneeling position, then until it takes you past kneeling and down on the other side. Roll and expand again. Extend your hand and foot when expanding.

Keep rolling. Contract your body and roll over your bottom. Experiment with different ways of contracting and expanding. Look for unexpected rolling patterns and put them in a sequence.

36 Chinese letters – developing into partner or trio exercise

Lie supine. Imagine a low ceiling, floating 30 centimetres above the floor. Without touching this low ceiling, form Chinese letters with your body. Build a sequence with several letters and the necessary transitions.
Dance your sequence with one or more dancers improvising with you, filling the empty spaces between your letters.
Repeat until a recurring pattern forms. Now you are allowed to break through the low ceiling every now and then. Try different moments in your sequence for your breakthroughs. Get somebody who watches your improvisation and decides which breakthrough moments to keep and develop further.

37 Waves

Lie on your back. Relax. Breathe. Let your weight sink into the floor. Approx. 20 minutes of guided relaxation.

Visualisation: You are lying on a beach. The waves are lapping your feet. Gently, pleasantly, your feet and legs are rocked by the waves. Imagine your body being moved by the water, without any effort from you. You can resist every now and then, and then relax into the rocking sensation again. Let it take over more and more of your body, until your whole body is following the rise and fall of the water.
This exercise can be developed further into contact improvisation, into space, or towards a theme. It needs a lot of empathy and time, but is a good tool to explore and gain trust in the floor. It is less suitable for developing movement sequences, though.

38 Twister

Chalk nine to twelve squares on the floor.

Create a movement combination in which different body parts touch different squares. This may result in some unexpected contortions – hence the name 'twister'.

IX. Group dynamics

39 Switching leaders

Form a circle. Somebody starts to move very slowly, the others try to move in unison. Then, without speaking, somebody else takes the lead. From an observer's perspective, it should be impossible to tell who is leading and who is following.

40 Collective decisions and reactions

Step 1
All dancers walk through the room. Without speaking and without instructions from outside, find a common tempo and vary it together: slow, fast, or full stop. The decision to speed up or slow down should be taken by everyone together, nobody runs ahead or just follows mindlessly. All dancers are responsible for evenly filling the dance floor.

While walking, try to use a 180° field of vision so you can perceive the whole group. Try to give 50% of your attention to the group and 50% to yourself. That means that everybody knows where they are and where the rest of the group are, what the current tempo is and whether he tends to follow the group's tempo or actively supports it. Try to find a medium level of energy where you neither push nor drag.

Step 2

Allow the spontaneous forming of smaller groups. They can move in the same direction together, as if they all were following the same path.

Step 3

The smaller groups can now take their own decisions: adding level changes, speed up or slow down, introducing arm movements etc. They have to keep travelling, though, and of course are not allowed to discuss what they want to do. The different groups then try to relate to each other.

Step 4

The groups dissolve, mix, and reform during the improvisation

41 Walking in a circle

The group forms a big circle. Throughout the exercise, the spacing between the dancers stays the same. As one, the circle starts moving: from standing to walking to maximum tempo and back. Try to speed up and slow down so evenly that the transition becomes almost invisible. The aim is to feel how the tempo constantly varies without anyone taking the lead. It sounds easier than it is, the challenge is to split your attention between your own forward movement and the tempo of the group. Some dancers will always have to restrain themselves so they don't push, while others will have to try hard not to wait for someone to push them.

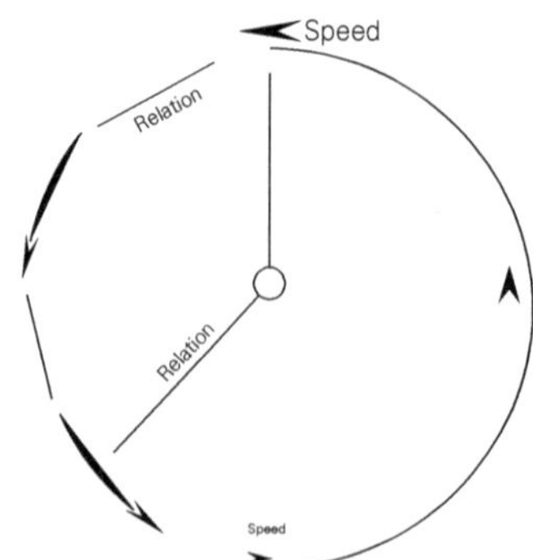

X. Music and movement

42 Relationship between beat and dance

Walk. Feel a four-four beat. Call out the first beat: Hey! Count 2, 3, and 4 silently in your mind. Keep up this rhythm while choosing an additional pattern for eight beats and clapping to it.

Experiment with different patterns. You can also split up the group and let one half provide the beat to which the other half improvises with movement.

43 Approaching a composition using graphical notes

Choose a multifaceted piece of music by a modern composer (e.g. Luciano Berio). Divide a sheet of paper in squares. To each square, assign a certain time span, let's say 15 seconds. Listen to the piece and draw everything you hear in the squares. You will have to listen to the piece many times until you find a graphical solution for every square. Once you have finished drawing, develop a spatial equivalent to your drawing, including emotion, rhythm, and dance.

44 Verbally defining a piece of music and isolated choreographing

Find a piece of music with a very distinct character. Describe that character in one word or in a sentence, for example 'restlessness' or 'spacious' etc. . Develop movements and an improvisation structure for your dancers according to this theme. Improvise without music first, fixing soli and group pieces, then start setting parts of the improvisation to music.

45 Transferring musical structures to dance

Meet up with a musician and together discuss the structure and composition of a piece of music. Transfer your insights onto a choreographic concept that matches the musical structure of the piece.

46 The music plays with the choreography

Dancer and musician agree on a theme. They then independently develop a basic structure. In a next step, they bring their work together.

47 Dialogue: musician - dancer

Action – reaction:
The musicians play a phrase. The dancers dances it, repeating in movement what the musicians played.

Vice versa:
The dancers dance a phrase. The musicians then play what they have seen.

Question and answer:
The dancers dance a sequence, the musicians answers, and vice versa.

Catching up:
The musicians improvise, and the dancers try to follow. Then switch the lead.

Switching leads between dance and music:
The lead of the improvisation switches between the musicians and the dancers. Repetition and variation of a theme are essential parts of the improvisation, the aim is to develop the theme together and also break the theme to find new motives.
Make sure you leave a few dancers to watch and give you feedback on what worked. They will also learn a lot from watching the improvisations of the other dancers.
If you don't have musicians available, or can't afford them, you can always work with your own voices. Just let some dancers take the part of the musicians – don't worry about singing beautifully, this is all about making creative sounds with your voice (see the following two exercises for ideas).

48 Sounds

Form a circle. Somebody utters a sound that is sent once around the circle until it returns to its sender (by which time it may sound quite different). Then another sound is released into the circle, and so on.

49 Vowels

Very slowly, sing the vowels a, o, u, e, i one after the other, creating a spheric droning sound. Randomly layer consonants and other sounds over this droning base. Because you are not training singers, it is enough to practise this until the dancers feel confident enough to make sounds for each other. Now you can make 'music' for each other's improvisations!

XI. Rhythm

50 Body percussion

Stand in a circle facing centre. One dancer starts by throwing a hand clap to his neighbour, and the neighbour passes the clap to her neighbour, and so on. Commit to receiving and passing the clap as if you were catching or throwing a ball. Once a clapping rhythm has established, you can start reversing the direction the clap is travelling, and add the option of throwing a clap through the centre of the circle to a dancer opposite you. You can then add an off-beat stomping of a foot that travels in opposition to the clap, or add random body percussion into the basic clapping rhythm.

51 Vocal rhythms

Two groups of four, one group are 'musicians', the other 'dancers'. Two musicians sit on chairs facing the audience, the other two stand behind them. The sitting musicians use their voices to make sounds, they are free to invent and improvise as they please. Again, don't worry about making it sound beautiful, the rhythm is more important. Repeat a sound several times. The silences between sounds is just as important as the sounds. The musicians who are standing repeat the sounds of the sitting musicians, they do not invent new sounds.

The dancers improvise to the musicians' vocal rhythms.
In my experience, it is not necessary to stop the exercise, as the group will naturally create a pattern of slowly rising rhythms, a melody, and a finale.

52 Rhythmical structure

Choose four pieces of music with different rhythms. Your students listen to the pieces and write down the rhythmical structures they hear. From these notes, they create short soli. Which choreographical elements do they use to translate the rhythmical structures into dance?

53 Vocal rhythms dominating the movement rhythms

In pairs. A dances a sequence, accompanied by B's vocal rhythms and body percussion. A rhythmically adapts her sequence to follow to B's rhythms. The sequence stays the same, but its tempo and phrasing changes according to B's sounds. Aim for two very different versions of the original sequence. You may slightly alter it if the rhythmic pattern asks for it.

Variation: The same starting point as above, but now the dancer opposes the music. She takes her own attitude towards the rhythms. The dance counters whatever the music says.

54 Rhythmic transformations

The group forms a big circle. One dancer improvises at the centre of the circle, keeping an even, clear rhythm. Another dancers joins him with a contrasting tempo and rhythm. Now the two dancers start communicating, taking over the other's rhythm and tempo for a few moments, then returning to their own.

You can have up to four dancers at the centre switching their tempi and rhythms, so that there is a continuous flow between the outside and the inside of the circle. To avoid confusion, you may consider to start first by just switching tempo, and later add switching rhythms.

55   Rhythmic observation and transfer

Watch a video of a good stand-up comedian, one of these professionals who seem to just stand there talking, and suddenly hit their audience with a punch line that has everybody clutching their bellies with laughter. Of course the comedian makes his spectators laugh with the content of his joke, but timing – rhythm! - is crucial. The same joke told with different phrasing may seem a lot less funny. The comedian knows exactly how to time his speech to build up tension, how to establish a rhythm and then break it, stopp, and surprise the audience with the punch line.

Draw the rhythmic structure of your comedian's different tempi, stops, breaks, etc., and transform it into a movement sequence.

56   Breaks

Draft a movement study that is entirely made up of breaks. Don't establish a rhythm, don't repeat phrases, keep breaking your material all the time. How many different breaks are possible? When does your intention become too obvious? How can you prevent it from becoming too obvious?
Use you dance repertoire, but also common everyday movements. Include your voice. If you want to use music, choose a piece that is not rhythmical. If you can, work live with a musician. Experiment, don't hold back. Anything goes!

57   Accents and inner impulses

If a choreography is rhythmically, dull, you can make it more interesting by inserting accents, i.e. changing the movement quality. The impulse comes from inside the dancer, from the muscles used to start and end the movement. You can fix unclear, vague motion by identifying and addressing the movement's point of origin in the dancer's body.

58 Impulses

Stand upright, let your arms hang. Twist your torso so that both your arms end up parallel to your left leg. Your hips stay facing front, creating a tension between shoulder and hip, like a spiral.

Now let go of the tension and let your arms swing to the right, and back to the left. Keep your hips centred, don't let them compensate the twisting motion. Stay in that swinging movement and change the impulse from the arms to your shoulders. Make it light, as if you were touching a key on a piano. Increase the intensity, making the impulse strong and hard, the movement very big and fast, until it becomes difficult to keep the hips centred. Now add another impulse to your swinging: an accent from your finger tips that pulls diagonally up and outwards. The first impulse from the shoulder now softens, the second impulse from your hands a hard accent.

Now let all power drain instantly from your swinging movement after each hand accent. You can let your hip follow the swing and see where it takes you, and how it changes the repetition of the swing.

Before you develop this into a full-blown piece, return to the beginning and start with small swings again. Now try to transfer the impulse to your head. The swinging motion stays the same, but now it is the head that turns first and pulls the shoulder after it. Then try to let the hips start the twist and the rest of the body follow. Now increase the impulse until it takes your body into movement through space. Observe the path your body follows during a swing, and try to vary it.

Once more return to your starting position. Now try an accent from your hands towards your body at the climax of each swing. Shorten the path of your arms by directly pulling your arms in towards your body. This will change the movement completely.
Experiment with other impulses and accents. Develop a study on the different possibilitis of a movement basing on your findings.

59 Translating two-dimensional rhythms into three dimensions

Choose a drawing or a painting.

Decide on directions in the painting, such as 'ascending diagonally from the bottom left corner to the centre and then straight up'.

Notice how different brush strokes give you a different sense of tempo, and what sense of tempo you get from the painting as a whole.

Transfer your findings from the two-dimensional space of the painting into the three-dimensional space of dance.

60 Musical lyrics and complementary elements

Choose an excerpt from a musical or an opera.

For example from 'Dance of the vampires': 'Sometimes at night, I have fantastic dreams...'

Now take one word from the lyrics, such as 'sometimes', and develop a movement to go with a word.

Then add another movement as a complementary element.

Do the same for the other words or clusters of words, noticing the rhythm of the words, and try to establish a dialogue between words and dance.

From this material, create a composition for a group.

Epilogue

As in all art forms, there are great masters in choreography. Some of them have a profound knowledge that they draw from to create dances of exceptional brilliance and power. Other masters have the same knowledge, but their dances draw their power from emotion. There are masters who break all rules without knowing them, and others who need to understand and analyse all limits of the art before surpassing them. However they approach dance, they all share a humbleness towards the elusive essence of dance. It is the awareness of this essence that keeps a sense of wonder fresh in a choreographer. No matter how versed we are in our craft, how intuitive or how skilled in both theory and practice, it is our sense of wonder that will always expand the possibilities of choreography with new spaces and new perspectives.

Wherever your path as a choreographer leads you - standing ovations, revolutionary art forms, reflection and expression through art, invitations from all around the world and big performances in renowned theatres – at the heart of it all, you will find the humbleness and the sense of wonder. It will help you to focus on the magic of movement and keep developing new approaches to one of the oldest expressive arts of man: dance.

About the author

Konstantin Tsakalidis, born 1966, studied acting, dance, and choreography in Stuttgart, Konstanz, Zürich and London.
He has worked as a choreographer, director, actor, and teacher for various theatres, film, TV and other events. He has taken part in productions with the Staatsschauspiel in Dresden, Berlin, London and Zürich, but has also choreographed for free ensembles and created solo performances. Since 1992, he has been presenting his work to audiences all over Europe.
Konstantin has been teaching choreography in various danceeducations for more than 20 years.

When I was about five years old, I heard the word 'choreography' for the first time. I asked my father what it means, and he said it was a Greek term which contained a word for 'circle'. The choreographer, he said, was the one who recorded and determined the circles of dance in a theatre. I knew straight away that this had to be a kind of magic. From that moment, this profession held a mystery for me, a profession which drew circles around things that were elusive and inexplicable. A lot of time has passed since then, and I have learnt how to draw different circles, how to let go of them, and always find them anew.

Notes

Many sources I couldn't trace any more. So many teachers and choreographers have shaped, developed and passed on inputs to each other that have never made into print before.

Here are a few of the most important books and methods I used for this book:

Humphrey, D. (1991). Die Kunst, Tänze zu machen: Zur Choreographie des modernen Tanzes. Ed. and trans. Karin Vial. Wilhelmshaven: Wilhelmshaven: Noetzel, Heinrichshofen-Bücher.

Kandorfer, P. (1984). DuMont's Lehrbuch der Filmgestaltung:Theoretisch-technische Grundlagen der Filmkunde. Köln: DuMont.

Hartley, L. Wisdom of the Body Moving: An Introduction to Body-Mind Centering. North Atlantic Books.

Braun, K.-H. (1987). Minidramen. Verlag der Autoren. 6. Aufl.

Thanks for your feedback

on one of the websites:

choreo-book.com

amazon.com

bod.com

Apple Books

Google Books

epubli.de

Photo directory

Page	Dancer	Photo
5	Verena Sommerer	Alf Ruge
20	Greta Bebenroth	Alf Ruge
25	Ariane Brandt	Alf Ruge
27	Greta Bebenroth	Alf Ruge
28	Ronny Kistler	Alf Ruge
34	Jérôme Gosset	Rolf Wrobel
39	Zaida Ballesteros, Vit Bartak, Stéphane Le Breton,	Rolf Wrobel
40	Zaida Ballesteros, Vit Bartak, Stéphane Le Breton,	Rolf Wrobel
51	Greta Bebenroth, Laura Stecher, Laura Jaeggi, Verena Sommerer	Alf Ruge
52	Zaida Ballesteros, Vit Bartak, Stéphane Le Breton,	Rolf Wrobel
61	Greta Bebenroth, Ariane Brandt, Laura Jaeggi, Verena Sommerer	Alf Ruge
63	Visuals	Alf Ruge
65	Silva Kirstein	Bernd Hänsch
66	Mia Kirsch, Lotte Brockmann	Konstantin Tsakalidis
70	Laura Jaeggi, Verena Sommerer	Alf Ruge
72	Laura Jaeggi, Verena Sommerer, Ronny Kistler	Alf Ruge
75	Laura Jaeggi, Verena Sommerer	Alf Ruge
80	Hanna Jacobi	Bernd Hänsch
82	Isaac Araujo	Vera Bandeira
89	Greta Bebenroth	Alf Ruge
90	Greta Bebenroth, Laura Stecher	Alf Ruge
92	Emily Kipp, Lisa Ludwig, Naby Oberbeck, Nadine Schwarz, Luise Tsakalidis	Konstantin Tsakalidis
93	Greta Bebenroth	Alf Ruge
94	Emily Kipp, Lisa Ludwig, Naby Oberbeck, Nadine Schwarz, Luise Tsakalidis	Konstantin Tsakalidis
96	Emily Kipp, Lisa Ludwig, Naby Oberbeck, Nadine Schwarz, Luise Tsakalidis	Konstantin Tsakalidis
101	Greta Bebenroth	Alf Ruge
106	Annika Wiessner,	Rolf Wrobel
110	Henrieke Zimmermann	Bernd Hänsch
111	Nathalie Zasada	Bernd Hänsch
112	Greta Bebenroth	Alf Ruge
116	Greta Bebenroth	Alf Ruge

119	Isabella Maria Grundei	Bernd Hänsch
123	Marie Holland	Bernd Hänsch
124	Isaac Araujo	Vera Bandeira
126	Kizzy Garcia Vale,Yasha Wang, Annika Wiessner	Rolf Wrobel
127	Kizzy Garcia Vale,Yasha Wang, Annika Wiessner	Rolf Wrobel
131	Isaac Araujo	Vera Bandeira
132	Verena Sommerer, Laura Stecher, Laura Jaeggi	Alf Ruge
134	Yasha Wang	Rolf Wrobel
135	Lara Wunsch	Konstantin Tsakalidis
136	Laura Stecher	Alf Ruge
138	Ronny Kistler, Verena Sommerer	Alf Ruge
145	Daniela Ciccolini	Bernd Hänsch
160	Greta Bebenroth, Laura Stecher	Alf Ruge
163	Jérôme Gosset	Rolf Wrobel
165	Visuals	Alf Ruge
169	Yuta Hamaguchi, Beatrice Kessi, Susanne Eder	Rolf Wrobel
177	Yasha Wang	Rolf Wrobel
184	Greta Bebenroth, Laura Stecher Ariane Brandt, Laura Jaeggi, Ronny Kistler, Verena Sommerer	Alf Ruge
185	Isaac Araujo	Vera Bandeira
187	Ariane Brandt, Laura Jaeggi,	Alf Ruge
193	Adina Eigenbrot, Sabine Fichter, Winfried Haas, Irka Plonski, Annegret Thiemann, Sabine Jordan	Konstantin Tsakalids
194	Yuta Hamaguchi, Beatrice Kessi,	Rolf Wrobel
195	Greta Bebenroth, Laura Stecher Ariane Brandt, Laura Jaeggi, Verena Sommerer	Alf Ruge
197	Melina Lauffs, Juliane Bittermann, Pia-Doreen Brandt, Laura Brosse, Edith Bürger, Petra Cavet, Alex Gesch, Silke Greiser, Carolin Hensel, Theresa Ivanovic, Tea Kolbe, Svenja Mertens, Judith Nüssler, Lena Pierskalla, Tina Scheigenpflug, Ida Schirok, Wera Stein, Céline Weigt, Henriette Rodemerk	Celine Weigt
198	Kizzy Garcia Vale,Yasha Wang, Annika Wiessner, Doriane Locatelli	Rolf Wrobel
200	Yasha Wang	Rolf Wrobel
201	Sebastian Mattner Laura Gestewitz	Bernd Hänsch
204	Kizzy Garcia Vale,Yasha Wang, Annika Wiessner, Doriane Locatelli, Jérôme Gosset, Konstantin Tsakalidis	Rolf Wrobel
205	Yuta Hamaguchi, Beatrice Kessi, Susanne Eder, Ahmed Soura, ,Yasha Wang, Doriane Locatelli	Rolf Wrobel
208	Greta Bebenroth, Ariane Brandt, Ronny Kistler,	Alf Ruge
209	Greta Bebenroth, Laura Stecher Laura Jaeggi,	

		Alf Ruge
210	Greta Bebenroth, Laura Stecher Laura Jaeggi,	Alf Ruge
211	Laura Stecher, Ariane Brandt, Ronny Kistler,	Alf Ruge
212	Fiona Wilke, Lara Wunsch, Franziska Becker, Henrieke Zimmermann.	Bernd Hänsch
213	Laura Stecher, Ariane Brandt, Ronny Kistler,	Alf Ruge
213	Zaida Ballesteros, Vit Bartak, Stéphane Le Breton,	Rolf Wrobel
215	Ann-Christin Hansen, Lisa Hofmann, Mona-Bawani Mühlhausen, Marie Holland, Hanna Jacobi,	Bernd Hänsch
216	Jose Maria Roquette Ortega	Konstantin Tsakalidis
216	Laura Stecher, Ariane Brandt, Ronny Kistler,	Alf Ruge
218	Jose Maria Roquette Ortega	Konstantin Tsakalidis
219	Nina Püschel, Cecilia Lerg	Felix Alexander Neudeck
220	Franziska Becker	Bernd Hänsch
221	Jose Maria Roquette Ortega	Konstantin Tsakalidis
223	Greta Bebenroth, Laura Stecher Ariane Brandt, Laura Jaeggi, Verena Sommerer	Alf Ruge
224	Kizzy Garcia Vale,Yasha Wang, Annika Wiessner, Doriane Locatelli, Jérôme Gosset	Rolf Wrobel
225	Franziska Becker	Bernd Hänsch
226	Greta Bebenroth, Laura Steche, Ariane Brandt, Laura Jaeggi, Verena Sommerer	Alf Ruge
228	Greta Bebenroth, Laura Steche, Ariane Brandt, Laura Jaeggi, Verena Sommerer	Alf Ruge
229	Greta Bebenroth	Alf Ruge
230	Greta Bebenroth, Laura Jaeggi, Ronny Kistler, Verena Sommerer	Alf Ruge
234	Greta Bebenroth, Ronny Kistler,	Alf Ruge
236	Daniela Ciccolini	Bernd Hänsch
240	Antonia Strobl, Fine Saeltzer, Silva Kirstein, Daniela Ciccolini	Bernd Hänsch
241	Greta Bebenroth, Laura Stecher	Alf Ruge
243	Henrieke Zimmermann	Bernd Hänsch
253	Lotte Brockmann, Mia Kirsch,	Bernd Hänsch
254	Johanne Uhle	Konstantin Tsakalidis
261	Isaac Araujo	Vera Bandeira
263	Alina Schneider	Ulf Leuteritz
264	Maria Ladopoulos	Betty Pabst
265	Miriam Arbach, Johanne Uhle	Betty Pabst
266	Maria Ladopoulos	Betty Pabst
267	Johanne Uhle	Betty Pabst
268	Miriam Arbach, Johanne Uhle	Betty Pabst

269	Miriam Arbach, Johanne Uhle	Betty Pabst
270	Maria Ladopoulos	Betty Pabst
271	Miriam Arbach,	Betty Pabst
272	Johanne Uhle	Betty Pabst
273	Miriam Arbach, Johanne Uhle	Betty Pabst
274	Mona-Bawani Mühlhausen	Betty Pabst
275	Mona-Bawani Mühlhausen	Betty Pabst
276	Johanne Uhle	Betty Pabst
277	Johanne Uhle	Betty Pabst
278	Johanne Uhle	Betty Pabst
279	Mona-Bawani Mühlhausen	Betty Pabst
280	Mona-Bawani Mühlhausen	Betty Pabst
281	Miriam Arbach, Mona-Bawani Mühlhausen	Betty Pabst
281	Jonathan Kolski	Konstantin Tsakalidis
282	Miriam Arbach, Maria Ladopoulos, Mona-Bawani Mühlhausen, Jilian Neuberger, Natalia Sesé Cabello, Daniela Wölfel,	Betty Pabst
283	Miriam Arbach, Maria Ladopoulos, Mona-Bawani Mühlhausen, Jilian Neuberger, Natalia Sesé Cabello, Daniela Wölfel,	Betty Pabst
285	Miriam Arbach, Mona-Bawani Mühlhausen,	Betty Pabst
287	Jana Quilitz, Diana Skripkina,	Betty Pabst
288	Mandy Unger, Diana Skripkina	Betty Pabst
292	Mona-Bawani Mühlhausen	Betty Pabst
295	Alessio Trevisani	Hai Vu Nguyen
297	Mona-Bawani Mühlhausen	Betty Pabst
300	Mona-Bawani Mühlhausen	Betty Pabst
301	Mona-Bawani Mühlhausen	Betty Pabst
303	Miriam Arbach, Mona-Bawani Mühlhausen	Betty Pabst
304	Miriam Arbach, Mona-Bawani Mühlhausen	Betty Pabst
305	Miriam Arbach, Mona-Bawani Mühlhausen	Betty Pabst
307	Vladimir Golubchyk	Betty Pabst
308	Vladimir Golubchyk	Betty Pabst
310	Miriam Arbach,	Betty Pabst
311	Miriam Arbach,	Betty Pabst
312	Miriam Arbach,	Betty Pabst
317	SLAM	Bernhard Mohr
319	Lotte Brockmann, Mia Kirsch,	Konstantin Tsakalidis
320	Lotte Brockmann	Konstantin Tsakalidis
323	Toni Zahaj	Holger Vocke
323	Elisabeth Krause	Florian Bornträger
330	Vladimir Golubchyk, Mona-Bawani Mühlhausen	Betty Pabst
331	Daniela Ciccolini	Bernd Hänsch

331	Vladimir Golubchyk, Mona-Bawani Mühlhausen	Betty Pabst
332	Daniela Ciccolini	Bernd Hänsch
335	Greta Bebenroth, Laura Stecher Ariane Brandt, Laura Jaeggi, Ronny Kistler, Verena Sommerer	Alf Ruge
336	Jérôme Gosset	Rolf Wrobel
341	Laura Stecher , Verena Sommerer	Alf Ruge
342	Laura Gestewitz	Bernd Hänsch
343	Konstantin Tsakalidis	Konstantin Tsakalidis
344	Greta Bebenroth, Laura Stecher Ariane Brandt, Laura Jaeggi, Ronny Kistler, Verena Sommerer	Alf Ruge
349	Yuta Hamaguchi, Beatrice Kessi, Susanne Eder, Ahmed Soura, ,Yasha Wang, Doriane Locatelli	Rolf Wrobel
350	Kizzy Garcia Vale,Yasha Wang, Annika Wiessner, Doriane Locatelli, Jérôme Gosset,	Konstantin Tsakalidis
355	Jo Kolski &Nolwenn Samson	Sophie Krabbe
355	GettyImages	GettyImages
356	Jan Sandro Berner	Konstantin Tsakalidis
357	Alice Bruder, Jan Sandro Berner	Konstantin Tsakalidis
361	Annika Wiessner	Konstantin Tsakalidis
362	Jo Kolski &Nolwenn Samson	Sophie Krabbe
363	Jasmin Potrafke	Nina Niestroy
363	Sabine Fichter	Konstantin Tsakalidis
364	Clair Dunn, Rowena Kinzett, Montserat Ventura	Konstantin Tsakalidis
377	Clair Dunn, Rowena Kinzett, Montserat Ventura	Konstantin Tsakalidis
379	Nina Püschel, Jana Schütze, Elisa Hahn, Laura Wolf, Dorothea Gack	Felix Alexander Neudeck
381	Clair Dunn, Rowena Kinzett, Montserat Ventura	Konstantin Tsakalidis
382	Ariane Brandt, Ronny Kistler	Alf Ruge
413	Konstantin Tsakalidis	Konstantin Tsakalidis

Alf Ruge – www.alf-ruge.de

Bernd Hänsch – www.beha-art.de

Betty Pabst – www.bettypabst.de

Felix Alexander Neudeck - www.felixalexander.net

Rolf Wrobel – www.rolf-wrobel.com

Vera Bandeira - www.verabandeira.com.br